GERMAN
LITERARY INFLUENCES
ON THE AMERICAN
TRANSCENDENTALISTS

BY STANLEY M. VOGEL

ARCHON BOOKS
1970

[*Yale Studies in English, Vol. 127*]

SBN: 208 00927 2
Library of Congress Catalog Card Number: 77-91192
Printed in the United States of America

Preface

THE purpose of this book is to present as fully as possible the profound debt which the American Transcendentalists owed to the literary forces of Germany. Although German philosophy came to them at first through secondary sources, the Transcendentalists read in the original, and discussed in their writings, the works of countless German poets, dramatists, and educators. Only when we take these factors into consideration can we obtain a correct insight into the nature of German influence.

The first part of the book traces the history of German literary criticism in New England outside the Transcendental circle. I have paid special attention to German scholarship in American books and periodicals during the years 1790 to 1845, when important persons like Bentley, Adams, Marsh, Everett, Ticknor, Bancroft, and Cogswell were active. In this section I have also discussed the careers of the major instructors of German in New England, since many of the Transcendentalists studied under their supervision. The second and main part of the book deals with German scholarship among the Transcendentalists themselves. Four major groups are represented: the men of letters—Emerson, Alcott, and Thoreau; the theologians—Channing, Hedge, Parker, and Ripley; the critics—Clarke and Margaret Fuller; and the translators—Dwight and Brooks. The appendix listing the German books in Emerson's personal library may prove useful to students of comparative literature.

In its original form this work was submitted to the Graduate School of Yale University in partial fulfillment of the requirements for the doctoral degree. The general subject was suggested by Stanley T. Williams, who first stimulated my interest in the Transcendentalists and under whose direction the study was originally prepared. It is a pleasure to acknowledge my indebtedness to Professor Williams whose wise counsel and patient advice are responsible for much that is substantial in this book.

For their kindness and cooperation in making available to me previously unpublished material I am grateful to Robert W. Hill of the New York Public Library, William A. Jackson of the Houghton Library at Harvard, James T. Babb of the Sterling Memorial Library at Yale, and James Freeman Clarke of Boston for allowing me to use the manuscripts, journals, and correspondence of his grandfather. I must express my appreciation for assistance given to me by Margaret Hackett, reference librarian at the Boston Athenaeum, and by the curators of the Emerson

House, the Old Manse, the Hawthorne House, the Alcott House, and the Antiquarian House in Concord. Edward W. Forbes was also most kind in permitting me to examine the Emerson library in Concord. Finally special thanks are due to Carl F. Schreiber of Yale University, who read the manuscript in its entirety and whose valuable observations enabled me to improve appreciably the interpretation and the presentation of my materials; to Benjamin C. Nangle, editor of the Yale Studies in English, for his aid in preparing the book for the press; to Neilson C. Hannay of Suffolk University for his many helpful suggestions; and to Ella M. Murphy of Suffolk University, not only for her scholarship and counsel but for sustaining me through many diffcult periods.

STANLEY M. VOGEL

Suffolk University
November, 1954

Contents

Abbreviations

For purposes of expediency I have abbreviated certain footnotes in this study as follows:

EMERSON, *Works*   Ralph Waldo Emerson. *The Complete Works of Ralph Waldo Emerson*. Centenary Edition.

EMERSON, *Journals*   *Journals of Ralph Waldo Emerson*. Edited by E. W. Emerson and W. E. Forbes.

EMERSON, *Letters*   *The Letters of Ralph Waldo Emerson*. Edited by Ralph L. Rusk.

Emerson-Grimm Correspondence   *Correspondence between Ralph Waldo Emerson and Herman Grimm*. Edited by F. W. Holls.

Emerson-Carlyle Correspondence   *The Correspondence of Thomas Carlyle and Ralph Waldo Emerson, 1834–72*. Edited by C. E. Norton.

THOREAU, *Writings*   Henry D. Thoreau. *The Writings of Henry David Thoreau*. Walden Edition.

FULLER, *Works*   Margaret Fuller. *Works*. Edited by A. B. Fuller.

As for the misspellings and faulty punctuation in the quotations, I have tried to preserve them faithfully, except when the sense of a passage was obscure. Necessary editings are indicated in the notes.

Introduction

THE unusual interest of American scholars in German literature during the early decades of the nineteenth century has been an incentive for detailed studies of German influence, but one finds no definitive work tracing the influence of German literature on the major American Transcendentalists when they were forming the doctrines first expressed in Emerson's *Nature*.

A few books and numerous articles have dealt with particular aspects of German-American Transcendental cross-currents. For example, the unpublished dissertation "German Backgrounds of American Transcendentalism: Prolegomena to the Study of Influence," by John H. Groth of the University of Washington, does not duplicate the material of this book. Mr. Groth was primarily interested in the influence of certain philosophical concepts, especially those of Jacobi, on the Transcendentalists, and the main part of his dissertation is a translation of one of Jacobi's little known works.

There have been, however, more helpful studies which in part relate to my subject. Frederick H. Wilkins published in 1899 a list of German literary works read in America from 1762 to 1825. Scott H. Goodnight in 1905 traced the appearance of German literature in American magazines prior to 1846. Bayard Quincy Morgan performed an invaluable service for all students of German-Americana when he produced his *Critical Bibliography of German Literature in English Translation*. Nor can one fail to mention the new *Bibliography of German Culture in America to 1940* by Henry A. Pochmann and Arthur Schultz (Madison, Wisconsin, 1953). More pertinent to this study was Harold S. Jantz's monograph, "German Thought and Literature in New England, 1620–1820," published in the *Journal of English and Germanic Philology* (1942), and Orie W. Long's *Literary Pioneers* dealing with the training of six early American educators and scholars at the University of Göttingen. Dissertations, such as *Emerson and Goethe* by Frederick B. Wahr (1915) or *Margaret Fuller and Goethe* by Frederick A. Braun (1910), have also been published, but much knowledge has come to light since these investigations were made. Important studies by Arthur Schultz and Henry A. Pochmann on Margaret Fuller's and George Ripley's German interests, the publication of Emerson's letters and Hawthorne's notebooks, and new biographies of Thoreau and Alcott have made these dissertations wholly inadequate. Yet even these later works have been individual studies. Not since 1915, when Emma Jaeck devoted to Americans who showed an interest in German scholarship one chapter in her book *Madame de Staël and the Spread of German Literature,* has anyone directed his attention primarily to the influence of German literature on the ideas of the whole Transcendental group.

A fault discernible in many of these studies is that the authors go too far in their theses. We are left with the idea that American Transcendentalism could not have existed without Jacobi, Goethe, or Madame de Staël, when in reality each of these influences was only part of a much larger trend of German influence. In fact, unlike many scholars, I do not contend that the German influence was solely responsible for the particular form of American Transcendentalism which developed. No one source, neither German, French, Oriental, nor English, can be given so much credit.

The question now arises whether we can make a distinction between the philosophical and the purely literary influences which came to these shores from Germany, for any discussion of Transcendentalism inevitably includes some aspects of German philosophy. Yet, in the case of the New England Transcendentalists, it is not impossible to make such a distinction, since they were not trained philosophers or profound students of theology. They gained their knowledge of the German philosophers and theologians through the essays of Samuel Taylor Coleridge and Thomas Carlyle or through the commentaries of the German men of letters. These New Englanders preferred Herder, Wieland, Schiller, and Goethe to Kant, Fichte, and Schelling. When the iron regulations of Calvinism began to hem them in, the Transcendentalists turned to these German literary men and not to the philosophers for inspiration.

Another important objective of this dissertation has been to prove that the avalanche of commentary dealing with German literature in the late 1830's and early 1840's was no sudden enthusiasm. It had its origins long before the series of essays by Carlyle and Coleridge. Even prior to the American Revolution our people were becoming aware of the merits of German literature. The poetry of Gessner, the dramas of Kotzebue, Schiller's *Die Räuber,* and Goethe's *Werther* were well known before the turn of the century. To be sure, New England had received some queer ideas from the French about Germans, prejudices which were hard to overcome.[1] By 1820, however, the attendance of American students at German universities caused an influx of ideas ranging from skepticism and rationalism in matters of religion to development of modern methods of education heretofore unknown in this country.

The rise of Transcendentalism, in particular, was identified with the interest in German philosophy and literature. Outsiders looked upon

1. In the *Polyanthos,* the character of the German was summed up in this fashion: in religion he was unbelieving; a pedant in the sciences; faithful in keeping his word; bearlike in courage; clownish in manners; a glutton in eating and drinking; and in diseases, infested with fleas. See *4* (May, 1814), 100-2.

Transcendentalism, as they looked upon all other things German, with a vague dislike, dread, or suspicion, and they closely connected it with infidelity and radicalism.[2] Perhaps Dickens in his *American Notes* summed up the current opinion best when he wrote, "I was given to understand [in Boston] that whatever was unintelligible would be certainly transcendental"[3] Hawthorne's description of the "Giant Transcendentalist" is even more colorful: "He is a German by birth, and is called Giant Transcendentalist; but as to his form, his features, his substance, and his nature generally, it is the chief peculiarity of this huge miscreant that neither he for himself, nor anybody for him, has ever been able to describe them. . . . He shouted after us, but in so strange a phraseology that we knew not what he meant, nor whether to be encouraged or affrighted."[4]

German influence was strongest in New England at a time when German philosophy was most metaphysical and German literature most romantic. Before the invasion of German idealism the thought and religion of New England, particularly Unitarianism, concerned itself with little more than the arid Methodism of eighteenth-century England. Its philosophy was based on the common-sense doctrines of John Locke and Dugald Stewart. It was a colorless philosophy with little power of inspiration; and the religion, of course, was similar. After the War of Independence a reaction against this cold and spiritless creed was so natural in New England that German ideas could easily take root on these shores. The new philosophy, with its individualism and fervid piety, was the very antithesis of the old. It threw men back upon themselves and bade them obey the inward voice of reason and conscience, the voice of deity, instead of conventional opinion.

There can be little doubt that Germany was the ultimate source of the language of Transcendentalism. Kant had originated the name and had systematically developed the transcendental conceptions. Kant's successors in turn gave literary and popular expression to the philosophy. The terminology then passed with little modification into the French and English languages.

Now if this terminology originated with Kant, we must still inquire how it reached Emerson and his circle and what debt they owed it. The Transcendentalists themselves were bothered by this question, and their answers were not always alike. Orestes Brownson wrote in the *Christian Examiner:*

2. Julia Ward Howe, for example, tells of her father's undertaking one day to read an English translation of *Faust*. He presently came to her and said, "My daughter, I hope that you have not read this wicked book!" See *Reminiscences* (Boston, Houghton Mifflin, 1899), pp. 59–60.

3. Charles Dickens, *American Notes* (Philadelphia, Lippincott, 1891), p. 66.

4. Nathaniel Hawthorne, *The Complete Writings of Nathaniel Hawthorne* (Boston, Houghton Mifflin, 1900), *4*, 274–5.

Men are classed together under the general term, Transcendentalist, who have scarcely anything in common but their fondness for philosophical pursuits. There are men among us who have a most hearty dislike for observation, who disregard experience, ask no aid of facts, and who deem themselves competent to construct a true philosophy of man and the universe by means of speculation alone. If they who condemn the Transcendentalists mean these, they are bound to say so; for there are others among us also called Transcendentalists, who adopt the psychological method, and pursue it with the most rigid fidelity, who will attach no scientific value to any metaphysical system, whatever its pretensions, which is not a legitimate induction from facts patiently collected, scrupulously analyzed, and accurately classed. These last are no more to be confounded with the first, than a modern chemist is to be confounded with an old alchemist, or a Bacon with a Paracelsus.[5]

The *Dial* also tried to deal with the problem in an article by J. A. Saxton called "Prophecy—Transcendentalism—Progress." He too gave credit to Kant, but then added:

I know nothing of the writings of Kant; but I find his doctrine thus clearly stated by one of his English interpreters. "Kant, instead of attempting to prove, which he considered vain, the existence of God, virtue, and immortal soul, by inferences drawn, as the *conclusion* of all philosophy, from the world of sense; he found these things written, as the *beginning* of all philosophy, in obscured, but ineffaceable characters, within our inmost being, and themselves first affording any certainty and clear meaning to that very world of sense, by which we endeavor to demonstrate them. God *is,* nay, alone *is;* for we cannot say with like emphasis, that anything else is. This is the absolute, the primitively true, which the philosopher seeks. Endeavoring, by logical argument, to prove the existence of God, the Kantist might say, would be like taking out a candle to look for the sun; nay gaze steadily into your candlelight, and the sun himself may be invisible.[6]

This statement was written as late as 1841. The writings of Kant, therefore, had not yet been translated in a way that would make them intelligible to the Transcendentalists no matter how conversant they might have been with metaphysical speculations. Yet, from Kant, through writers like Coleridge and Goethe, they seemed to draw the idea that the good, the true, the beautiful—all things of which they instinctively approved—were somehow connected together and were really one thing; that our appreciation of them was in its essence the recognition of a law; that this law and the very idea of law was a subjective experience.

5. *Christian Examiner, 22* (May, 1837), 188.
6. The *Dial, 5* (July, 1841), 91.

Moreover, Kant's intimations concerning the Practical Reason, as an impulse urging us to enlarge the conceptions of the Understanding, appear to agree well enough with Emerson's definition of Transcendentalism as "the feeling of the Infinite."

The value of this German philosophy to these New Englanders, however, 'v not in obtaining an exact doctrine but in the authorization it gave to their own ideas, and especially the presence of God in the individual heart. As one critic put it, "What the Americans wanted was not so much an itinerary as a passport. They asked from the Germans, what their Puritan ancestors had asked from James I—a charter. The less they knew of the details of the patent, the more free they felt to pursue their own objects in their own way." [7] Finally, it must be remembered that Transcendentalism was a faith rather than a philosophy, and it went to Germany to find confirmation of that faith.[8]

7. O. W. Firkins, *Ralph Waldo Emerson* (Boston, Houghton Mifflin, 1915), p. 63.
8. See Vernon Parrington, *Main Currents in American Thought* (New York, Harcourt, Brace, 1927), *2, 382*.

PART I

German Scholarship Outside the Transcendental Circle

I

The Nature of German Literature in New England
before 1800

EW literary movements or literary influences have a sudden beginning, and the German influence on American writing is no exception. Before 1800 a knowledge of German literature in New
England was far more limited than in New York and Pennsylvania,
where emigrants from central Europe had settled in greater numbers. In
other sections of the country German culture flourished decades before
most New Englanders became in any real sense aware of German literature.[1] The purpose of the early chapters in this study, however, is not to
analyze the German response in various parts of America. Mention of
affairs in Philadelphia or New York is justified only in terms of their
influence on the New Englanders. Nor are these first chapters intended
as an exhaustive treatment of pre-Revolutionary interest in German
literature.[2] At the most, one can consider them a summary or brief introduction to German scholarship in New England, which in turn influenced the major figures of the Transcendental movement.

German scholarship was not absent even from our first colony in New
England. Settlers at Plymouth actually had German books in their
libraries, although these books dealt mainly with theological subjects.
William Brewster's inventory of 1644 included a large number of Ger-

1. In the eighteenth century, for example, Benjamin Franklin, a Bostonian by birth
but a resident of Philadelphia, was one of the few famous persons who had a deep
interest in the Germans and their culture. To him should be given the credit of having
issued in the year 1732 the first German newspaper in America, *Die Philadelphia Zeitung*
(see L. Viereck, "German Instruction in American Schools," *Report of the Commissioner
of Education for the Year 1900–1901* [Washington, 1902], *1*, 541). What is more important, in consideration of the trend fifty years later, Franklin decided to visit the
University of Göttingen, and his presence at a meeting of the Royal Society of Science
was reported in the Göttingen *Anzeiger* of September 13, 1766 (see I. M. Hays, *The
Chronology of Benjamin Franklin, 1706–90* [Philadelphia, 1904], p. 14). For the benefit
of German settlers Franklin issued from his printing press religious literature, such as
hymn books (the first in 1730), prayer books, and catechisms. He was also responsible
for the introduction of German into the curriculum of the Academy at Philadelphia. The
people of Pennsylvania recognized Franklin's devotion to the spread of German culture,
and in 1787, when they agreed to establish a German college at Lancaster, they named
it Franklin College (now Franklin and Marshall) in his honor.

2. For a detailed study of German influence in colonial America to which I am particularly indebted see Harold S. Jantz, "German Thought and Literature in New England, 1620–1820," *Journal of English and Germanic Philology*, 41 (1942), 1–45.

man theological works; Myles Standish owned several volumes of German history; and isolated items of German origin were also to be found in the collections of William Bradford and Samuel Fuller. The library of the Massachusetts Bay Company, in its inventory of 1629, listed sixteen German volumes by outstanding theological scholars. John Harvard's library contained more books by Germans than by Dutch, Italian, and French writers combined, and these were presented to the newly established college in 1638.[3]

Among persons of note in early New England John Winthrop the Younger (1606–76), governor of Connecticut, was especially concerned with German scholarship. After settling in this country in 1631, he maintained an active exchange of information on scientific subjects with numerous Germans or Englishmen with German connections. No less significant persons than the astronomer Johann Kepler the Younger and the chemist Johann Rudolph Glauber, as well as Germans living in England like Prince Rupert of the Palatinate, Samuel Hartlib, and Henry Oldenburg, were among his correspondents. Winthrop purchased German books and publications throughout his life, even checking the catalogues of the Frankfurt book fairs. The predominance of chemical and mineralogical treatises in his library shows the importance of German scholarship in scientific fields which were of special interest to Winthrop. Since these books were mainly in the German tongue rather than in Latin or English, it is obvious that Winthrop must have had an adequate knowledge of the language.[4]

Nor was Winthrop an isolated case. His friend, Nathaniel Ward of Ipswich, satirist and author of *The Simple Cobbler of Aggawam in America,* had been a pastor in Germany, at Elbing, Prussia, and had also lived in Heidelberg.[5] In *The Simple Cobbler* Ward referred to persons of German origin like Paracelsus and Frederick Duke of Saxony. Michael Wigglesworth, author of the *Day of Doom,* also owned a number of

3. The early records of the Harvard Library reveal interesting trends so far as German books are concerned. Although a few German learned periodicals and isolated volumes were purchased, the collection continued to show an absence of German literature throughout the greater part of the eighteenth century. The first catalogue (1723) lists Hebrew, Latin, and French grammars published in Germany, a Luther New Testament, and the works of Jacob Boehme in German. Even the catalogue of 1790 lists mainly works of a scientific or theological nature.

Yale's record is similar to Harvard's. In its 1790 library catalogue, we find listed a German Grammar by John King (London, 1758), and in 1808 a second German Grammar by John James Bachmair (London, 1752). A few theological titles are also found in the Yale collection of 1808 but nothing which could be called German literature.

4. Professor Jantz, in his examination of the Winthrop collection, found over sixty publications entirely in the German language and several more partly in German. *German Thought,* p. 10.

5. See S. E. Morison, *Builders of the Bay Colony* (Boston, Houghton Mifflin, 1930), pp. 220–1.

German theological and scientific treatises which could have affected his writings.[6] More important, however, was Increase Mather, who, with his son Cotton, built up a formidable collection of German books. As in John Harvard's library, the German volumes outnumbered those in other modern tongues. Not only did their collection contain countless German theological and scientific works, but also German books dealing with the occult sciences, which must have been studied avidly during the witchcraft trials. A third German element in the Mather collection was books of a pietistic and missionary nature. Cotton Mather showed a particular interest in German charities and childhood training, and corresponded with the theologian August Hermann Francke of Halle on such matters.[7]

German pietism and mysticism may also have connections with the Quaker movement. Groups of Quakers had settled in Rhode Island and Nantucket, and although their doctrines were of English origin, some of their ideas closely parallel those of Germans like Jacob Boehme. The interest in pietism fostered by the Mathers reached a high point, however, with the arrival of John Wesley and George Whitefield. Wesley stimulated emotional religion in America, which followed a pattern similar to that in Germany.[8] His familiarity with German theology is evident in his translations of German tracts and hymns.

It is not surprising then that before the nineteenth century German literature in America was predominantly religious. Even in Europe Lessing, Goethe, and Schiller were not acclaimed until late in the eighteenth century. To look for any substantial interest in German literature before the American Revolution is, therefore, wholly unprofitable. After the Peace of Paris in 1783 the interest in German culture remained stagnant. This situation can be accounted for. Obviously the popularity of Lafayette and the French, in contrast with the dislike of Hessian soldiers who fought for the British, was partly responsible. Secondly, there was a noticeable decrease during this period in the number of German emigrants coming to America.[9] The Germans who had reached our shores settled in the ports of New York and Philadelphia rather than Boston, and even in those sections where they congregated, their influence was stronger in the political than in the literary and scholarly

6. See John Ward Dean, *Sketch of the Life of Michael Wigglesworth* (Albany, J. Munsell, 1863), p. 16.

7. See Kuno Francke, "Cotton Mather and August Hermann Francke," *Harvard Studies and Notes in Philology and Literature, 5* (1896), 57–67. Also *Americana Germanica, 1* (1897), 31–66 and *Philological Quarterly, 5* (1926), 193–5.

8. For German influence on Wesley and Whitefield see the *Princeton Theological Review, 5* (1907), 49–70 and 210–41.

9. *Report of the Commissioner of Education for the Year 1897–1898, 1,* 607 and *1900–1901, 1,* 546.

sphere. Puritan New England almost entirely ignored them until the beginning of the nineteenth century.

Americans realized only in the last decade of the eighteenth century that culture could be found in Europe beyond the confines of France and England. In the *Columbian Magazine* for 1788 [1] an article on "The Literary Wit and Taste of the European Nations" mentioned no single German author or work. Moreover, in New England magazines one finds no important references to German authors before the Revolution other than to Frederick the Great, whose poems show the influence of Voltaire and French literature far more than that of German writers.[2] As a German, however, Frederick was well known in New England because of his early recognition of America and his support of American commerce. Anecdotes about him often appeared in the American periodicals of the day.

German books of travel and English accounts of travel in Germany also began to make their appearance in the latter part of the eighteenth century. They gave New Englanders a more precise idea of the nature of German society and culture. Such books were Baron Riesbeck's *Travels through Germany,* William Coxe's *Travels in Switzerland,* and Charles Burney's *Present State of Music in Germany,* which had much to say about German literature as well. Along with these travel books and journals appeared translations of mid-eighteenth-century German literature, available for the first time. Then with the close of the war, contact with Germans in other states like New York and Pennsylvania helped to bring about greater understanding, although the process remained sluggish until after 1800.[3] Only scholars who had studied the German language and had become familiar with its literature were eager to praise it. In contrast, the people who were ignorant of German culture were the first to be suspicious of it, and to criticize it adversely. In New England, where the German language was still comparatively unknown and opportunities to learn it relatively few, any knowledge of

1. *Columbian Magazine, 2* (July, 1788), 384–8 and (August, 1788), 423–30.

2. Professor Goodnight drew up these interesting statistics. In the magazines prior to 1795 which he examined, there occur, aside from the references to Frederick the Great, eleven to Lavater, eight to Luther, seven to Goethe's *Werther,* six to Gessner, two to Lessing, and one each to Haller, Wieland, Klopstock, and Gellert. He found no reference to Gottsched, Herder, Bürger, or Schiller, although *The Robbers* had been reprinted in 1793, and none to any work of Goethe other than *Werther.* From 1795 to 1800 appear the names of Bürger, Goethe, Herder, Jacobi, Kant, Kotzebue, Niebuhr, Schiller, Stolberg, and Zimmermann. If we examine a complete list of references from 1800 to 1845, he says, "Scarcely a name found in the index of a modern history of German literature for that period, would be missing, and a large number of writings, wholly forgotten today, are represented by translations, biographical notices and criticisms." See S. H. Goodnight, *German Literature in American Magazines prior to 1846* (Madison, Wisconsin, University of Wisconsin, 1908), pp. 17, 18.

3. Dr. Benjamin Rush's essay, "An Account of the Manners of the German Inhabitants of Pennsylvania" (1789), particularly impressed New Englanders.

German literature had to filter in through English and French translations and résumés.[4] The tone of the criticism remained, therefore, unfriendly. We have no better guide to this criticism than the comments which appeared in the various periodicals of the day.[5]

In the *New England Quarterly Magazine* a note on German literature suggested that we should avoid it, since it was engaged in the cause of vice and infidelity.[6] A brief article on Kant recorded this interesting but completely false statement: "The difficulty, and even the danger, attending the study of the higher branches of philosophy and metaphysics, has become more and more evident; and the number of metaphysical writers seems to have again decreased in Germany." [7]

The progress, however, among Germans in classical scholarship was beginning to be recognized. The *Monthly Anthology and Boston Review* (June, 1810) praised the labors of the German literati in the different departments of Greek literature.[8] Among the Germans, it contended, the classical spirit of Greece seemed to have revived. The article then defended the Greek and German Dictionary of Professor Schneider of Frankfurt, and proved that German is more accurately translated into Greek than is Latin. German was, therefore, indispensable for the Hellenist who wished to be thoroughly acquainted with his science. The next issue added to this praise: "The labours of the learned men of Germany, their recent advances in this sort of critick [Biblical criticism], the connection of these researches with the subject of the oriental and most ancient mythology, in short, this whole grand subject of biblical exegesis, is worthy of the highest degree of attention from the learned men and thinkers of every country, whatever may be in other respects their religious opinions." [9] Praise of this type began to appear more frequently, although the puritanical element, especially in New England, continued to complain of the lack of moral quality in German literature.

If current opinion maintained that German literature did not measure up to the ethical standards of American readers, one may wonder which German books were approved of by the great majority of people, and what causes brought about a change of taste in their choice of reading

4. We must remember that Harvard offered no instruction in German until 1825 when Charles Follen began to teach there.

5. E. Z. Davis in his monograph *Translations of German Poetry in American Magazines* points out that German authors were seldom introduced for the first time to American readers in book form. Translations and reviews of their works appeared in magazines, usually before the copies of an English translation in book form reached these shores. This was especially true of poetry. Abridged versions of Klopstock's *Messiah* or Gessner's *Death of Abel* were printed along with collections of short lyric poems.

6. *2* (July, August, and September, 1802), 262.

7. See the *Emerald or Miscellany of Literature, 1* (December, 1806), 382.

8. *8*, 429.

9. *9* (July, 1810), 55.

material. Obviously in the early years Goethe and Schiller did not appeal to New England. On the contrary, the idyllic, bucolic, and edifying
works of Gessner and the moralistic writings of Lavater, Zollikofer,
and Zimmermann were known long before the authors of *Werther* and
Die Räuber, whose works were generally considered vicious.

The first German writings to gain a favorable reputation in this
country were by Salomon Gessner, a native not of Germany but Switzerland. From the time of the earliest American reprint (Boston, 1762)
until 1820 Gessner's idyls and poems, such as *The Death of Abel,* maintained a steady popularity.[1] The first magazine contributions attributed
to a German author were three idyls by Gessner appearing in the years
1774, 1775, and 1785.[2] Since religious literature appealed far more to
the readers of that day, one will not be surprised by the popularity
of Gessner's writings. They even popularized another religious work of
greater significance, Klopstock's *Messiah;* the English translator of
the latter work advertised it as being "in the manner of *The Death of
Abel.*"[3]

Gessner's works continued to maintain their high standing during
the first decade of the nineteenth century. In 1805 the *Literary Miscellany* (Cambridge) wrote of him:

> As a pastoral poet, Gessner is undoubtedly entitled to a very dis-
> tinguished rank; and we may justly say, that, if he has been equalled
> by any, he has been excelled by none. It is commonly believed, that
> pastoral poetry is very limited and confined; but those, who read the
> works of Gessner, will be convinced, that it is susceptible of much
> variety, when treated by the hand of a master. . . . His language is
> that of the graces, and the chastest ear may listen to the love, which
> he has created. If he has sometimes the humor of Sterne and Fon-
> taine, it is without their licentiousness.[4]

By 1814, however, the works of Gessner were beginning to outlive
their fame. The *Quarterly Review* admitted this change of taste when
it described Gessner as amiable and accomplished in private life, but
deficient in nerve as an author. In his place, the article stated, had arisen
the mighty names of Klopstock, Schiller, and Goethe, a triumvirate
which no country perhaps, except England, could equal, and whose
splendors were as yet but little known by the English reader.[5]

1. For a list of early American editions of German works see F. H. Wilkens, *German
Literature in America 1762–1825* (New York, Macmillan, 1900), pp. 63–100.
2. The first recorded edition of Gessner's *Idyls* was not printed until 1802.
3. Wilkens tells us that since Gessner was especially popular with the ladies, it is
not surprising to find that a lady wrote a work in imitation of *The Death of Abel,* called
The Death of Cain (London, 1790?). This work found its way to America and was reprinted together with *The Death of Abel* (Wilkens, p. 9).
4. *I,* 81.
5. See *10* (January, 1814), 379. Yet as late as 1816, in an article "On the State of

Another German religious writer, Friedrich Klopstock, enjoyed a reputation in America similar to that of Gessner. His poem *Messiah* was popular for a longer time than many other religious works because of its moral tone and genuine poetic quality.[6] Although the *Messiah* did not appear in Boston until 1811, it had been printed earlier in New York and Philadelphia, and was known through the reviews and notices in Boston periodicals. In 1810, the preceding year, the bookstores in Philadelphia, Baltimore, and Boston were also selling Friedrich and Margaret Klopstock's *Memoirs,* and the response was favorable.

Among other works of religious inspiration familiar to American readers were Lavater's *Maxims and Aphorisms on Man*[7] and Zimmermann's *Thoughts on the Influence of Solitude on the Heart.*[8] The writings of the German divines Zollikofer and Sturm had even greater appeal. Sturm's work *Reflections on the Works of God* could have been found on many a bookshelf in New England, and Zollikofer's sermons served as models of eloquence worthy of imitation.[9]

Although Americans were reading these moral and semireligious works, they knew little of German scholarship in the first years of the century, and the critics, for the most part, condemned all Germans as atheists and skeptics. One article asserted that at Berlin, and at all the courts of Germany, the fashionable philosophy had made such a rapid progress that "those who had confessedly no part of the kingdom of God in their hearts, were ready to take refuge in infidelity, and to treat the religion of Jesus with contempt." Then it added piously, "It [Christianity] hath survived their Pagan predecessors, and it will live and flourish, when all its revilers shall fade as the leaf."[1]

When Madame de Staël's book *De l'Allemagne* appeared in 1813, its chapters devoted to German philosophy, although highly superficial, helped to mitigate the general condemnation then prevalent. The *Quarterly Review* also admitted that everywhere but in their native land the

Polite Literature in Germany," Gessner was rated superior to Goethe, Schiller, Lessing, Kotzebue, and Bürger, and of all these writers he alone was not considered as "hopelessly deficient in the matter of taste." See the *Portico* (Baltimore), *2* (July, 1816), 17.

6. "Klopstock's Messiah," said the *Literary Magazine and American Register,* "will ever remain the first and grandest poetic monument for the German nation. . . . To this work Germany is indebted for the honor of not yielding, to any modern nation at least, in the higher department of epic poetry, and of maintaining a superiority over most. The religious epopee is carried in the Messiah to higher perfection than in Milton's Paradise Lost. . . . No German poet has ever reached the variety, fulness, and harmony of Klopstock's hexameters." See *7* (June, 1807), 343–5.

7. *Aphorisms on Man* was printed in Boston in 1790. Goodnight lists fifteen references to Lavater in periodicals prior to 1800, and in this regard he leads all the others.

8. It was reprinted in America in 1793. Two more editions appeared before 1800, but the Boston reprint did not appear until 1804.

9. Between 1806 and 1810 three different collections of Zollikofer's sermons appeared in Boston.

1. *New York Missionary Magazine, 1* (1800), 318.

metaphysicians of Germany had been depreciated far more than they deserved, and that the charge of extravagance should have been confined to the imitators of Kant, since the founder of the school had undoubtedly "the merit of calm and cautious investigation." [2]

New Englanders frowned upon the purely secular literature of Germany, but they must have read much of it, judging from the variety of translations published in this country. They preferred poetry and drama to novels and romances. In New England, especially before the year 1800, they seem to have ignored the German romances.[3] Matthew Gregory Lewis' translation of Zschokke's *Abaellino, the Bravo of Venice* was the only prose romance reprinted in Boston before 1809. They also read the educational novels of Jean Paul Richter, which should be singled out from the general group of German romances, since Americans believed that Richter had a high, moral purpose. In 1802 the *New England Quarterly Magazine* sketched Richter as being "all soul." [4] It praised his conversation for abounding in wit and humor, and compared him with Voltaire, who never opened his mouth without a witticism. The article ended optimistically: "When he shall have learned to confine within due bonds his exuberant fancy, and to give to his works a more pleasing form, he will rank as the first romance-writer of his country. He is not translatable into any other language; but it is worth the while to learn German on his account alone." [5] While such sentiments seem to us now completely out of proportion to his literary worth, at that time his popularity was assured. During the first four decades of the century, critics continually sang his praises. Even the Transcendentalists, partly conditioned by the opinions of Carlyle, commented favorably on his writings.[6]

Among the German poets, Bürger and Wieland were adequately translated both in England and America. Bürger's *Lenore* was especially popular, and Sotheby's translation of Wieland's *Oberon* (1798) made that work accessible to both English and American readers.[7] John Quincy Adams translated Wieland's *Oberon* just before Sotheby's version was published. In a letter to Charles Follen he said that his German teacher had sent a copy of the translation to Wieland himself, and asked him his opinion. Wieland compared it with the recently published translation of Sotheby, and frankly admitted that although Sotheby was

---

2. *10* (January, 1814), 392.

3. A few works of German fiction gained some prominence in Philadelphia and New York, among them Schiller's *Geisterseher,* Vulpius' *Rinaldo Rinaldini,* and Lafontaine's *Familienromane.*

4. *2* (July, August, and September, 1802), 57.

5. *Ibid.,* p. 58.

6. Charles T. Brooks translated and published many of Richter's works. For a discussion of his interest in Richter see pp. 152–3.

7. Sotheby's translation was not reprinted in Boston until 1810.

the greater poet Adams was more faithful to the original, a decision which Adams fully confirmed.[8]

The *Monthly Anthology and Boston Review* also reflected in this statement the general praise which Wieland continually received:

> From the variety and number of the writings of Wieland, he has been justly called the Voltaire of Germany. . . . But, however much we may admire the wonders of his invention and the skill of his arrangement, it must be conceded that he has studied too much in the school of the wild and Colossal, and too little in that of nature. . . . Yet amidst these occasional defects the spirit of poetry shines forth with surpassing splendour, and the Oberon, considered as a whole, exhibits an exuberance of imagination, unparalleled in modern poetry.[9]

German drama before 1800 fared far better in popularity than the other forms of literature with the exception of religious works. Modern taste would find little to its palate in the choice of dramas produced on the stage and published, although the first German play to hold the stage anywhere in America was Lessing's *Minna von Barnhelm,* performed in Charleston, South Carolina, February 18, 1795.[1] A translation of Lessing's *Miss Sarah Sampson* appeared in 1789 or 1790, but the play was not produced on the stage at that time. The first German play on any New York stage was Schiller's *Die Räuber,* first acted on May 14, 1795.[2] A dramatization of Goethe's *Werther* by Reynolds was produced at New York and Boston in 1796 and 1797.[3] Yet neither Lessing nor Schiller nor Goethe held first place in popularity among German playwrights. In Boston as well as in New York and Philadelphia the plays of August von Kotzebue monopolized the stage for decades.[4]

8. See *The Works of Charles Follen* (Boston, Hilliard, Gray, 1841), *1,* 306-7.
9. *9* (September, 1810), 193-4. Similar praise is found in the *Analectic Magazine:* "To no writer of the age, perhaps, are the literature, the language, and the public taste of the Germans under such great obligations as to Wieland, whose talents have for half a century been the boast and admiration of the country which gave him birth. Few authors of any nation have written so much; but what constitutes a far more honourable distinction, still fewer have written so well. . . . It is impossible that his merits can be fairly appreciated in this country, where so few of his numerous works have yet found their way before the public." See *2* (November, 1813), 418-19.
1. C. F. Brede, *The German Drama in English on the Philadelphia Stage from 1794 to 1830* (Philadelphia, Americana Germanica Press, 1918), p. 4.
2. G. O. Seilhamer, *History of the American Theatre, 1792-1797* (Philadelphia, Globe Printing House, 1888-91), *3,* 111.
3. *Ibid.,* p. 369.
4. In the periodicals Kotzebue's name first appeared in the New York *Monthly Magazine, 1* (April, 1799), 76. His talents and powers of observation were highly praised, but the writer believed that because of differences in national taste it was not likely that any other of his dramatic compositions [he was referring to *The Stranger*] would ever be brought on the English stage. How much this correspondent was mistaken may be seen by the fact that in America thirty of his plays were published in English translation before 1820.

The labors of William Dunlap, manager of the Park Street Theater in New York, were partly responsible for this vogue. Although Dunlap and the German influence in New York are outside the scope of this study, his popularization of Kotzebue spread quickly to Boston and therefore deserves to be mentioned. As early as 1798 Dunlap brought out a translation of *Menschenhass und Reue* as *The Stranger*. When the play won acclaim, Dunlap decided to study German in earnest. The following year, on March 11, 1799, he produced his version of Kotzebue's *Das Kind der Liebe* under the title, *Lovers' Vows*, succeeded a month later by *Count Benjowsky*. We know that Kotzebue proposed to sell to Dunlap a number of his unpublished plays, with the stipulation that they should not be printed. So far as we know Dunlap did not accept the offer.[5] In 1800 Dunlap produced fourteen new plays of Kotzebue, proving his words that "the necessity for producing" Kotzebue's plays "rendered *Hamlet* and *Macbeth,* and all the glories of the drama, for the time a dead letter." [6] This epidemic of Kotzebue may have been caused by the sentimental material used in the plays as well as by Dunlap's unaffected style and facile translation. His English rivals, in contrast, "embalmed Kotzebue's easy conventional style in the somewhat elaborate and artificial English prose style of the eighteenth century." [7]

Kotzebue's plays were printed in Boston as early as 1799, when *The Constant Lover* and *Self Immolation* appeared. The next year *Count Benjowsky* came into print, and in 1809 *Pizarro*.[8] During the same decade Kotzebue's *Virgin of the Sun* was produced on the Boston stage with no less interesting actors in the main roles than the parents of Edgar Allan Poe—Elizabeth acting the part of Cora, the heroine, and David, Ataliba, the King of Quito.[9]

Kotzebue's works both on the stage and in print remained popular during the first two decades of the nineteenth century, although the praise was not universal. Puritan New England refused to sanction his work in spite of the general acclaim. In a criticism of *Pizarro* the *Monthly Anthology and Boston Review* asserted: "The chief purposes of the *illuminated* author of this play evidently are to dazzle and seduce a romantick fancy, to raise delightful and exalted notions of a savage state of nature, and, by partial delineation and false colouring, degrade and calumniate the mild doctrines of Christianity." [1]

5. Wilkens, p. 16.
6. W. Dunlap, *History of the American Theatre* (New York, Harper, 1832), 2, 124.
7. Wilkens, p. 24.
8. *Pizarro* again appeared in 1818.
9. On April 18, 1808, Mrs. Poe also played Amelia to her husband's Francis, the villain in Schiller's *Die Räuber*. See Arthur H. Quinn, *Edgar Allan Poe* (New York, Appleton-Century, 1941), p. 28.
1. 5 (February, 1808), 97. Joseph Dennie, editor of the *Portfolio* of Philadelphia, who damned the work in no uncertain terms, was in accord with this review. He wrote: "Of the noxious tendency of the German drama, little doubt is now entertained among the

It seems singular to link Schiller's work with that of Kotzebue, but at that time Schiller was known only by his early productions, especially *Die Räuber* and possibly *Kabale und Liebe*. Although *Die Räuber* was not produced so frequently as Kotzebue's plays, and in spite of the hostility of the periodicals, *Die Räuber* clung to the standard repertoire. Dunlap offered the public an abridged version of Schiller's *Don Carlos* as early as May 6, 1799, apparently without success. The first biographical sketch of Schiller, which also appeared in 1799, was biased and highly superficial.[2] The reviewer, after attacking all of Schiller's early dramas, contended that even Germany regarded him as a second-rate artist.

Apart from the drama of Schiller and Kotzebue, Goethe was the only other German writer whose name began to appear with greater frequency, seldom with favorable criticism. The only work of Goethe to receive recognition before 1800 was *Die Leiden des jungen Werther,* of which six editions in translation were issued in this country between 1784 and 1807.[3] To this day a picture representing an incident from *Werther's Sorrows* hangs in Washington's home, Mount Vernon, an indication of the popularity of the book in the young republic.[4] In spite of its fame this novel received its share of critical abuse. Doctor Benjamin Rush, for instance, blasted it as an exaggerated and insincere portrait of life causing young ladies to "weep away a whole forenoon over the criminal sorrows of a fictitious Charlotte or Werter." Yet at three o'clock they would turn with disdain from the sight of a beggar.[5] Within a period of four years, 1787 to 1791, seven poems highly sym-

---

lovers of sense, and Shakespeare, and the advocates of Truth and Virtue. When we range over the waste of this German's writings, from the licentious *Stranger* to the dashing *Pizarro,* from Rolla to Cora, from his *Wildgoose* to his Wanton Women, we find little of the beautiful, and still less of the true. . . . Those readers, whose purer taste has been formed on the correct models of the old classic school, see, with indignation and astonishment, the Huns and the Vandals once more overpowering the Greeks and the Romans." See *1* (September, 1801), 283.

2. *Monthly Magazine* (New York), *1*, 153.

3. The Boston reprints appeared in 1798 and 1807, but Boston was not the only place in New England where this little work was popular. Listed among American editions in the Speck Collection at Yale are the following copies all printed before 1840:

1789 *The Sorrows of Werter,* published by Thomas Collier, Litchfield, Connecticut.
1814 *The Sorrows of Werter,* published by William Fessenden, Brattleborough, Vermont.
1824 *The Sorrows of Werter,* published by Jacob B. Moore, Concord, New Hampshire.
1824 *The Sorrows of Werter,* published by Silas Andrus, Hartford, Connecticut.
1829 *The Sorrows of Werter,* published by Silas Andrus, Hartford, Connecticut.
1830? *The Sorrows of Werter,* published by Andrus and Judd, Hartford, Connecticut.
1839 *The Sorrows of Werter,* published by Andrus, Judd, and Franklin, Hartford, Connecticut.

4. John A. Walz, *German Influence in American Education and Culture* (Philadelphia, Carl Schurz Memorial Foundation, 1936), p. 8.

5. B. Rush, *Essays Literary Moral and Philosophical* (Philadelphia, printed by Thomas and William Bradford, 1806), p. 82.

pathetic to *Werther* appeared in American magazines, proving that America like Europe was touched by the Werther fever.[6] Denunciations, however, did not subside. In 1806 *Werther* was condemned anew as one of those books "which no parent should suffer to enter the hands of her child; which no bookseller should sell . . . a book more read than any of its kind by the young, and which has proved the bane of more than one family." [7] Aside from other strictures on *Werther* there were few objective comments on Goethe before 1812, when an anonymous review of *Die Wahlverwandtschaften* appeared.[8] Americans still nourished themselves on English criticisms in periodicals such as the *Quarterly Review,* which superficially criticized Goethe in a comparison with Gay, Swift, Sterne, Scott, and Southey. It completely denied any similarity to Shakespeare. The following statement typifies this mode of criticism: "His smaller poems, numerous as the sands of the sea, we have neither time nor inclination to criticise in detail. Most of them have some sort of whimsical originality. Many have considerable pathos, and all are more or less immoral." [9] Concerning *Faust* it makes the comment that with all its horrors it may be read without danger, though not without a painful feeling.

We should not condemn these criticisms too quickly when we remember the circumstances under which they were written. German books were still not available, and even if they had been, almost no one, as we shall see, knew enough of the language to read them with any accuracy. The few translations which had been printed were inaccurate, unscholarly, and limited, for the most part, to second- and third-rate German writings. We have no right, therefore, to expect an unbiased opinion of a foreign literature when that opinion had to be based on a handful of semireligious books, lurid dramas, and sentimental romances.

6. Goodnight, p. 24.
7. *Literary Magazine and American Register, 6* (December, 1806), 451.
8. *Walsh's American Review* (Philadelphia), *3,* 51. There also appeared in Richmond in 1805 a reprint of Holcroft's translation of Goethe's *Hermann und Dorothea,* but it is doubtful whether it was considered any greater than Gessner's *Idyls.*
9. *10* (January, 1814), 355.

2

The Trend toward Favorable Criticism

THE growing familiarity with German literature and the gradual changes of taste are best reflected in the early nineteenth-century periodicals which the Transcendentalists were reading. During the years when American scholars who had studied at Göttingen exerted most influence, the *North American Review* and the *Christian Examiner,* largely under their domination, laid new stress on the writings of Goethe, Schiller, Herder, Klopstock, Wieland, and the Schlegels. Although we miss the criticism of many important German writers, we breathe a sigh of relief at the decrease in the popularity of Gessner, Lavater, Kotzebue, and Zimmermann.[1] Numerous translations of lyrical poems as well as sentimental, homely, and moralizing stories also appeared in these periodicals. They corresponded closely to the type of literature written in America or imported from England. Although the fight to recognize genius in German writing was not won without a struggle, we can observe that the unrelenting condemnation of earlier years gradually disappeared. Bitter foes like Andrews Norton and his magazine the *Select Journal of Foreign Periodical Literature* remained, but these were exceptions.[2]

In Boston the *North American Review* was without any doubt the most powerful disseminator of German culture. Göttingen men, such as Edward Everett and George Bancroft, were not the only contributors of articles on German literature.[3] In April, 1823, the Reverend Mr. Frothingham criticized Grillparzer's *Das Goldene Vliess,* a review unusual in two respects: first, it was one of the few comments on Grillparzer in these years; and second, it recognized Grillparzer's superiority to Werner, Kotzebue, Klinger, and others. Frothingham contended that by these inferior dramatists and their imitators could be chronicled the reign of false taste and turgid style, "faithful to the dignity of the drama, to its approved rules and noblest models." Grillparzer, in contrast to the other writers, wrote drama with great freedom and spirit,

---

1. One finds, however, little or no mention at this time of writers such as Kleist and Hölderlin.
2. For Norton's relations with German literature and the Transcendentalists see pp. 73.
3. For articles on German literature by the Göttingen scholars see pp. 24ff.

full of action, though the leading incidents which formed its materials were few, and the incidents familiar to the reader.[4]

In the same year Alexander Everett's review of the *Life of Schiller* appeared. Unlike the other commentators, Everett analyzed the merits of *Die Räuber* as well as its defects, although even he could not resist bemoaning its supposed immorality. Everett by no means condemned Schiller as an immoral poet. He said of him:

> It is much to his honor, that all his writings are distinguished by a pure morality, and an elevated tone of thought and feeling. In making this remark, we mean, of course, to except the Robbers, for reasons, which we have already explained at length. Though not, strictly speaking, licentious, the moral of this play is certainly exceptionable. —The rest of his works, whether in prose or verse, are uniformly fitted to encourage the noblest and most amiable sentiments. . . . His two great contemporaries, Goethe and Wieland, for example, are by no means so pure as Schiller, though the tendency of their work is, in general, far from being absolutely vicious. . . . It is therefore a great happiness for a nation, when a writer like Schiller, whose talents secure him an unbounded popularity and influence, has the grace to exert them uniformly in the great cause of virtue and human happiness.[5]

The *North American Review* also assessed Fouqué's *Undine,* a short German romance, which, the editors said, would give pleasure to any who were willing to be pleased by a consistent, though fanciful narration; from it they were "content to receive gratification without attempting to analyze its causes." [6] In January, 1825, a friendly criticism of Herder's works appeared,[7] and in October, 1828, an article on John Russell's book *A Tour in Germany* accented the University of Göttingen and the work of the German theologians, two topics of prime interest

---

4. *16* (April, 1823), 283.

5. *16* (April, 1823), 424.

6. *18* (April, 1824), 412. Another favorable review of *Undine* is found in the *United States Literary Gazette, 1* (June, 1824), 50, but one which has greater literary ramifications was written by no less a person than Edgar Allan Poe when he was editing *Burton's Gentleman's Magazine* in September, 1839. Poe praised the republication of *Undine* "in the very teeth of our anti-romantic national character." He then proceeded to give a most lively résumé of the plot, followed by an analysis of the style. Poe pointed out that the book was crowded with incident, but beneath all, there ran a mystic or undercurrent of meaning, simple, yet richly philosophical. *Undine* was "a model of models," on which he could have written volumes about its various beauties. Its unity he found absolute with everything attended to and nothing out of time or out of place. In fact, he called it the finest romance in existence. "Were we to pick out *points* for admiration in *Undine*" he concluded, "we should pick out the greater portion of the story. We cannot say whether the novelty of its conception, or the loftiness of its ideality, or its intense pathos, or its rigorous simplicity, or that high artistical talent with which all are combined, is the particular to be chiefly admired."

7. *20*, 138.

among American scholars.[8] In July, 1834, when Carlyle's *Life of Frie-drich Schiller* was reviewed, the false ideas prevalent in earlier years about Schiller and Goethe were clearly stated, and the German authors completely vindicated. By July, 1836, the *North American Review* had come to the defense even of Heinrich Heine. The reviewer dared to say of his work *Letters auxilliary to the History of Modern Polite Literature in Germany* [*Die romantische Schule*] :

> Whatever we may think of the moral character, motives, and inten-tions of the author of this book, it claims attention as exhibiting the views and opinions of a man of uncommon talent on a subject, which cannot but be interesting to every person of liberal education,—the condition of German literature during the last forty or fifty years. . . .
>
> Does any one ask, Of what use, then, is the perusal of the writings of such a man? Of very little, indeed, if we look solely for lessons of virtue; but of great importance, . . . when we consider that this same man is not only a witness testifying to what he has seen and what he knows, but to some extent himself an actor in the great drama which is going on, and surely no despicable actor in a state of society where books are the most powerful engines for good or evil. Men of Mr. Heine's stamp may be opposed, their opinions refuted, and their influence counteracted; but they cannot be silenced. Any at-tempt to conceal their influence only enhances the danger. They are, and are active; and it is impossible to form a complete and correct idea of the present social condition of Germany, and its prospect, of which they constitute an element, without being acquainted with them and their agency.
>
> Besides, Mr. Heine has excellences as well as faults; and, although we are far from considering them as amends for his errors, we are equally far from denying or concealing their existence. . . . We are far from advocating or even excusing his political, theological, and philosophical opinions; but we would in fairness acknowledge the correctness, justice, and originality of many of his criticisms.[9]

When the *North American Review* pronounced so dispassionately upon Heine, whose name was still anathema among most God-fearing people, it demonstrated the steady progress which this periodical had made in developing a liberal attitude toward German literature. During these early decades New England scholars were apparently gaining a clearer perspective through an ever growing study of German literature. No longer did they laud minor literary figures merely because they mouthed pious platitudes. Literature for its own sake was beginning to speak up.

8. The same topics were discussed in the review of Henry E. Dwight's *Travels in the North of Germany, 19* (October, 1829), 389.
9. *43*, 163-6.

By the 1830's the New England intelligentsia had finally accorded the profound thinkers of Germany some recognition.

The *Christian Disciple,* later published under the title the *Christian Examiner,* was hardly less instrumental than the *North American Review* in forming an opinion of German literature.[1] A review of Herder's *Letters Relating to the Study of Divinity* thus summed up the progress of German literature in this country:

> Herder, though one of the most celebrated writers of the last part of the last century in Germany, has been very little known abroad. The chief cause of this probably is, that all his writings are composed in his own tongue; and the language and literature of the Germans have not till lately been much attended to by foreigners. It is a singular fact, that while scarcely a work of note, either in letters or the sciences, appears in English, without soon issuing in translation from the German press; our own language has been put in possession of little in return, except a few strange plays and extravagant fictions. The prejudices, which those loose writings had a great part in creating, are however wearing away fast; and men are beginning to believe that there is not a science in the whole circle, which does not owe great obligations to German genius and research.[2]

In May, 1830, the *Christian Examiner* published Professor C. C. Felton's review of Goethe's *Iphigenie auf Tauris.* Felton, who, suffering from the New England conscience, attacked the morals of Goethe, nevertheless recognized him as the greatest genius in German letters. Certainly the following passage shows his admiration: "Schiller, Wieland, Klopstock, and those other literary giants who have made Weimar the Athens of Modern Europe, have long rested in the silence of the tomb. Of that constellation, one star only, but that the brightest of all, yet remains, shining on with a pure and steady lustre, amidst the flood of softened and reflected light that still lingers over the horizon where those kindred stars have set." [3]

The *Athenaeum* was a third Boston periodical during these years to feature German literature. In 1817 and 1818 it published criticisms of Körner and Schiller with translations of their poems, excerpts from Goethe's autobiography, and biographical sketches of Kotzebue.[4] In January, 1820, it served up a review of Müllner's drama *Guilt* [*Die Schuld*], and in February, 1821, it reprinted from Baldwin's *London*

1. Unlike the *North American Review,* however, the *Examiner* took no positive stand with regard to German literature. Not all its criticism was favorable. In fact, one of the most vicious attacks on Goethe was written for this periodical by George Bancroft in July, 1839.
2. *8* (July and August, 1820), 233.
3. *Christian Examiner, 8* (May, 1830), 188.
4. *3, 48; 5, 321, 358.*

Magazine a very sympathetic article on Goethe's *Faust*.[5] A review of Grimm's *Fairy Tales* in the *Athenaeum* took this modern stand toward children's books:

> It is the vice of parents now-a-days to load their children's minds with useful books—books of travels, geography, botany, and history only, and to torture young thoughts with a weight beyond its strength. Why should little children have grown-up minds?—Why should the dawning imagination be clouded and destroyed in its first trembling light? Is the imagination a thing given to be destroyed?—Oh no!—Let the man and the woman have the dry book—the useful leaves—for their food; but give to childhood the tender green and flowers for its yeanling imagination.[6]

Indeed, from 1820 to 1830 the names of Schiller, Goethe, Fouqué, Körner, Bürger, A. W. Schlegel, Richter, Herder, Arndt, and the translations of Carlyle appeared in this periodical with ever increasing frequency.[7]

In 1833 the *Select Journal of Foreign Periodical Literature* made its debut in Boston, and although its life span was brief, it figured with no little importance in the German controversy. Its editor, Andrews Norton, was so hostile to any phase of German culture that he would not allow his son to study the language at Harvard.[8] Naturally his comments on Goethe and other German writers were biased. The utter condemnation and hostile feelings toward Goethe and his admirers which he displayed are hard to understand at so late a date as 1833.[9] Even the ar-

5. The review is significant, for at that time most of the comments to be found on *Faust* were derogatory.

6. *13* (April, 1823), 20.

7. See Series 1: *6*, 289, 353, 358; *8*, 491; *9*, 94, 106, 209; *10*, 72, 154; *11*, 144, 310, 368; *13*, 20; *14*, 284, 439; Series 2: *5*, 42, 464; *6*, 1, 137, 455; Series 3: *4*, 158, 269; *5*, 142.

8. Norton's connections with the Transcendental controversy will call for further discussion later, but in reviewing the material available in Boston periodicals, it is not out of place to speak of him at this time.

9. He said of Goethe: "He was . . . a very extraordinary man, extraordinary from the character and circumstances which enabled him to hold such a despotic power over many German minds. But that he should ever attain a corresponding influence out of his own country, and especially among English readers, is not to be apprehended. It would imply a revolution of taste, of moral sentiments, of philosophy, and of religious faith, as improbable as it would be disastrous. . . .

"The blessed era to be brought about by this most extraordinary man, who, during a great part of his life was 'filled full with skepticism, bitterness, hollowness, and thousand-fold contradictions,' is to be effected, we must presume, from what is said, not by his Werter or Faust, but by Wilhelm Meister's Apprenticeship, and his later poems. We are not told what part in this grand renovation is to be accomplished by his other novel, entitled 'Elective Affinities,' which, to most English readers, if ever translated, will appear only a cold, disgusting story of complicated adultery. Werter and Faust may well be put out of the question. The day of the former has passed. The weakest of sentimentalists, at least out of Germany, would now regard it as a book too silly to cry over. As to Faust, the most zealous of its admirers must allow that the moral renovation which it is adapted to produce is of a very questionable kind. . . .

ticles in Norton's periodical chosen from foreign magazines were cold
toward German literature. A review of Goethe's *Faust, Part II*, reprinted from the London *Foreign Quarterly Review*, No. 23, gave
Goethe some grudging praise, but this was the only exception.[1] A critical
notice of Richter's *Vision* was unfavorable both to Carlyle and to Goethe,[2]
and in an article on religion in Germany Goethe was held responsible for
the prevailing spirit of doubt.[3] In reviewing Börne's *Briefe aus Paris*,
abridged from the London *Foreign Quarterly Review*, No. 19, the editor
said:

> When we first read the article in the Foreign Quarterly Review . . .
> we concluded not to select it for republication. The names of Boerne
> and Heine have been little known in our country; and the review it-
> self is written in a tone of irony which does not seem to us very
> happy. . . . The barbarous and unmeaning jargon of the metaphysics
> taught by these men, their absolute irreligion, their contempt of all
> that is established in morals, their public outrages upon decency, their
> violent and false theories concerning the relations of man to man in
> civil society, and the new and monstrous forms of literature which
> have hence resulted, are producing the most disastrous effects.[4]

In spite of his efforts, Norton could not stem the rushing tide which
was constantly swelling through the efforts of the Göttingen men, the
German department at Harvard, and the editors, printers, and publishers in and around Boston. This interest in German learning affected
even the smaller periodicals of the day. The *New England Magazine*
presented German poems and stories in all its volumes; the Boston
Ladies' Magazine printed excerpts from Schiller, Wieland, and Herder
along with notices of other German works. The Boston *Weekly Messenger* reprinted German poems and sketches of Körner, Kleist, Blücher,

"We have no intention of discussing the character or the genius of Goethe; or the
causes of the extraordinary ascendency which he has attained over the minds of many
of his countrymen. We have been led to make the preceding remarks from a consideration of what seems to us the tendency of his writings and the influence of his character,
considered under a moral and religious aspect. We are not, however, among the admirers
of his works, considered merely as literary productions. We doubt whether a cultivated
English reader of correct principles and good taste could unhesitatingly lay his hand
upon any one of them, and say that it would have been a loss to mankind had it never
appeared.
"We ought, however, to remark that it is rather the outrageous admiration which has
been bestowed on Goethe, than any thing in his own character or writings, which we
regard as likely to be very pernicious, at least to English readers. Upon their minds
his writings can have little hold. An artificial and diseased taste must be created before
they can read them, without much weariness and dislike." See *1* (April, 1833), 250–62.
   1. *3* (January, 1834), 16.
   2. *Ibid.*, p. 124.
   3. *4* (July, 1834), 115.
   4. *4* (October, 1834), 222. This was no impartial judgment of Heine like the one
in the *North American Review* of 1836.

and Görres.[5] The Boston *Missionary Herald* contributed letters on Luther.[6] The *Quarterly Review,* reprinted in Boston, advertised works of Fouqué, Goethe, Wetzler, Schiller, and Grimm.[7] The *New Monthly Magazine,* reprinted in New York and Boston, contained long criticisms of Schiller's *Don Carlos,* Grimm's tales, Kotzebue's and Iffland's plays, and translations of poems such as Goethe's "Heidenröslein." [8]

This résumé of the growth of German literature in the books and periodicals of New England from the Revolution until the 1830's is by no means exhaustive. It suffices, however, to show that before 1800 German literature received little recognition in this country, in contrast with French literature. Even where it was read, the German literature chosen was but a poor sampling of the best available material. Not only did the comparatively minor religious and moral writers hold first place, but in drama, poetry, and fiction, the second- and third-rate writers were preferred. Of the great German writers Goethe and Schiller, only their least mature works were known. To make matters worse, the few American scholars who could read German were hampered by the lack of German books, and translations were inadequate both in quantity and quality. As yet Americans had little conception of the progress which German scholarship was making in the study of the classics, and the only information which they had concerning new treatises on philosophy and theology were vague rumors that the Germans were atheistic and immoral. When we consider all these factors, it is not surprising that most American critics condemned German literature as unintelligible, bombastic, and vulgar.

With the more frequent appearance of translations in the periodicals and the publication of German books both here and in England, condemnation of German literature in the early years of the nineteenth century gradually disappeared. As time went on readers were also beginning to prefer Goethe, Schiller, and other more important writers of German literature rather than the semireligious writers of the eighteenth century. Even the most puritanical critics reached the point where they could praise, or at least tolerate, such writers as Börne and Heine. By the 1830's scarcely a magazine in New England failed to include some comment or notice of German literature, good evidence of the spread of German influence.

5. *5,* 94; *6,* 207; *9,* 78; and *9,* 229.
6. *17,* 94.
7. See the Boston reprint of the *Quarterly Review* from 1821 to 1829.
8. See the Boston reprint of the *New Monthly Magazine* for 1823, 1824, and 1826.

3

New England Scholars and the Study of German

BEFORE 1800 several celebrated scholars discovered what German culture had to offer.[1] Such a person was William Bentley of Salem. While still at Harvard and later as a pastor in Salem, Bentley acquired an enormous amount of knowledge including a mastery of the important European languages as well as several of the Orient.[2] As a student of theology and history he became familiar with the best of German scholarship and literature, and collected one of the finest and largest scholar's libraries in the country. In his *Diary* (September, 1806) he expressed his delight upon finding a book store in Boston where German classical and critical works were being imported from Leyden. "I believe," he wrote, "this to be the first importation of the kind in America. Books, chiefly of devotion, have been sent from Germany, and whenever any public notice has been given, I have directed enquiries and have always found them rather promises than any thing done upon any regular scale." [3]

Bentley's library included not only Biblical and classical scholarship but also an excellent collection of German periodicals and German literary writers from Klopstock to Schiller. Even though his collection was weak in Goethe and the romantic writers, it was unique for its time. No wonder then that this interest soon spread among his friends, such as William Jenks, a tutor at Harvard, who exchanged German books with him. Bentley also wrote or reprinted countless articles on German culture in the Salem papers and made translations of German prose

1. Several detailed studies to which I shall refer have already been written on the major figures of this chapter, but since these New England scholars had relations with the Transcendentalists, it is necessary to restate their accomplishments.

2. In the catalogue of Bentley's books put up for sale on June 14 and 15, 1820, at Blake and Cunningham's in Boston, one finds listed not only numerous Latin, Greek, French, and German dictionaries but also Portuguese, Russian, and Old English grammars and spelling books (see *Catalogues of Private Libraries,* a collection of pamphlets bound together, Boston Athenaeum). Bentley's biographer, Joseph G. Waters, stated that in Bentley's collection were also rare Persian, Arabic, and Chinese manuscripts (see *The Diary of William Bentley, D.D.,* Salem, Essex Institute, 1905–14, *1,* xxi).

3. *Ibid., 3,* 247. The American Antiquarian Society at Worcester received most of Bentley's German books, but even in the catalogue of his books sold in 1820 one finds, in addition to the countless editions of Greek, Latin, and theological volumes published in Germany, a goodly number of books by Gessner, Klopstock, Humboldt, Wieland, Schiller, Goethe, and Kant.

and poetry. He even used his knowledge of German to correct Noah Webster's errors in discussing the origin of the English language.

Bentley's correspondence with Christoph Daniel Ebeling, whose name appears often as one of the greatest collectors of Americana in his time, is of special importance.[4] Ebeling had met a number of Americans at Hamburg, where New England trade brought frequent visitors,[5] and soon became interested in Americana. In 1794 he was elected to the Massachusetts Historical Society and later to the American Antiquarian Society, which received from him valuable German publications. His most important correspondent, however, was Bentley, for they had the same interests at heart. Ebeling was especially fond of Klopstock, and he sent Bentley nearly all his works.[6] Bentley, in turn, furnished Ebeling with materials for his history and geography of the United States, one volume of which is dedicated to Bentley. The friendship was thus one of mutual profit and pleasure.

Toward the end of the century Bentley and his friends became involved in the controversy over German orthodoxy in philosophy and theology. In their brilliant polemics they completely refuted the statements of Professors Tappan and Pearson of Harvard, Jedidiah Morse, and others whose knowledge of German was almost nonexistent. More important was the fact that the controversy made many Americans, for the first time, aware of what German culture had to offer.

A better known name among New Englanders who at this time demonstrated an enthusiastic interest in Germany was John Quincy Adams. He has already been mentioned in connection with his translation of Wieland's *Oberon*. In 1800 he traveled through Silesia and described his experiences in a series of letters to his brother.[7] Evidently he enjoyed his associations with the German people and felt sympathetic toward them. As ambassador to Russia Adams was able to increase his acquaintance with German literature, because the German influence was strong in St. Petersburg. He also purchased German books for his library. When Adams deposited his books at the Boston Athenaeum, Ticknor borrowed his friend's copy of *Werther* and, incidentally, never returned it.[8]

4. For an account of Ebeling's library which was given to Harvard in 1819 see p. 169.

5. Joel Barlow, Aaron Burr, Edward Everett, and Joseph Cogswell were only a few of the famous Americans who visited him.

6. Ebeling had known Klopstock intimately during the poet's last years and had collaborated with him on the German text of Händel's *Messiah*.

7. They were published in the weekly issues of the *Portfolio* in 1801, under the title *Journal of a Tour Through Silesia*.

8. Albert Bernhardt Faust edited the translation of Wieland's *Oberon* which John Quincy Adams began in 1799 (New York, F. S. Crofts, 1940). The catalogue of the John Adams Collection now in the Boston Public Library also lists Schiller's *Geschichte des Abfalls der vereinigten Niederlände von der Spanischen Regierung* (Leipzig, 1801).

Years later, on October 24, 1831, Adams wrote to Charles Follen, newly appointed Professor of German Literature at Harvard:

The perusal of your discourse has renewed the gratification with which I heard it, and my pleasure, both at the institution of the professorship of the German Language and Literature, and at the selection of the Professor. I am the more flattered, at the introduction of the names of Klopstock and Wieland into the list of eminent writers of various literature, because, on my mentioning to you, that I had noticed their omission, you observed, that Klopstock should have been included in your list, but expressed a doubt whether Wieland was entitled to the same honor.

Thirty years have passed away since a residence of four years at Berlin, and excursions into Saxony and Silesia, had given me an enthusiastic relish for German literature. At that time, Wieland was *there* I think decidedly the most popular of the German poets, and although there was in his genius neither the originality nor the deep pathos of Göthe, or Klopstock, or Schiller, there was something in the playfulness of his imagination, in the tenderness of his sensibility, in the sunny cheerfulness of his philosophy, and in the harmony of his versification, which, to me were inexpressibly delightful. . . .

As I took the liberty of naming to you two German poets, with whose works I was acquainted, I now take that of inquiring what are the writings of Richter and Tieck, which have given them celebrity. I have some knowledge of Voss, and Musaeus, and Auguste La Fontaine, and, above all, Bürger.[9]

With Adams in Russia was Alexander H. Everett, who served as his private secretary. As early as 1813 Everett wrote in the *General Repository and Review* that he considered German literature on a par with that of England and France.[1] Everett also underscored in this article the philological importance of German. Although French, Latin, and Greek, he wrote, may have enriched our language, it derived its strength and stamina from the Teutonic element. We should, therefore, carefully study this important part of the English tongue. In drama, he believed, the Germans had not only equalled the modern productions of France and England, but were already beginning to surpass them. To prove this assertion one merely had to mention the names of Goethe, Schiller, and Lessing. In conclusion, he denied that the German language was difficult to learn. Even if it were true, Everett said, it might be sufficient to quote the ancient saying, "Labor is the price that the Gods have affixed to the attainment of everything valuable."

These were rash statements to make at a time when most people did

9. C. Follen, *Works, 1,* 305–7.
1. *4* (July, 1813), 91ff.

not seem to realize that the Germans could boast of any literature besides Luther's Bible, but Everett did not stop here. While his brother Edward edited the *North American Review* (1820–24) and during his own editorship (1829–33) he contributed numerous articles on German literature, including criticisms of Madame de Staël and Schiller. Of the Schiller review, which appeared in April, 1823, Professor Goodnight says, "A large share of the credit for having rectified the former conception of Schiller,—that of a writer of turgid, incoherent and blasphemous extravagance under the name of drama, and of having established in its place the real Schiller is due to the two scholarly essays of A. H. Everett and George Bancroft." [2] In July, 1829, Alexander Everett published the important article "The History of Intellectual Philosophy" in which he discussed the theories of Kant, Fichte, Leibnitz, and Wolff.[3] He also wrote articles on German literature for the *Boston Quarterly Review,* the *United States Democratic Review,* the *Boston Miscellany,* and the *Southern Review.*

Another scholar who studied German literature early in the nineteenth century and whose influence may have been more important was Moses Stuart, Professor of Theology at Andover Seminary. When Stuart could find no teacher of German available, he refused to be thwarted. In two weeks' time he read by himself the Gospel of John in German, and through a friend he obtained Seiler's *Biblische Hermeneutik,* which introduced him to a wide range of German literature.[4] Years later in the September issue of the *Christian Review* for 1841 Stuart wrote of this struggle to learn German:

> Time was, when, for years together, I was almost alone in the study of German, in our country. There were indeed, and always have been, native Germans in some places, who of course pursued reading of this kind. There was here and there a solitary individual, who had been prompted by accident, or moved by curiosity, or led by peculiar circumstances, to the study of German. There were some at Boston and Cambridge, who had begun to make inquiries respecting it. But among all our Clergy, the deed was undone; and even the bare attempt to do it was regarded as a matter of idle curiosity, or as a kind of excrescence or monstrosity in respect to the body of sound and healthy literature.[5]

We must, therefore, credit Stuart for having extended the wealth of German scholarship in the field of Biblical and theological learning.

With the language mastered, Stuart began to collect German Bibli-

2. Goodnight, p. 98.
3. *North American Review, 29,* 67ff.
4. See E. A. Park, *A Discourse Delivered at the Funeral of Professor Moses Stuart* (Boston, Tappan and Whittemore, 1852), p. 27.
5. *6,* 454.

cal literature. In a short time he built up at the Andover Seminary one of the finest collections of its type. His colleagues' fears that these German studies would undermine Stuart's orthodoxy were not justified. Stuart, in fact, used his knowledge of German theology and philosophy to combat the Unitarianism of Doctor Channing.[6] Not only did he himself learn German to unlock this huge thesaurus of intellectual endeavor, but he urged his students to imitate him. Stuart suggested to Edward Everett as early as 1812 that he translate Herder's *Briefe das Studium der Theologie betreffend*. He said of it, "There is a vivacity, a beauty, an enchanting something, *je ne sais quoi,* which will please you, I am sure." [7] To Stuart also belongs the credit for having influenced Theodore Parker's study of German.[8]

One of Stuart's protégés, James Marsh (1794–1842), was equally influential in spreading the knowledge of German theology and philosophy. While still a theological student at Andover, he devoted much of his leisure time to the study of modern languages. On February 21, 1821, he wrote in his journal : "Of my progress in the German language, I have been more conscious than ever before, and begin to feel as if I had conquered it. On Saturday in the forenoon I read in the regular course of my studies about fifty pages, and read it well." [9] While at the seminary he also undertook to translate for publication Bellermann's work on the geography of the Scriptures, since an understanding of Biblical criticism demanded that book.[1]

His biographer Joseph Torrey stated that with the aid of Coleridge and Madame de Staël he began to consult Kant's *Critique of Pure Reason,* then a *terra incognita* to American scholars.[2] A few years later, in 1829 to be exact. Marsh republished Coleridge's *Aids to Reflection,* a work which was to have direct bearing on the Transcendentalists' knowledge of German philosophy.[3]

No doubt there were in the early decades of the century other isolated New England scholars of German literature besides Bentley, Adams,

6. Park, pp. 29–30.

7. O. W. Long, *Literary Pioneers* (Cambridge, Harvard University Press, 1935) pp. 63–4.

8. See letter of Dr. W. T. Harris quoted in *Report of the Commissioner of Education for the Year 1897–1898,* p. 613.

9. J. Torrey, *Memoir of Rev. James Marsh* (Boston, Crocker and Brothers, 1843), p. 37.

1. *Ibid.,* p. 56.

2. *Ibid.,* p. 43.

3. Marsh was recognized by both Coleridge and his nephew as the principal disciple of Coleridge in America. See C. F. Thwing, *The American and the German University* (New York, Macmillan, 1928), p. 204. He was also one of the first to translate Herder's works for publication in America. In 1833 appeared his edition of Herder's *Spirit of Hebrew Poetry,* which was popular with the Transcendentalists. See O. B. Frothingham, *Transcendentalism in New England* (New York, Putnam, 1876), p. 48.

A. H. Everett, Stuart, and Marsh.[4] The first evidence, however, of a group of men developing an interest in German culture can be found in the desire of American students to attend the universities of Germany rather than those of France and England. This fact may seem strange when one remembers that French literature had been popular in New England long before the American Revolution, but the reasons why Americans should have turned to German universities, and especially to Göttingen, for inspiration are obvious. First, able teachers were on the faculty; [5] second, methods of instruction were both wise and progressive; and third, Göttingen had one of the finest libraries in Europe. In contrast, French libraries were difficult to use; and although the French were famous for the clarity of their language and thinking, American students were less impressed by this quality than by the German accumulation of facts. The atheistic tendencies of the French Revolution also may have turned away Puritan New Englanders.

This new movement began in the years 1815 to 1820 when George Ticknor, Edward Everett, George Bancroft, and Joseph G. Cogswell decided to study at the University of Göttingen.[6] The embargo of continental Europe—an embargo which had taken different forms from 1793 to 1815—had now been lifted. During the previous quarter century few Americans had the opportunity to travel in Germany. It is true that there were notable exceptions. Joel Barlow lived in Hamburg in 1794–95. Joseph Buckminster, who brought back German books from Europe in 1807, had been studying German in preparation for his professorship in Biblical criticism at Harvard, but he died in 1812 soon after his appointment.[7] During these somewhat barren years another interest-

---

4. A typical and noteworthy example of such an isolated spirit is James Gates Percival (1795–1856), the forgotten American poet from New Haven, who maintained a passionate interest in German scholarship. He too never studied in Germany, but he imported vast numbers of German books and became, in his time, one of the most versatile students of philology in America. In fact, he was the proofreader for Noah Webster's *Dictionary* begun in 1827, and corresponded with George Ticknor about such matters. Through Ticknor, Percival also met Professor Follen at Harvard and discussed with him the study of Middle High German poetry, for which there was not even an adequate glossary. A full discussion of Percival's interest in German and a study of his countless translations of German poetry appears in the unpublished thesis, "James Gates Percival, a Pioneer Student of German Culture," by Frederick Lehnert, Yale University, 1934.

5. It was at Göttingen that Heeren lectured on history, the Grimms on philology, Otfried Müller and Carl F. Hermann on classics, Evald and Michaelis on Biblical and Oriental scholarship, and Blumenbach on natural history.

6. These men were not the first Americans to study at the University of Göttingen. Benjamin Smith Barton (1766–1815), a physician of Philadelphia, received a doctor's degree in 1799 from the university. See *Report of the Commissioner of Education for the Year 1897–1898*, p. 607.

7. See *Sermons of the Late Rev. J. S. Buckminster* (Boston, 1814), p. xxxii. Buckminster's library, sold in Boston in 1812, contained several maps, grammars, and dic-

ing American visitor to Germany, although not a New Englander, was Aaron Burr, who toured the European continent during 1809 and 1810, calling upon important scholars like Ebeling, Wieland, and Goethe.[8]

In the decade 1820–30 Motley, Calvert, William Emerson, and Longfellow followed the older men to Göttingen, thereby increasing the knowledge of German scholarship in this country.[9] Thomas W. Higginson, himself a Transcendentalist, said that these Americans who attended Göttingen took our whole educational system away from the English tradition, substituted German methods, and laid the foundation for non-English training not only in Boston but in America.[1] Ticknor's reforms in the system at Harvard, Everett's address on the "Objects of a University Education" based on the ideas of Humboldt, Fichte, and Schleiermacher, and Bancroft and Cogswell's experiments at the Round Hill School demonstrate this influence. These men also persuaded German political refugees to come to our shores and teach in American schools, a factor which was of utmost importance in the diffusion of German culture.[2] To trace the experiences of the Americans who studied at Göttingen is not one of the objects of this work. Orie W. Long has already studied the prominent figures in his book *Literary Pioneers*. Yet it is important to comment on the results of the movement, and show its influence on the Transcendentalists.

George Ticknor, like many of the Transcendentalists, first became acquainted with the German language and universities by reading Madame de Staël's work on Germany.[3] In addition to this source his friend, the Reverend Samuel C. Thacher, gave him an account of the superlative library at Göttingen. Ticknor stated in his letters that at first he could discover no other information on the subject, nor any one in Boston to teach him German.[4] At Jamaica Plain he finally found a

---

tionaries in German as well as numerous theological works by Germans like Michaelis and Zollikofer, and German editions of Latin and Greek classics (see *Catalogues of Private Libraries*, Boston Athenaeum).

8. *The Private Journal of Aaron Burr,* ed. M. L. Davis (New York, Harper, 1838), *I, 337*ff. and 386.

9. Between 1815 and 1850 several hundred American students attended German centers of learning, at first Göttingen and later Berlin, Halle, Leipzig, Bonn, and Heidelberg. One hundred and thirty-seven of the two hundred and twenty-five American students at German universities, became professors in American colleges. For a complete list of American students at Göttingen, see *Report of the Commissioner of Education for the Year 1897–1898,* pp. 610–11, and for additional statistics, see A. B. Faust, *The German Element in the United States* (New York, Steuben Society of America, 1927), p. 211.

1. *Atlantic Monthly, 79* (April, 1897), 490.

2. Among them were Charles Follen, Carl Beck, and Francis Lieber.

3. G. Ticknor, *Life, Letters, and Journals* (Boston, Houghton Mifflin, 1880), *I*, 11. Ticknor was to visit Madame de Staël in Paris and become a close friend and correspondent of Auguste de Staël, her eldest son.

4. As has been pointed out by Harold Jantz (p. 2) and Frank Ryder (*Ticknor's Werter,* Chapel Hill, North Carolina, 1948, p. xv), these statements of Ticknor on the conditions of German scholarship in Boston at that time merit examination. Other

native of Strasbourg, Dr. Brosius, who instructed him in German, but Brosius was not accurate in his pronunciation, and Ticknor could not find any books to correct his teacher's errors. His only aids were a Meidinger's grammar in French and German borrowed from Edward Everett and a German dictionary sent from New Hampshire. He finally obtained, through Mr. William S. Shaw's connivance, a copy of Goethe's *Werther* in German from John Quincy Adams' books.[5] Ticknor, therefore, got so far as to write a translation of *Werther* but no further.[6]

This translation of *Werther,* recently published by Frank G. Ryder, deserves comment. In a letter to Jefferson, October 14, 1815, Ticknor remarked that *Werther* was "known in English only by a miserable imitation of a garbled French translation made by someone who understood neither the languages." Why Ticknor with his Puritan and classical background should have been so fond of this work remains a mystery, but he was fond of it and he poured into it his creative inspiration. I should not go so far as Mr. Ryder, however, in saying that it was a misfortune for American letters when Ticknor did not publish the result of his labor, for although this translation increases our knowledge of Ticknor's interest in German, other versions of *Werther* were already popular, as is proven by the numerous printings in New England. Even if Ticknor did lavish upon it all his feeling for the beauties and dignity of the English tongue, the translation is far from perfect. As to verbal accuracy, it is, at times, actually inaccurate and pedestrian.

When Ticknor finally reached Germany, his journals and letters overflowed with praise for the culture that he found there. He considered the instruction completely satisfactory,[7] and was delighted with the library of 200,000 volumes where, unlike conditions in certain American college libraries, few restrictions were placed on the use of the books.[8] In Göttingen Ticknor's enthusiasm for German literature, already stimulated in America, found ample opportunity for growth. He wrote to C. S. Daveis of Portland on February 29, 1816: "Narrow as the circle is, and though the strictness of posterity will perhaps make it yet narrower, still I know of none in the modern languages—except our own—where one so interesting can be found as the circle of German

---

scholars had studied German. The Reverend William Bentley, for example, took lessons in pronunciation from Frederick Jordy, who advertised in the *Imperial Register* in 1800. It is true, however, that German books on the language and German instruction were certainly not common.

5. On going to Europe, Adams had deposited his library in the Athenaeum under Mr. Shaw's care.

6. Ticknor, *Life, Letters, and Journals, 1,* 12–13.

7. He wrote to Elisha Ticknor, November 5, 1815: "Even while I was struggling with the language, and of course was cut off from half the means and opportunities the University could afford,—even then the conviction was continually pressing upon me of the superiority of their instructions and modes of teaching. Now I know it." *Ibid.,* p. 79.

8. *Ibid.,* pp. 70–2.

literature. It has all the freshness and faithfulness of poetry of the early ages, when words were still the representatives of sensible objects, and simple, sensible feelings rather than of abstractions and generalities; and yet, having flourished so late, it is by no means wanting in modern refinement and regularity." [9]

We find a far more ardent defense in his letter to Edward T. Channing, November 16, 1816:

If anybody chooses to say the literature of Germany is poor, feeble, good for nothing, etc., I have no disposition to disturb him in his opinion,—*chacun à son goût*. He cannot enjoy what I can,—and I, on the other hand, no doubt, am incapable of some pleasures which he perceives. But when a man comes out like the author of a "Review of Goethe's Life," and says Schiller is the first genius Germany has produced, or, like yourself, that German poetry is obscure, artificial, etc., I am bold to say, with all due respect, the man knows nothing about the matter. Again, if a man says, "I am going to give an account of Goethe's life, as he himself represents it," and then draws a caricature of it, as is done by the Edinburgh Review, I say he is dishonest, without entering into the question whether the book is defensible. Or, if, like the author of the "Review of the Ancient German Poetry," he says, Bouterweck's book on this subject is indifferent, I reply, without inquiring whether the judgment be accidentally right or not, that the man is a scoundrel, for *every* fact and *every* opinion in his Review is pilfered from this very book, and he evidently knows nothing of the early history of German literature which he has not found in it. Yet this is the way the Germans are every day judged by foreign nations. Fortunately, however, the grounds of accusation are so different that all cannot be true, and their incoherence and inconsistency are the best possible testimony to the ignorance of the persons who make them. . . .

Perhaps you will ask what I mean by all this tirade against other people's mistakes. I mean to show you by foreign proof that the German literature is a peculiar national literature, which, like the miraculous creation of Deucalion, has sprung directly from their own soil, and is so intimately connected with their character, that it is very difficult for a stranger to understand it. A Frenchman, or indeed any one of the Roman nations, generally makes as bad work with it as Voltaire with Shakespeare, and for the same reasons; for it deals with a class of feelings and ideas which are entirely without the periphery of his conceptions. An Englishman, too, if he studies it at home only, generally succeeds about as well,—but show me the man who, like

9. *Ibid.,* p. 89.

Walter Scott, has studied it as it deserves, or, like Coleridge, has been in the country, and who has gone home and laughed at it. . . .

After all, however, you will come round upon me with the old question, "And what *are* your Germans, after all?" They are a people who, in forty years, have created to themselves a literature such as no other nation ever created in two centuries; and they are a people who, at this moment, have more mental activity than any other existing. I have no disposition to conceal that this literature has many faults, but if you had read Goethe's Tasso, or his Iphigenia, or his ballads, you would never have said their poetry lacks simplicity; or if you had read the tales of Musaeus, or Wieland's Oberon,—even in Sotheby,—or fifty other things, you would not have said "the Germans do not know how to tell stories." I am not at all disposed to conceal from you that this mental activity is in my opinion very often misdirected and unenlightened,—but, even when in error, you see that it is the dark gropings of Polyphemus round his cave, and that when such ponderous strength comes to light, it will leave no common monuments of its power and success behind it.[1]

Ticknor soon realized that his knowledge of German was useful to him for purposes other than the reading of German literature. He could not even study his Greek without depending entirely upon German commentaries and handbooks, and he told Elisha Ticknor that such German texts excelled anything found in English or even in Latin.[2] To Jefferson he wrote: "Within forty years the scholars of this country, I am persuaded, have done more toward the final understanding of the classicks, than all Europe had done during the century that preceded, not by imitating the minute and tedious accuracy of the Dutch commentators, but by reducing the whole study of antiquity to a philosophical system, in which one part assists to explain the other and all together form a harmonious whole." [3]

Ticknor also seized advantage of every opportunity to meet German authors of whom he had already heard in America. His interesting account of these visits in his journals and letters reflects the literature which was popular in New England at that time. Among these writers moved the Schlegel brothers, whose brilliance he idolized. When he met Friedrich Schlegel on March 29, 1817, at Frankfort, he praised him together with Luden of Jena as the only men whose conversation reminded him of "the genuine, hearty flow of English conversation."[4]

1. *Ibid.*, pp. 118–20.
2. *Ibid.*, p. 82.
3. Long, p. 23. In July, 1816, Ticknor sent Jefferson editions of Homer and Virgil by Heyne, of Aeschylus by Schultze, of Juvenal by Ruperti, and of Tacitus by Oberlin.
4. Ticknor, *Life, Letters, and Journals*, *1*, 122.

On April 14 he left his calling card with August W. Schlegel, and after this visit, decided to see him often if possible.[5] He paid a call on Voss at Heidelberg on April 2, where he discussed the vivacity and freshness of *Luise*, a work comparatively well known in this country. Of Voss himself Ticknor recorded that he was pleased with his neat appearance, "unlike most German men of letters."[6] When Ticknor came to Germany in 1835 and 1836, he spent many hours with Ludwig Tieck,[7] whose stories, poems, and satires were becoming household words to Americans during the 1830's.[8]

Ticknor's companion at the University of Göttingen was Edward Everett, who had been appointed Professor of Greek at Harvard, and had come to Germany to prepare himself under the supervision of German scholars. After a period of almost five years, two of which were spent in Göttingen, he returned to America infected with an ardent enthusiasm for German culture.[9] He also brought back with him a large collection of German books, later to form the nucleus of a German library at Harvard. Everett's enthusiasm for German literature was apparent in his letters to his family and friends. He wrote to Theodore Lyman on March 1, 1816, that if he really wished to gain a thorough knowledge of Greek and Latin, he would do well to spend six months studying the German language, which from the humblest grammar up to the highest commentary was for its store of critical aids as far beyond England, as England America. Denying that German was tediously prolix and dull, he styled such a criticism an absurd prejudice. In the German language he found "more manuals, abridgments, popular views, and every sort of device to make learning attractive and easy than in all the other European languages together," and even the accounts of English literature he considered superior to those written in English.[1]

Under Professor Eichhorn's supervision Everett read German literature such as Winckelmann's works, Schiller's poetry, and Voss's *Luise*. He was also attracted to Klopstock, whose *Messiah* he attempted to translate. In a letter to his brother, Everett suggested that they each translate ten books of this work, since he thought it "very easy."[2] In January, 1816, Everett reviewed Heeren's *Life of Christian Gottlob Heyne* in the *North American Review*, and in 1817 he demonstrated his

5. *Ibid.*, p. 127.

6. Ticknor visited him again in 1835, and found him still absorbed in his Sanscrit as well as in modern politics. *Ibid.*, p. 435.

7. He visited Tieck a number of times in the latter part of November, 1835, and again in January, 1836. For comments on Tieck see *ibid.*, pp. 457 and 473.

8. Even Hawthorne who was living at the Old Manse was reading them.

9. While traveling in England in 1818, he wrote home that Americans had more to gain from the German universities than from the English.

1. Long, p. 65.

2. *Ibid.*, p. 56.

familiarity with Goethe's works by criticizing *Dichtung und Wahrheit*.[3] Once more he pointed out the inadequate knowledge of Goethe in America, where the German savant had been known almost entirely by a poor translation of *Werther* and by the work of Madame de Staël. "One could wish," Everett wrote, "that such works, as that before us, might be read in America, were it only to cross the race of English and French literature, which has been propagated so long among us, that it is in danger of running out." [4] Unlike preceding critics, Everett singled out *Faust* as Goethe's masterpiece. He apologized for the mangled version of the passages which appeared in Madame de Staël's work, and blamed the French language which he said was as inadequate to render the German of *Faust*, as the dialect of our Indians had been to render the Bible. Although he did not give his *imprimatur* to the complete work, he stated boldly that there were flights and touches not easily matched since Shakespeare.[5]

During the years 1819 to 1824 Everett found his knowledge of German scholarship extremely useful to him as Eliot Professor of Greek at Harvard. For the benefit of his students, he translated Buttmann's *Greek Grammar* from the German, and edited a Greek reader based on one by C. F. Jacobs. The best proof of the effect which Everett's German background had on his students is found in Emerson's writings. "Germany," Emerson commented, "had created criticism in vain for us until 1820, when Edward Everett returned from his five years in Europe, and brought to Cambridge his rich results. . . . He made us for

3. *North American Review, 4* (January, 1817), 217ff. This review has been called the first significant paper on Goethe in any American journal. See Long, p. 68.

4. *North American Review, 4* (January, 1817), 261–2.

5. Both Ticknor and Everett visited Goethe, and the accounts of these visits are extremely interesting in their variations. Everett was more critical of Goethe than was Ticknor. He wrote to his brother: "The next morning we sent our letters, and asked at what time we should wait upon him, and were told at eleven. At the appointed time we went. He was very stiff and cold, not to say gauche and awkward. . . . He was oppressed at feeling that we were gazing at him, looked restlessly out of the window, at which he sat, and talked low and anxiously. . . . I forgot to say that the day after our call on G., George sent him Byron's "Siege of Corinth," which had been mentioned in the interview, of which he did not even acknowledge the receipt. And thus ended our introduction to Goethe." See Long, p. 69.

Ticknor wrote much more enthusiastically in his Journal dated Weimar, October 25: "We sent our letters to Goethe this morning, and he returned for answer the message that he would be happy to see us at eleven o'clock. We went punctually, and he was ready to receive us. . . . Taken together, his person is not only respectable, but imposing. In his manners, he is simple. He received us without ceremony, but with care and elegance, and made no German compliments. The conversation of course, rested in his hands, and was various. . . . Once his genius kindled, and in spite of himself he grew almost fervent as he deplored the want of extemporary eloquence in Germany. . . . We remained with him nearly an hour, and when we came away he accompanied us as far as the parlor door with the same simplicity with which he received us, without any German congratulations." See Ticknor, *Life, Letters, and Journals, 1,* 113–14.

the first time acquainted with Wolff's theory of the Homeric writings, with the criticism of Heyne." [6]

Of the American students who studied at Göttingen, perhaps the one who had the greatest knowledge of German literature was George Bancroft. After graduation from Harvard in 1817 he became a roving student at Göttingen, Heidelberg, and Berlin.[7] Since it was believed that he might train himself both for the ministry and for an instructorship at Harvard, President Kirkland gave the following information to Professor Eichhorn: "They [the trustees] wish him to attend especially to philology, the ancient languages and Oriental literature that he may thus be qualified to pursue theological studies to the greatest benefit, to give instruction as any opening may occur and invite, and become an accomplished philologian and biblical critic, able to expound and defend the Revelation of God." [8]

His program at Göttingen was very similar to Ticknor's and Everett's, since he studied under the same professors: Benecke, Eichhorn, Planck, Heeren, Blumenbach, and Dissen. After receiving his degree of Doctor of Philosophy in 1820, he decided to continue his studies at Berlin, where he met Schleiermacher, Wilhelm von Humboldt, Savigny, Lappenberg, and Varnhagen von Ense. Then he went to Heidelberg to study under Schlosser.

Having made the acquaintance of German literature and having met many of its leading thinkers and writers, including Goethe,[9] Bancroft

6. See R. W. Emerson, "Historic Notes of Life and Letters in New England," *Works, 10*, 312–16. Emerson also attended Ticknor's lectures at Harvard. See Emerson MS Journal, *The Wide World*, No. 2, p. 23.

7. Professor Sidney Willard, self-taught and with no notion of German pronunciation, gave Bancroft his first knowledge of German. See Lowell's address before the Modern Language Association in 1890, *Publications of the Modern Language Association, 5,* 5.

8. President Kirkland recognized Bancroft's brilliant record as a student and chose him to study at a German university in preparation for an eventual berth on the college board. Bancroft received a traveling scholarship of seven hundred dollars per year for three years. See Bancroft's letter to President Eliot of Harvard, July 4, 1871, quoted in the *Report of the Commissioner of Education for the Year 1897–1898*, p. 615. For letter quoted above see M. A. DeWolfe Howe, *The Life and Letters of George Bancroft* (New York, Scribner, 1908), *1*, 33.

9. When Bancroft was in Jena on October 12, 1819, he visited Goethe, and recorded his impressions in his diary. He found Goethe talkative, and eager to speak of America, a topic about which he seemed to think he was quite well acquainted. As in his conversation with Ticknor and Everett, Goethe praised Byron in the highest terms, declaring himself one of a large party in Germany who admired him greatly. Goethe also offered Bancroft a letter allowing the young American to examine his private library at Weimar. *Ibid.*, pp. 67–8.

On March 7, 1821, Bancroft again visited Goethe in Weimar and remained a half hour with him. He wrote in his diary: "I felt the vast difference between [Goethe] and the many scholars whom I have lately seen. Goethe has the ease of a gentleman, speaks with liveliness and energy, but does not seem to take any longer a lively interest in the affairs of the world." Bancroft tried to bring him to talk of the German writers such as Tieck and the Schlegels, but Goethe remained silent. He was always anxious to talk

soon gave up the idea of studying for the ministry. In a letter to President Kirkland, he wrote:

I add one word about German Theology. I have nothing to do with it, except so far as it is merely *critical*. Of their infidel systems I hear not a word; and I trust I have been too long under your eye, and too long a member of the Theological Institution under your inspection to be in danger of being led away from the religion of my Fathers. I have too much love and esteem for my friends at home, and too little for those, who can trifle with the hopes of thousands, to suffer myself to be overpowered by a jest or a sophism. I say this explicitly, because before I left home I heard frequently expressed fears, lest I should join the German school.[1]

On August 1, 1819, he said to Edward Everett: " 'Tis out of the question to expect, that in any American University whatsoever the station of Professor of theology would be offered me or anyone else, who had gotten his theology in Germany." [2] Yet less than six weeks before, on June 27, 1819, he had "the boldness in daring" to deliver a sermon in the German language. To his own amazement the audience was uncommonly attentive, and on leaving the pulpit, he was overwhelmed with congratulations.[3]

Bancroft's comments on German literature, especially his preference for Schiller rather than Goethe, are first found in his diary and letters written while he was still a student at Göttingen. Like many of the Transcendentalists, Bancroft was hindered from expressing an impartial opinion, because he placed too much emphasis on the moral and too little on the aesthetic qualities of German literature.[4] Goethe, of course, shocked him. He wrote in his diary: "I am only more and more astonished at the indecency and immorality of the latter [Goethe]. He appears to prefer to represent vice as lovely and exciting sympathy, than virtue, and would rather take for his heroine a prostitute or a profligate, than

---

of Byron, however, with his American and English acquaintances. *Ibid.*, pp. 97–8. On the whole, both of these meetings with Goethe passed pleasantly, and contrast sharply with the bitter remarks which Bancroft was to make later about Goethe's writings.

1. Howe, *1*, 55.
2. *Ibid.*, p. 65.
3. *Ibid.*, p. 62.
4. This meticulous concern with purity was nothing innate in his character, but rather was the result of continual preaching by his Puritan elders in New England. After three years in Europe Bancroft had the good sense to express himself on this subject in the following letter to Andrews Norton: "You are right to warn me against the vice of Europe. Yet as far as I have been in the world, I find one place nearly as bad as another. I mean by that; there are everywhere the means of indulgence offered to the dissolute. The number of the dissolute is of course unequal. But after all, is Amsterdam worse than Hamburgh, or is Paris worse than Amsterdam? And can Naples exceed Paris? He that will be vicious can be so in any part of Europe. Weimar is the only place I know of, worthy of commemoration for its staid morality." *Ibid.*, p. 111.

give birth to that purity of thought and loftiness of soul, which it is the peculiar duty of the poet to raise, by connecting his inventions with the actions of heroes, and embodying in verse the merits of the benefactors of mankind." [5] Even more captious was this statement: "I do not love Goethe. He is too dirty, too bestial in his conceptions. There is nothing of a noble, high, enthusiastic soul in him. His genius is admirable. His knowledge of life wonderful. But the whole is spoilt by the immorality of his writings, by the vulgarity of his characters. It may be, that all this happens in the world, but at any rate, this remains a blot on his fame, which all the waters of the ocean cannot make white and which justify in his censures a moral man, who cannot find in him a single work of genius." [6]

Back in America, Bancroft published these comments in a series of articles and translations appearing in the *North American Review* and other periodicals.[7] Perhaps the most famous was his criticism of *Schiller's Minor Poems* in the *North American Review,* October, 1823. He found him "no less distinguished for his genius and the purity of his taste, than for the perfection of his style." He emphasized the fact that Schiller never inclined to the demoralizing principles which distinguished many of his poetical contemporaries. On the contrary, he preserved the purest character throughout all his writings, and never hesitated to show reverence for the sanctity of religion and the domestic affections. This, he felt, was no small praise in a poet who was almost contemporary with Wieland and Voltaire, and who lived in a period when unexampled popularity was obtained by writers who knew how to join licentiousness and profaneness to wit. Bancroft then drew the inevitable contrast between Goethe and Schiller. Goethe, he said, "reflects in his problems the feelings of others; Schiller felt deeply himself, and knew how to embody his feelings in verse. . . . The person of Goethe is never seen through his verse; that of Schiller presents itself

5. *Ibid.,* p. 38.

6. Long, pp. 116–17. The fact that Bancroft was pompous in his display of morality is evident in many of his letters on German society. One is apt to smile today when one reads that Bancroft was shocked to see the German ladies sew, knit, or waltz on Sunday evening or drink rum in their tea. See Howe, *1,* 52. He wrote to Andrews Norton: "I would give you a specimen or two of the high language of Germany, if it did not sound so flatly like blasphemy or vulgarity in English. Nay, then, I will write you some of them in the order of rank, and in German. *Ach, Gott,*—used chiefly by very young girls, and very old women; *ach, der Herr Gott; ach, allmächtiger Gott; ach, du lieber Gott; Gott im Himmel; Jesus—ach, der Herr Jesus,* or by contraction, *ach, du Herr Je— Gott, Gott, Gott, Gott.* These are some of the expressions under which the good and pious ladies of Göttingen express their feelings. The last, however, I never heard but once, and then from a Professor; the rest are on the tongue of every maiden or wife in Göttingen." See Howe, *1,* 52–3.

7. Later they were slightly revised and published in his volume, *Literary and Historical Miscellanies* (New York, Harper, 1855), pp. 103–246.

constantly. . . . We may learn from Goethe what the world is; but Schiller teaches us what it should be."

In October, 1824, his essay "The Life and Genius of Goethe" appeared in the same magazine. This article made a claim for German literature which is worth comparing with Alexander Everett's [8] written a dozen years before:

> The most eminent German writers have often been misunderstood, and their claims to admiration unjustly represented. The time is yet remembered, when German sentiment and German metaphysics were common expressions of a disdainful criticism, and when the German poetry, though allowed to be original and various, was also proscribed as unnatural and exaggerated. If the principles of reciprocity and mutual justice are to be applied in the world of letters, there is no nation, which so signally merits a fair and impartial judgment from foreigners. In poetry, no less than in matters of science, they have been careful to become familiar with the best productions of the human mind, whatever may have been their origin, and by means of excellent translations they have incorporated them into their own literature. . . .
>
> A foreign literature will seldom be in strict harmony with the taste and associations acquired at home; but this, far from being any objection to its excellence, confers on it an additional claim to attention. . . . The literature of each nation is national, and the true critic must endeavor to regard it from the same point of view with the nation, on which it was designed to produce an effect. The whole sphere of the fine arts becomes changed by differences of climate, of situation, of national character. It is the same as to each particular effort; its purpose must be known before its merit can be estimated.
>
> If on first acquaintance it [the literature of Germany] offend, or seem strange and unnatural, this is nothing more than might have been expected; for the culture, and consequently the productions of the Germans, have much that is original and peculiar; and every peculiarity, both in the forms and in the subjects of their works, only makes them more worthy of respect.[9]

Bancroft voiced quite a different opinion of Goethe himself from the earlier remarks in his journal and letters.[1] Now he found him "the most national poet of the Germans, the most fit representative of their litera-

---

8. See the *General Repository and Review,* 4 (July, 1813), 91.

9. *19* (October, 1824), 303–5.

1. In spite of this praise, Bancroft's criticism of Goethe became increasingly hostile. In 1839 his review in the *Christian Examiner* of Dwight's *Select Minor Poems from the German of Goethe and Schiller* contained a bitter attack on Goethe's character, and accused him of having "no philosophy, no creed, no principles."

ture, and, more nearly than any other, the universal favorite of his countrymen." He went on to say:

> The works of Goethe are not without lessons of practical morality. Though he makes no boasts of being himself a religious man, he acknowledges religion to be essentially the best foundation of a good character and considers cooperation with others in works of practical utility, and in the execution of just and righteous designs, the safest and happiest course. He has also drawn many exquisite and elevating pictures of female excellence, has illustrated the superiority of domestic life, and has given the noblest encomiums to that sex, which knows how to establish order and economy, to feel, and to endure. "Ye call women fickle," says he, "ye err; she but roams in search of a steadfast man." [2]

When Goethe received a copy of this essay from George Calvert, he sent a letter of thanks to Bancroft, saying, "This essay has a good effect upon everybody: so much intellect and insight, joined with a youthfully cheerful enjoyment in writing, excites a certain sympathetic, pleasant feeling." [3]

During the next decade Bancroft's articles on German literature became so well known that already in February, 1824, Jared Sparks wrote to Bancroft: "Some of the old school here have expressed to me their apprehensions since your last article, that the North American is becoming too partial to the Germans, at the expense of our worthy brethren the English." [4] Sparks asked Bancroft to write the article on Herder which appeared in the issue of January, 1825.[5] In July, 1826, Bancroft wrote an essay on Frederick Augustus Wolf,[6] and in June, 1830, he reviewed William Taylor's *Historic Survey of German Poetry,* which he censured as "a wanton and officious exhibition of his indifference to religion." He did not approve of Taylor's flattering comments on the works of Bürger, Wieland, and Kotzebue. Wieland's works, Bancroft said, showed "neither a wise, practical philosophy of life, nor the proof of poetic genius. Strike from literature the entire work of Wieland, and nothing would be lost to the world." Kotzebue's plays he called "ludicrously extravagant . . . a repertory of moral curiosities, a museum of moral monsters," in which the characters were "neither Christian, pagan nor men." [7]

We should also mention Bancroft's various guides to the study of

2. *19* (October, 1824), 324.

3. Howe, *1*, 182.

4. *Correspondence of George Bancroft and Jared Sparks, 1823–1832* (Northampton, Massachusetts, 1917), p. 73.

5. It may be the first account of Herder to appear in an American periodical.

6. *North American Review, 23*, 146.

7. *American Quarterly Review, 7*, 436–49.

the classics. In 1824 when his version of Heeren's *Reflections on the Politics of Ancient Greece* appeared, Everett wrote of it in the *North American Review:* "Mr. Bancroft deserves the public thanks for translating this volume. . . . This translation implies a command, not only of the German language, such as few possess, but an accomplishment of still greater value, a good knowledge of the English tongue." [8] From the German, Bancroft translated Ch. F. Jacobs' *Latin Reader* (1825), C. G. Zumpt's *Latin Grammar* (1829), and adapted for English use the German edition of Cornelius Nepos (1835). Of far greater importance was his experiment with the Round Hill School, a project stemming directly from his observations in Germany.[9]

Another New England scholar who studied at Göttingen was Joseph Green Cogswell. After having gone to Europe in November, 1826, as tutor to Augustus Thorndike, Cogswell joined Ticknor and Everett at Göttingen. Over thirty at that time, he did not feel entirely at home among his younger contemporaries.[1] But it was not long before he succumbed so completely to the charm of Germany that during a vacation in Rome he wrote to a friend: "Italy is a tame country, to one who had known the delights of Germany: yes, life to me in this supposed paradise . . . is weariness compared with the vigor I felt and the spirits I had when leaping from cliff to cliff amid German clouds." [2]

At the suggestion of Ticknor, he decided to study library classification under the supervision of Professor Benecke. Since Göttingen had at that time one of the finest libraries in Europe, not only from the point of view of its collection but also because of its organization and administration, Cogswell could not have chosen a better place for bibliographical training. He put this knowledge to use later when he organized the Astor Library in New York.

Like his friends, Ticknor and Everett, Cogswell toured various parts of Germany, meeting many German celebrities. He went to Weimar in 1817 for the sole purpose of seeing Goethe, and when he found that this famous man was absent on a visit to Jena, he pursued him to obtain an audience. Cogswell's American friends had led him to expect a "most repulsive reception." When, on the contrary, he received quite differ-

8. *18* (April, 1824), 406.
9. For a discussion of the Round Hill experiment see pp. 40–2.
1. He wrote to his friend, Charles S. Daveis, February 16, 1817: "When I saw myself, fitted out in the style of a German student, with a large portfolio under my arm, trudging off to my lesson, with the regularity and punctuality of a school boy who fears the birch, it seemed that I must have gone back several years in life. At first I knew not how to reconcile myself to the situation of another period of pupilage, but habit effects anything. I soon made my tasks, construed my German and submitted to correction, with as much docility as if I had never known what it was to be myself a teacher and a governor." See A. E. Ticknor, *Life of Joseph Green Cogswell as Sketched in His Letters* (Cambridge, Riverside Press, 1874), p. 51.
2. *Ibid.*, p. 77.

ent treatment, he felt not a little flattered. Their common passion for mineralogy also gave them a far closer tie than that which existed between Goethe and any of the other American visitors.[3] At this time Goethe and Cogswell began to correspond concerning the gift of Goethe's works to the Harvard College library.[4] In 1819 Cogswell made two more visits to Goethe, one at Weimar on May 10 [5] and the other at Jena on August 17.[6]

Upon his return to America in 1821 Cogswell was appointed librarian at Harvard and professor of mineralogy and geology. Yet although progressive educators like Ticknor praised Cogswell's innovations in reorganizing the Harvard library along the lines of the Göttingen library, the overseers were only lukewarm toward his efforts.[7] Disgusted with their conservative attitude, Cogswell decided in 1823 to join his former pupil and intimate friend, George Bancroft, in the educational experiment at Round Hill.

Bancroft, who had not been successful as a tutor at Harvard, desired to experiment with a school where, unharassed by conservative superiors, he could utilize the knowledge of education he had acquired in Germany. According to Bancroft's correspondence, as early as August 1, 1819, he was projecting such a school. He wrote to Edward Everett from Göttingen:

3. Cogswell described this visit in a letter to C. S. Daveis: "I sent him my letters of introduction, with a note, asking when he would allow me to wait upon him. . . . Soon after being introduced to him, with the politeness of a real gentleman, he turned the conversation to America, and spoke of its hopes and promises, in a manner that showed it had been the subject of his inquiries, and made juster and more rational observations, upon its literary pretensions and character, than I ever heard from any man in Europe. We talked, also, of English and German literature. I told him of the interest we were now taking in the latter, and found a very convenient opportunity to introduce a few words of compliment to himself, which was the least return I could make for his civility." *Ibid.*, pp. 56–7.

4. See pp. 169–70.

5. Of the May 10 visit Cogswell wrote to Ticknor: "He was not merely gracious, but affectionate and playful even,—but he is breaking, and will never do much more to increase his fame. I spent all my time in Weimar with him, which was one evening only: at supper he was unusually gay. . . . We sat till midnight, and of course you will conclude he must have been in glee, as such things are not often done in Germany. . . . He was enthusiastic in his praises of Byron, pronounced him the greatest and the only living poet, which was no small gratification to me, from its coincidence with my own opinion." *Ibid.*, pp. 97–8.

6. He wrote to Mrs. Prescott of the August 17 visit: "They say in Germany that he is proud and has no heart, but it has ever been my good fortune to see him when he showed none of his pride, and to be received by him as if he had a heart, and a feeling one too." *Ibid.*, p. 104.

7. Ticknor wrote in April, 1822: "Cogswell is doing much good in the library, reforming it utterly." In February, 1823, however, he added: "Cogswell has put the library in perfect order, and is now finishing his catalogue of it, but the corporation neither comprehend what he has done, nor respect him enough for his great disinterested labor." *Ibid.*, pp. 133–5.

Several Gentlemen in Boston are desirous, I should become acquainted with the German Schulwesen, and on coming home set up a high school, on the European plan. I hardly know what to say to this. The labour of a school is nothing alluring; but it must be confessed, this would be the way of doing most good. A school might be established, and then instructors sent for from Germany. I would not wish, however, to give many years of my own life to an immediate connection with it. I am now between eighteen and nineteen years old, and before I am two and twenty shall probably be in America. I should be too young to begin anything, that would decide my destiny for life, and could perhaps for five years do nought better than attempt to establish a learned school.[8]

He expressed his continued admiration of the Prussian school system in a letter to President Kirkland, November 5, 1820:

I need not say, how fine the schools of Prussia are; they are acknowledged to be the finest in Germany. Here in Berlin a great many new ideas are going into application; and the indistinct forebodings of Pestalozzi, and the eloquent discourses of Fichte have not been without lasting fruits. I need not assure you how happy I am in having an opportunity of studying the science of education in a city, where it has been the subject of so much discussion and where the Government have done so much, have done everything they could do, to realize the vast advantages about to result from the reform in the institutions of instruction. No Government knows so well how to create Universities and high schools as the Prussian. The new Academy at Bonn rivals already the oldest Universities.[9]

Both Bancroft and Cogswell, who had visited the schools of Pestalozzi at Yverdon and Fellenberg at Hofwyl, were impressed by the success of these innovators in methods of education.[1] Among the shocking innovations were companionship and individual attention given to each pupil by the teacher. Bancroft and Cogswell also had other aims. They wished to give instruction in modern languages, especially German,[2] to stress

8. Howe, *1*, 65–6.
9. *Ibid.*, p. 90.
1. Many years later, in July, 1838, Cogswell wrote in the *New York Review* that Germany was the only country where the science of education had been thoroughly and faithfully carried into practice. Of all modern languages, he said, German should receive the most attention, since although French may be of more worldly value, a single shelf of German literature was more worth to the scholar than a whole French library. See *3*, 149–94.
2. In the Prospectus for the Round Hill School was this statement on the teaching of German: "Its value is now recognized, and while we cannot promise to teach it to all our pupils, those who are distinguished for the faculties requisite for acquiring lan-

physical as well as mental education, and to abolish fear and the rod. To develop the student's critical powers was the goal rather than the parroting of facts. Finally, a new importance given to physical culture introduced into the curriculum skating, fencing, riding, and swimming, along with sketching, model farming, and house building. Cogswell and the boys indulged in many of these activities during vacation trips made in the typical German fashion.

In the years 1823 to 1831 two hundred ninety-three pupils from nineteen states and four foreign countries came to Round Hill.[3] Such distinguished persons as Lafayette and Duke Bernard of Saxe-Weimar visited the school.[4] Although unsuccessful from a financial point of view, the Round Hill experiment remains one of the earliest and most important attempts to improve the antiquated methods of education prevalent at the time. It also forecast the various educational experiments by Bronson Alcott, the Brook Farmers, Elizabeth Peabody, and other Transcendentalists.

A slightly younger group including John Lothrop Motley, Henry E. Dwight, William Emerson, George Calvert, and Henry W. Longfellow soon followed these pioneers in early German scholarship. As these people were closer contemporaries with the Transcendentalists, we should take into account the extent of their interest in German culture.

Inspired by the instruction of Charles Follen, John Lothrop Motley turned to Germany to complete his education. While still a senior at Harvard, he composed a brilliant essay on "The Genius and Character of Goethe," which delighted both his professors and fellow-students. Motley's former teacher, Cogswell, sent a copy of it to Goethe's daughter-in-law, Ottilie, who was rumored to have said upon reading it, "I wish to see the first book that young man will write." [5] Later when Motley was cordially received by Ottilie in Weimar, his greatest regret was that he had not come to Germany while Goethe was still alive.

Unlike his predecessors, Motley was not impressed by Göttingen. Most of the professors who had bequeathed to the University its great name were either dead or inactive. The town itself he found excessively dull.[6]

---

guages, must not be left without the possession of this, which will introduce them to so much good literature, accurate thought and profound erudition." See p. 14.

3. In New Haven a gymnasium conducted by Henry E. and Sereno Dwight existed from 1829 to 1831, and also stressed German methods of instruction.

4. Among the teachers at Round Hill were the two famous German scholars, Carl Beck and Charles Follen, of whom we shall have more to say later. Carl Beck taught Latin and established at Round Hill the first indoor gymnasium in this country. Follen, through Ticknor's influence, was soon transferred to Harvard.

5. O. W. Holmes, *John Lothrop Motley, A Memoir* (London, Osgood, 1878), p. 15. In the Speck Collection at Yale University one can still see Motley's *Commonplace Book* in which is to be found most of the material for his essay on Goethe.

6. G. W. Curtis, ed., *The Correspondence of John Lothrop Motley* (New York, Harper, 1889), *1*, 25.

He was enthusiastic, however, about one literary figure in Germany, Ludwig Tieck, whom he had met in Dresden. He wrote of him to his mother:

> I do not know if many of Tieck's works have been translated into English. If they have, you will get them at the Athenaeum. Inquire for "Fantasas" or "Puss in Boots" or the "World Upside down," or Tieck's novels (which last are a set of exquisite little tales, novels in the original meaning of the word), full of old German legends and superstitions, and the authorship of which will entitle him to the title of German "Boccaccio." The other works are the old nursery tales of "Fortunatus," "Puss in Boots," "Blue Beard," etc., etc., done into plays (not for the stage), and as full of playful and sharp satire, poetry and plain sense as they can hold. If they have not been translated we shall have a chance of reading them together one of these days. I was invited by Tieck to tea on Sunday evening, when there was a small party. He is at present just about finishing his translation of Shakespeare (in company with Schlegel), and is in the habit of reading a play aloud to a party of select auditors. I did not hear him, and rather regret it, because he seems to be rather vain of his elocution. . . . His conversation was like his books, playful, full of *bonhomie,* good-natured sort of satire, and perhaps a little childish vanity.[7]

While Margaret Fuller, John Dwight, and others in the Transcendental group were publishing translations and reviews of Goethe's works, Motley wrote two articles presenting the German writer in a sympathetic light. In a review of *Aus Meinem Leben, Dichtung und Wahrheit,* which appeared in the *New York Review,*[8] he denied the charge of egotism so prevalent in American and English criticism of Goethe, and called it a rather novel accusation against an autobiography. Goethe, he said, "has not only given us a most interesting, detailed, and vivid history of his own inner and outer development—a history written in old age, yet possessing all the freshness, the vivacity, the naïveté of a child's narrative, but his work is a picture of the age. . . . And if the author is himself the central point around which all seem to revolve, this is in conformity with the idea of an autobiography, and is necessary to unity of design."

Immorality in Goethe's writings was the second charge he tried to combat. If this charge rested on the lack of a distinct moral aim, he found Goethe fully justified on the ground that morals and aesthetics constitute two distinct provinces. "A work of art is perfect," he said, "when

---

7. *Ibid.,* pp. 35–6. Another American outside the scope of this study, but one who had most interesting connections with the Tieck circle in Dresden, was Washington Irving. See Stanley Williams, *Life of Washington Irving* (New York, Oxford University Press, 1935), *1*, 215–54.

8. *3* (October, 1838), 397.

it is perfectly conformed to the rules of art. With the laws of morality it has nothing to do, except so far as they are implied in those of art. It is absurd to demand of an artist that his work should inculcate a moral."

Just as Motley defended Goethe, another young New Englander, Henry Edwin Dwight (1797–1832), son of the famous president of Yale, Timothy Dwight, was defending Schiller's works against the usual judgment based upon an imperfect knowledge.[9] In 1829 Americans knew Schiller only by Coleridge's matchless translation of *Wallenstein* and by his play *Die Räuber,* which, written at the age of seventeen, should have been considered merely as a juvenile effort when compared with the productions of his manhood. Americans, who had not read the other works of Schiller, regarded his mind as a blending of all that was wild and extravagant. In Germany, Dwight pointed out, Schiller had created a national drama, and in a country, too, where Shakespeare was as much read and admired as in England and the United States.[1]

A second topic of prime importance which Dwight discussed in his book *Travels in the North of Germany* was the state of the German universities and their libraries. The *North American Review,* numbering among its contributors Everett, Bancroft, and Hedge, extolled these remarks, and confessed to the deficiency of our own university libraries. Not so the *Christian Spectator* of New Haven, whose editor felt that Dwight's criticism had been aimed directly at Yale. One could hardly find a better example of a prejudiced point of view than in the following excerpt from the *Spectator:*

> Mr. Dwight has occasionally introduced comparisons between the German universities, and those of his own country, much to the advantage of the former. . . .
>
> The first great defect of our literary institutions, upon which Mr. Dwight comments at large, is the smallness of their libraries. In this respect, our highest seminaries, when brought into comparison with those of Europe, certainly appear to great disadvantage. . . . We agree with Mr. Dwight as to the importance of books in an institu-

9. After studying at Yale and at Andover, where he was exposed to a German influence under the instruction of Professor Marsh, Dwight followed the footsteps of the Americans already discussed and went to Göttingen, where he remained from 1824 to 1828. Like the others, he combined his studies with trips through Germany, which he recorded and published under the title *Travels in the North of Germany* (New York, Carvill, 1829).

1. Dwight was not wrong in assuming that Schiller was still known mainly by his most youthful productions such as *Die Räuber,* although Madame de Staël had devoted seventy pages to his life and works in *De l'Allemagne.* The first American reprint of Coleridge's translation of *Die Piccolomini* and *Wallensteins Tod* did not appear until 1831, when *The Poetical Works of Coleridge, Shelley, and Keats* were published in Philadelphia.

tion where the arts and sciences are to be taught on a liberal scale; and have, perhaps, had occasion to lament, hardly less frequently than himself, the deficiencies of the libraries to which we have had access. But allowing our great inferiority in the number of books, we see no reason for believing, that we are of course inferior, in the same proportion, in every other respect. . . .

Mr. Dwight shows no backwardness to do full justice to foreign universities, in respect to their libraries, but in his references to the libraries of the institutions of his own country, we think he hardly allows them their due. This is at least the case so far as our own knowledge extends. "Almost one hundred and fifty years ago," says Mr. Dwight, "the library of Yale College was founded: there are now eight thousand volumes." Yale College library has not yet been founded one hundred and thirty years, and the number of volumes it contains is nearer nine thousand than eight; but these mistakes are not very important. . . .

But it seems our libraries are not only small, but not sufficiently accessible. . . . If this is true, it is an evil, which ought to be remedied; but so far as we are acquainted with the facts, no such state of things exists in the United States. . . . Besides, we have it from good authority, that the instructors in Yale College entertain the opinion, that miscellaneous reading among undergraduates is not much to be encouraged. They go even so far as to say, that according to their experience the knowledge of this class of students is generally in an inverse ratio to the number of volumes which they take from the library;—with the exception of a very limited number of books, connected immediately with the course of their studies. . . . They believe, that students may see the backs of many books without knowing much of their contents, and read title-pages throughout their whole course without increasing their wisdom. But however this may be, the complaint of illiberality in the management of our public libraries, so far as Yale College is concerned, is wholly unsupported by facts; and we have reason to believe, that Mr. Dwight has as little ground for his unfavorable representations in respect to other similar establishments of the country.[2]

With Dwight at Göttingen was William Emerson, brother of Ralph Waldo Emerson. William, like Dwight, visited Goethe in 1824 and described the experience in his journal. Although the account is rather long, it should be quoted in its entirety, since William may have influenced Ralph Waldo Emerson's interest in German culture:

We soon left Erfurt for Weimar, and I must forget all the scenery, to hurry forward to that, which rendered this an ever memorable day

2. *1* (December, 1829), 638ff.

to me. As I felt much at a loss for time, in arranging my journey from Göttingen, nothing but the hope of seeing Göthe would have induced me to take this circular route. I knew that he was very seldom visible to strangers, but resolved to hazard the attempt. We arrived in the pleasant town of Weimar at noon, and I immediately repaired to his house, and sent up my card, on which I had previously added "Boston, N. America" to my name. He sent me word that he was then surrounded with company, but if I would call at 4, he would see me. It may be supposed, that I did not forget the appointment. I was shown into a room, that was filled with works of art. A huge bust of Minerva was placed over one of the doors. A large case with books, which from their great size, must have been drawings, stood in one corner. Göthe, the gentle and venerable poet, entered almost immediately. I was so struck with the difference between him who came into the room, and the formidable portrait that is commonly to be seen of this great man, that I almost expected to see another person behind him. His address and manner were perfectly simple and unconstrained. After finding out my profession, he led the conversation immediately upon the state of religion in the U. S. and afterwards upon the state and hopes of our country in general. His tone became gradually that of an instructor, and yet it ceased not to be unassuming, but all was uttered quietly, as a mere private opinion. He said he thought we had nothing to do with the different systems of philosophy, but that the highest aim of life should be for each one to accommodate himself perfectly as possible to the station in which he was placed. He asked many questions, and talked willingly, yet seemed not loath to be interrupted. The only thing that was American in my possession, a number of the Palladium, I ventured to offer him, as our papers are a great curiosity in Germany. He accepted the trifle very graciously, and said it was 2 years since he had seen one. He shook me kindly by the hand when I took leave. I left Weimar immediately, but I shall not hastily forget this exceedingly interesting visit. He was of the common size, with pleasing but not striking features; his dress was a blue surtout, over a white vest, I should not have judged him to be more than 65, yet he is said to be about 10 years older.[3]

We know, however, that William did not take Goethe's advice, but deciding to obey his conscience, gave up the ministry for a law career. Emma Jaeck surmises that this episode "made a lasting impression on

3. See R. L. Rusk, *The Letters of Ralph Waldo Emerson* (New York, Columbia University Press, 1939), *1*, 161. Goethe recorded in his diary on September 19, 1824: "Will. Emerson aus Boston, Nordamerika, in Göttingen studirend, protestantischer Theolog. Blieb für mich." *Goethes Werke* (Weimar, 1887ff.), *9*, part III, 271. Quoted in Rusk, *1*, 162.

the young Ralph, and kept him from reading Goethe's writings." [4] Emerson, she believed, could not have approved of the acquiescent attitude which Goethe adopted in as important a matter as one's religious convictions. Evidence for such an opinion is weak. The reasons for Emerson's delay in the reading of Goethe, as we shall see later, were not of such a personal nature. Even if it were true, it seems ironical that he should have become a leading interpreter of Goethe among the Transcendentalists.[5]

Two more Americans who studied at Göttingen should be mentioned. The first was George H. Calvert, who was spurred on by Follen at Harvard to complete his education in Germany. Like his fellow students he decided that he could not leave that country without meeting Goethe, and, as usual, this German writer made a striking impression upon his American visitor. Calvert wrote of him in his book *First Years in Europe:*

> Of the transcendent glory of Frankfort among German cities I then had hardly a faint apprehension; for I had not happened to have read —what alone of Goethe was in that day accessible to foreigners— "The Sorrows of Werther," the English translation of which having been made from a loose French one, would stand to the original as would the refuse from the reeky tub of a sluttish washerwoman, stinted in water, to the clear abundant current of a bubbling spring. Goethe was remote and nebulous. The sweet, sightly, succulent ears of his wisdom lay buried to me in the multiplex husks of German verbs, adjectives, nouns, adverbs. Even when, on leaving Germany, I brought away a key to all the riches of a great language, its deepest treasure could only be partially valued; for it is a profound virtue of this poet-sage that his meanings reveal themselves but dimly to the young and the uncultivated.[6]

Later in the book he added: "Goethe was one of the most richly-endowed of the sons of men, many-sided and broad-sided and bright-sided. Having the supreme gift of imaginative transfiguration, he gives to truth winged bodies of beauty, wherewith to hover over and attract, and delight awhile, instructing, the more capable of his fellows; he having first, through this high power of imagination, gained insights that purged his nature and his knowledge and gave a symmetry to his thought while it stimulated its vast fertility. Goethe's thought is not for Germans only but for men." [7]

4. E. G. Jaeck, *Madame de Staël and the Spread of German Literature* (New York, Oxford University Press, 1915), p. 384.
5. For further discussion of Emerson and German literature see pp. 79–108.
6. *First Years in Europe* (Boston, Spencer, 1866), pp. 82–3.
7. *Ibid.,* p. 205.

German literature was not merely a fugitive interest for Calvert. In 1834 he published a metrical version of Schiller's *Don Carlos*.[8] The *North American Review* praised this translation and Calvert's general knowledge of German when it reviewed a lecture on German literature which he gave before the Athenaeum Society of Baltimore on February 11, 1836:

> The author of this Lecture has been favorably known by his contributions to our periodical literature, and by his general scholarship, for several years. His translation of Schiller's "Don Carlos" shows an accurate knowledge of the German language, and an uncommon power of rendering German poetry faithfully into English. In some passages that translation is rather stiff, but it is always true to the original. It sometimes fails of being idiomatic English, but never of giving the sense of the German.
>
> This Lecture shows a wide acquaintance with German literature, and an enthusiastic love of it. The author begins from the earliest German poetry, which he characterizes in a brief but satisfactory manner, and then follows its course down to the present times, diversifying the general views he presents to us with short biographical notes, and criticisms of particular works, which show a minute knowledge of the subject.[9]

The last important New Englander outside the Transcendental circle who studied German was Henry Wadsworth Longfellow. Although he was hardly a pioneer, not having reached Germany until 1829, as a commentator on German literature his relations with the Transcendentalists were closer than we might at first suppose. One cannot accept without some limitation Professor Long's statement that Longfellow was the first important interpreter of Goethe's genius and fame. That he was the first to teach *Faust* in the college classroom is true,[1] but by the year 1838 many of the Transcendentalists, including Margaret Fuller and Emerson, had also made themselves heard.

The development of his interest in Germany, however, mirrors the trend in New England at the time. When Longfellow hesitated whether he should study in Spain, Italy, or Germany, George Ticknor pointed out the growing importance of the German language. The elder Longfellow spoke of it in a letter to his son:

8. He also reviewed the book, *Wahrheit aus Jean Pauls Leben,* in the *New York Review, I* (October, 1837), 272.

9. *43* (October, 1836), 528.

1. In the article, "Goethes Verbindung mit Amerika," by Ludwig Frankel which appeared in the *Goethe-Jahrbuch, 15,* 288 the author says, "Im Jahre 1838 unternahm es der berühmte Dichter H. W. Longfellow als Professor der neueren Sprachen am Harvard College Goethes 'Faust' in akademischen Vorlesungen zu behandeln und zu erklären: der erste derartige Versuch an einer amerikanischen Universität."

I have recently seen Mr. Ticknor, who appears very anxious that you should go to Germany. He says the acquisition of the German language will be of more importance to you as a literary man than any two other languages within his knowledge, as it unlocks a vast store of learning and you find in that language the best treatises on French, Spanish, and even English literature that are to be found in any language. Although you may be correct in your supposition that generally speaking a situation in a private family in a retired town would be better than a university, I should doubt whether a seclusion of that kind in Germany would be so advantageous to you as a residence at the University of Göttingen. Mr. Ticknor says the advantages there for perfecting your knowledge of all the languages are very great, and the expenses are much less than at any other place in Europe.[2]

Mrs. Longfellow, however, was not too pleased, since she had heard that the Göttingen students were very licentious, unrestrained by the government, and extremely addicted to duelling.[3]

Once settled in Göttingen and well pleased with his situation, Longfellow launched himself on a study of modern languages and literature. From his letters and journals of this first trip to Europe there is not much evidence that he read a great deal of German literature.[4] Only after he had begun his duties as Professor of Modern Languages at Harvard in 1836 did he study German intensively. His views of Goethe were by no means original. In *Hyperion* he still followed the conservative notions of his time when he objected to "the old gentleman's sensuality," called the *Römische Elegien* immoral, spoke of *Die Wahlverwandtschaften* as "that monstrous book," and summed up his opinion in these words: "The artist shows his character in the choice of his subject. Goethe never sculptured an Apollo, nor painted a Madonna. He gives us only sinful Magdalens and rampant Fauns." [5] Yet in spite of this criticism, he had a lasting regard for Goethe, and placed him above his other favorite German writers, Heine, Richter, and Uhland.

2. Long, p. 163.
3. J. T. Hatfield, *New Light on Longfellow* (Boston, Houghton Mifflin, 1933), p. 4.
4. Professor Long found only one reference to Goethe. See Long, p. 168.
5. See *The Works of Henry Wadsworth Longfellow* (Boston, Houghton Mifflin, 1886), *8*, 120–2.

4

German Instructors in New England

WITH the exception of the Round Hill School, formal teaching of the German language in New England schools and colleges did not begin until 1825, when Harvard appointed as instructor in German Charles Follen (1796–1840), a political exile from Germany.[1] Follen was no ordinary person. Already in his student days at the University of Giessen he joined an uprising of the German people against Napoleon and fought on French soil. Having been exposed to the teachings of Kant and Fichte, in which supremacy of the moral law and a strict obedience to the inner voice of duty were of prime importance, Follen played an active role in the patriotic *Burschenschaft* movement. Republican ideals and the overthrow of the old feudal order were his aims, and soon he became a leader among the radical youths. Although Follen himself was absent from the demonstrations at the Wartburg Fest in 1817, he was, without doubt, one of its main organizers. Even after his appointment to a lectureship at the University of Jena, Follen remained active in revolutionary circles. It was not surprising, therefore, that when Kotzebue, a reactionary writer, was assassinated by Follen's friend, Karl Sand, in March, 1819, he should have been arrested as an accomplice in the plot. Although Follen was acquitted, he was dismissed from the university, his career temporarily interrupted. Follen then took refuge in Paris, where he met Lafayette, who suggested that he go to America. Instead, he turned his steps to Switzerland, where for three years he lectured at the University of Basel, but his efforts were in vain. Once more his own government charged him with subversion, and he had no choice but to flee. With his friend Carl Beck, in November, 1824, Follen set sail for America.

The lot of a refugee is not an easy one, and Follen's was no exception. Once more, however, Lafayette befriended the young man. He

1. The University of Pennsylvania was the first institution of higher education to offer courses in the German language. This event took place in 1780, when a German professor of philology taught Latin and Greek in the German language. Columbia University also offered German instruction as early as 1784, but it was discontinued in 1795 and not taken up again until 1830. See L. Viereck, *Zwei Jahrhunderte Deutschen Unterrichts in den Vereinigten Staaten* (Braunschweig, 1903), p. 12, and Wm. H. Carpenter in *Columbia University Bulletin* (March, 1897), p. 82.

informed George Ticknor that Follen was living in Philadelphia and studying the English language and customs.[2] Ticknor, after an interview with Follen, recommended him to the Harvard overseers, and in December, 1825, this man, who had passed through so many crises, began his duties as instructor of German. So dynamic was his personality and of such significance did his efforts appear to his contemporaries that a number of comments were written about him and his work. Henry Ingersoll Bowditch said of Follen: "During my entire school and college life I never met but one man who, *as my teacher,* presented any high ideal before me of my opportunities and my duties as a pupil, or, in other words, tried to make me a better youth or man. Charles Follen, when he gently and almost imperceptibly led me to study German for my own sake, and without the least reference to my position in the class, became one of the greatest benefactors of my life; and so far as his influence went, amended my character."[3]

Of greater interest, although certainly exaggerated, is the account of Andrew Peabody, a former student of Follen, who described the first German class at Harvard in his book *Harvard Reminiscences:*

German had never been taught in college before; and it was with no little difficulty that a volunteer class of eight was found, desirous, or at least willing, to avail themselves of his services. I was one of that class. We were looked upon with very much the amazement with which a class in some obscure tribal dialect of the remotest Orient would be now regarded. We knew of but two or three persons in New England who could read German; though there were probably many more, of whom we did not know.[4] There were no German books in the bookstores. A friend gave me a copy of Schiller's "Wallenstein," which I read as soon as I was able to do so, and then passed it from hand to hand among those who could obtain nothing else to read. There was no attainable classbook that could be used as a "Reader." A few copies of Noehden's Grammar were imported, and a few copies of I forget whose "Pocket Dictionary," fortunately too copious for an Anglo-Saxon pocket, and suggesting the generous amplitude of the Low Dutch costume, as described in Irving's mythical "History of New York." The "German Reader for Beginners," compiled by our teacher, was furnished to the class in single sheets as

2. Follen wrote to his parents from Philadelphia, January 13, 1825: "I know the country and the people too little, at present, to be able to determine what occupation I should now take up. One, however, presents itself already, namely, the German language and literature, which there is much inclination to study in many parts of the United States." See C. Follen, *Works, 1,* 145.

3. V. Y. Bowditch, *Life and Correspondence of Henry Ingersoll Bowditch* (Boston, Houghton Mifflin, 1902), *2,* 295.

4. Obviously, many prominent scholars of German in New England had not communicated their knowledge to this group at Harvard.

it was needed, and was printed in Roman type, there being no German type within easy reach. There could not have been a happier introduction to German literature than this little volume. It contained choice extracts in prose, all from writers that still hold an unchallenged place in the hierarchy of genius, and poems from Schiller, Goethe, Herder, and several other poets of kindred, if inferior, fame. But in the entire volume, Dr. Follen rejoiced especially in several battle-pieces from Körner, the soldier and martyr of liberty, whom we then supposed to have been our teacher's fellow-soldier, though, in fact, he fell in battle when Dr. Follen was just entering the University. I never have heard recitations which impressed me so strongly as the reading of those pieces by Dr. Follen, who would put into them all of the heart and soul that had made him too much a lover of his country to be suffered to dwell in it. . . .

Dr. Follen was the best of teachers. Under him we learned the grammar of the language, in great part, *in situ,*—forms and constructions, except the most elementary, being explained to us as we met them in our reading-lessons, and explained with a clearness and emphasis that made it hard to forget them. . . . He bestowed great pains in bringing our untried organs into use in the more difficult details of pronunciation, particularly in the *ö,* the *ü,* the *r,* and the *ch,* on which he took us each separately in hand. His pronunciation was singularly smooth and euphonious.[5]

Several statements in this account call for further comment. The textbook of which Peabody spoke was mentioned by Follen as early as December 22, 1825, in a letter to Dr. Beck: "I want a German Reader. Professor Ticknor is of the same opinion as I, that we two should make a German Chrestomathy, which might, at the same time, serve as a sketch of the history of German literature. Professor Ticknor possesses, as you know, a very rich library. If we add to this what may be obtained in other places, we might furnish something useful. Ask Mr. Bancroft for his opinion. The book must be such, that it may be introduced into other institutions, and thus at least pay its expenses." [6] According to the preface, the textbook had a double purpose: to furnish the teacher with reading matter from recognized German masterpieces and to illustrate the rules and peculiarities of the language. A general sketch of the history of German literature was included in the book for Americans who had no accurate conception of it. The text itself contained about one hundred fifty pages of prose and twenty of poetry, chosen from the most famous classical and romantic German writers and embracing the period from Lessing to Körner.[7]

5. *Harvard Reminiscences* (Boston, Ticknor, 1888), pp. 117–20.
6. Follen, *Works, 1,* 160.
7. Among the selections he chose for the first edition were extracts from Lessing's early

The vogue of the work is manifested by the hospitality it received in the periodicals of the day. The *United States Literary Gazette* found the book "much needed" and valuable to beginners, since it would supply "a deficiency hitherto much felt." In addition to this praise, the review included the following ardent defense of German culture:

An acquaintance with this language is becoming daily more important to every man who wishes to keep pace with the progress of knowledge. In all its departments, German students are the most assiduous labourers, and, as a body, furnish the largest contributions to its stock. The literary treasures of this nation are vast, varied, and rapidly multiplying, and demand the attentive study of every one who desires to excel in any branch of intellectual labour. The metaphysician will find it the very home of profound speculation, the native land of intellectual, as truly as of physical gymnastics. For the lover of natural science, the patient research of the German character has accumulated a rich storehouse of facts. The classical scholar has been long familiar with its massy erudition, and, more lately with its deep investigation into the spirit of antiquity. The professional man, the student of law, physic, or theology, may satisfy the keenest appetite with the fruits of German toil. The lover of belles lettres will here meet with a fresh and beautiful literature, formed by, and breathing the spirit of the age, exulting in the consciousness of vigour and progress, not made up of beautiful relics, but of the finished productions of modern art, equally splendid, and better suited to the wants and the taste of the times. New, rich, and rapidly increasing, it opens a wide and important field to the scholar of every nation, more especially to the nations of German origin.[8]

The *North American Review* also thought highly of Follen's book: "This is one of the pleasantest and best selections we are acquainted with, for the purpose of introducing a beginner to the knowledge of a foreign language. . . . This object is, we think, well attained; and though a task of no very formidable nature, yet it is one not unworthy

Fabeln. Herder's *Paramythien,* Schiller's *Geisterseher,* Wackenroder's *Herzensergiessungen eines Kunstliebenden Klosterbruders,* Goethe's *Italienische Reise* and *Wilhelm Meister,* Schlegel's lecture on *Macbeth,* and Körner's poems. His selections depended a good deal upon the material available in this country. Follen himself had brought over no library from Germany, and therefore utilized his friends' collections. He wrote in his journal, February 20, 1826: "I have taken the extracts, with the aid of Professor Ticknor and his library, from the principal authors since Lessing. I wish I had some fables of Pestalozzi's. There is no extract from Novalis, because I have nothing of him." The second edition of the book contained new material, such as a passage from Novalis' *Heinrich von Ofterdingen,* and Gothic type was substituted for the Roman. The Speck Collection includes copies of these volumes.

8. *4* (September, 1826), 458.

of the attention of the learned scholar who has prepared the book, and to whom we are indebted for contributing his efforts to increase the means of cultivating one of the most useful and important languages of the present day." [9]

Follen's latest biographer, George W. Spindler, believes that a second volume, which was printed in Cambridge in 1833 containing texts of *Maria Stuart, Tasso,* and *Egmont,* also may have been edited by Follen, since the "advertisement" stated that the text was adapted to follow the *Lesebuch.*[1] Another book which Follen published under his name and of equal importance to his students and contemporaries was his *German Grammar.* Having a knowledge of Grimm's work in philology, he produced this volume, which passed through many revised editions.[2]

Always an ardent admirer of Schiller, Follen highlighted Schiller's writings in his lectures.[3] He often included whole scenes of the plays in his own English version, and in his remarks on the German poet, he did not hesitate to disagree with the opinions of Schlegel and Carlyle. William Henry Channing said that these lectures were delivered before the best audiences in New York and Boston, and that the translations of the passages were as poetical as they were accurate.[4] His love for Schiller, however, threw off balance his opinion of Goethe. Like many Americans, Follen could not brook Goethe's lack of moral enthusiasm and his seeming indifference to the struggle of his countrymen in the cause of freedom. Perhaps this attitude toward Goethe could be traced to Follen's early years in Jena when Goethe was the nominal head of the university. At a later time "Das Junge Deutschland," which sympathized strongly with many of Follen's ideas, often raised the question, "Who is the greater, Goethe or Schiller?" Follen's attitude toward Goethe also suited Americans who preferred the sugary, moral, and

9. *24* (January, 1827), 251.

1. See G. W. Spindler, *Karl Follen; A Biographical Study* (Chicago, University of Illinois, 1917), p. 101. This is also the theory of E. Parry, *Friedrich Schiller in America,* p. 30. From my own examination of the Follen material, I see no reason to disagree with this statement.

2. Follen had this *Grammar* in mind as early as December, 1825, when he inquired of Dr. Beck whether he had done anything in the way of producing one. Follen obviously did not wish to infringe on a project which Beck had already considered. See Follen, *Works, I,* 160. The *Grammar* was just as popular as the *Reader,* and was to be found in the libraries of almost all the New Englanders interested in German culture. Emerson owned the first edition of this book.

3. After his death Mrs. Follen published these lectures in which Follen wrote of Schiller: "Among all the writers of my native land who were the light and the companions of my early days, there is no one who stands so near my heart, and with whom I would wish you so much, to be not merely superficially acquainted, but firmly and intimately connected, as the chaste, elevated, enlightened, tender, and enthusiastic Schiller, —the friend of the young in spirit, the delight of the pure in heart." *Ibid., 4,* 6–7.

4. *Christian Examiner, 33* (September, 1842), 33–56.

political qualities rather than the artistic in the literature which they read.[5]

In addition to his books and lectures, Follen gained fame at Harvard, because his personality appealed to his colleagues and students. Ticknor wrote of him to his friend Charles Daveis as early as 1826 "Our German teacher, Dr. Follen . . . a young man who left his country from political troubles . . . is a fine fellow, an excellent scholar, and teaches German admirably. . . . He is a modest, thorough, faithful German scholar, who will do good among us, and be worth your knowing." [6] At Ticknor's home Follen passed many pleasant hours with the books and friends he loved. Almost immediately he became an arbiter in matters of German culture. The *Goethe-Jahrbuch* credits him with founding the German Society in Boston, which numbered among its members S. A. Eliot, G. Ticknor, S. H. Perkins, Wm. T. Andrews, F. C. Gray, J. Pickering, N. I. Bowditch, E. Wigglesworth, F. Lieber, Mr. Miesegalo, T. Searle, and J. M. Robbins.[7]

Elizabeth Peabody also said in her biography of William Ellery Channing that German literature began to be studied extensively in Boston only after Follen came.[8] Nor was this activity limited to the men. Mrs. Follen wrote in a *Memoir* of her husband:

A small number of ladies, of whom I was one, had just formed a little party to meet once a week for the purpose of improvement in the art of reading well. We invited Dr. Follen to join us. He gladly accepted the invitation. At the first meeting, when called upon to read in his turn, he objected, on the ground that he could not read any thing in English well, without previously studying it. I asked him to recite a German poem. No one present will ever forget his recitation

5. Camillo von Klenze believed that since Follen's personal prejudices hindered an impartial opinion of German literature, his influence cannot be regarded as "uniformly beneficient." See *Brooks and the Genteel Tradition* (Boston, D. C. Heath, 1937), p. 18. I do not agree, for if we consider the reputation of Schiller in America prior to Follen's arrival, we can see how far he advanced the popularity of Schiller's works. Not only had Schiller been criticized for writing *Die Räuber*, but the mere fact that he had written for the stage blackened his name in the eyes of New England. Even Frederic Henry Hedge regretted "that a writer of Schiller's standing in this age of the world should have devoted the principal part of his life to a department of art so questionable in its tendency and so surely destined to decay as the drama." See the *Christian Examiner, 16* (July, 1834), 391. Follen helped to change this attitude and no doubt influenced the preference for Schiller rather than Goethe among the Transcendentalists who attended his lectures. Charles T. Brooks's first German translations were from Schiller's *Jungfrau von Orleans, Maria Stuart,* and *Wilhelm Tell.*

6. Ticknor, *Life, Letters, and Journals, 1,* 352.

7. "Eine bedeutendere Gesellschaft," says the *Goethe-Jahrbuch,* "konnte es damals dort nicht gegeben haben" (*25,* 23–4). The only record of this club is found on the paper covers of an old German book printed in 1829. Follen's name heads the list of members. See the *Harvard Graduates' Magazine, 11* (March, 1903), 492.

8. *Reminiscences of Rev. Wm. Ellery Channing* (Boston, Roberts, 1880), p. 339.

of Goethe's "Kennst du das Land," especially the tender accents of his voice when repeating the words,

"Dahin! dahin!
Möcht' ich mit dir, O mein Geliebter, ziehn."

It was indeed the cry of the homesick spirit after its fatherland.[9] On December 6, 1827, Follen himself recorded: "In the evening I went to Miss C——'s, where Miss R—— was. I read to them some extracts from Faust, translated by Gower, so as to give an idea of the whole. I had to take some pains to avert all prejudice with respect to the supposed immorality of the piece. . . . It seemed to produce a great effect on my hearers."[1] The "hearers" were certainly unaware that they were listening to a most inadequate version of *Faust*. In fact, the Gower translation is so poor that one could doubt Follen's mastery of English.[2]

Meanwhile his classes were steadily growing.[3] From the first group of eight students in 1825 the number of men studying under his direction increased to sixty by 1830. This unexpected success led Follen's friends to establish a full professorship of the German language and literature and endow it for five years.[4] His inaugural address, delivered before the University, September 3, 1831, constitutes a landmark in the history of German culture in New England. After pointing out in this address the treasures to be found in German literature, Follen helped to exonerate them from the charges of obscurity, irreverence, and skepticism. He flatly denied the accusation that the German language was almost impossible to learn. Edward Livingston remarked of the address in a letter to Follen: "It marks a new era in our classical course of education; and the introduction of the German literature and language cannot but have a powerful effect on our own."[5]

Follen did not by any means limit his activities to teaching the Ger-

9. Follen, *Works, 1,* 164.
1. *Ibid.,* pp. 209–10.
2. For a discussion of the Gower translation see Adolf I. Frantz, *Half a hundred Thralls to Faust* (Chapel Hill, University of North Carolina Press, 1949), pp. 4–11.
3. In a letter to his father in 1829 he wrote: "The study of the German language and literature is steadily increasing. Many young Americans, particularly theological students, who have finished their studies here, are travelling to Germany, in order to begin there anew, and then to make the dead riches of German learning live here anew in this free air." *Ibid.,* p. 265.
4. Mrs. Follen contended that Follen's anti-slavery sentiments were the cause of his severance with Harvard at the end of this five-year period. In 1834 the corporation informed him that they could not renew his appointment as professor, but that if he wished to stay on as instructor of the German language, he could do so at a salary of five hundred dollars. Having no other income, Follen had no alternative but to resign and look for more profitable employment.
5. Follen, *Works, 1,* 30.

man language. As instructor of ethics and ecclesiastical history at the Harvard Divinity School, he promoted the study of German philosophy. To prepare for this work he wrote a series of lectures, which he read before an enthusiastic Boston audience during the winter of 1830–31.[6] His views of Kant and Fichte were to have special significance in his associations with the Transcendentalists. We can assume that Emerson, Ripley, Alcott, Parker, Clarke, and Margaret Fuller both attended and read his lectures. Emerson was living in Divinity Hall when Follen was teaching at Harvard, and Emerson's letter to Carlyle in 1835 shows that he valued Follen's work.[7] George Ripley also may have met Follen as early as 1827, since as friends of Channing, both men were frequent visitors in the Channing household. Theodore Parker, who entered Harvard in 1830, the same year in which Follen became Professor of German Literature, attended his lectures. James Freeman Clarke, another student of Follen, passed on Follen's opinions of Schiller, Körner, Richter, and Goethe to Margaret Fuller.[8] Even when Bronson Alcott established his infant school in Boston, he consulted Follen about German methods of education.

One other aspect of Follen's work should be mentioned. Having been a disciple of "Turnvater" Jahn in Germany, founder of societies for gymnastics and patriotism, Follen began a physical training program with the students at Harvard, and set up the first college gymnasium in this country.[9] He had to use one of the dining halls, but the enthusiasm both of the students and the people of Boston made up for the lack of facilities and equipment.[1]

The popularity of gymnastics brought to Boston another political refugee and famous teacher of German culture, Francis Lieber.[2] In 1819 he had been arrested in Germany as a dangerous character, but after his release, he resumed his studies at Jena. When the war of liberation in Greece broke out, Lieber, as a liberal, felt that he had to partake in the struggle. He sailed for Greece, only to suffer disillusionment and despair. Lieber returned to Germany but once more found himself un-

6. Spindler, p. 123.
7. For quotation from this letter see p. 66.
8. Miss Fuller also met the German professor at Channing's home and in the ladies' reading circle.
9. Almost all the early scholars who came from Germany had a deep interest in the two widely different fields of theology and physical training. Follen, Lieber, and Beck were among the men who devoted their time to both activities.
1. See letter to Beck in Follen's *Works, I,* 161.
2. Julius Goebel comments on him in *Das Deutschtum in den Vereinigten Staaten von Nord-Amerika:* "Als Freiwilliger hatte er den Feldzug von 1815 mitgemacht, aber als Schüler Jahns und als Burschenschaftler hatte er den Hass der preussischen Regierung auf sich gezogen und entging nur durch Niebuhrs freundliche Bemühungen einer langen Gefangenschaft. Im Jahre 1827 kam er nach Amerika, gründete zunächst eine Schwimmschule in Boston und übersetzte das Brockhaussche Konversationslexikon" (p. 48).

comfortable. After a year in England, where he taught languages and wrote for German periodicals, he received a request to come to Boston, where he landed in June, 1827.

Once established in this country, Lieber helped determine fundamental academic traditions in our colleges. Almost immediately he prepared a swimming school modeled on the establishments of General Pfuel in German cities, and thus intensified Follen's physical training program.[3] Nor were his activities limited to the schools. As correspondent to the *Allgemeine Zeitung*, he was able to inform the Germans about America, a service which aided friendly relations between the peoples of both countries. In addition to his gymnastic duties he also undertook the more arduous work of editing the *Encyclopedia Americana*. This tremendous task, a translation and adaptation of Brockhaus's famous *Conversations-Lexikon*, was accomplished by the best scholars in Boston, working nearly five years under Lieber's direction. To enhance its usefulness information of interest only to Germans was omitted, and American subjects were substituted. Edward Everett, George Bancroft, Charles Follen, and Moses Stuart were among the scholars who aided Lieber. When the work was published in 1832, it was recognized as the first real encyclopedia to originate in this country.[4]

Two more German instructors should be mentioned. The first was Carl Beck, who came to New York with Follen, and was recommended by Ticknor for the position of Latin instructor at the Round Hill School. Beck was the step-son of the famous theologian De Wette, Biblical critic and professor at Heidelberg and Berlin. Beck too was involved in the murder of Kotzebue because his step-father had written a letter to the mother of the murderer, Karl Sand. De Wette and his family, therefore, were forced to leave Berlin and take refuge in Switzerland, where young Carl finished his theological studies. There he became a close friend of Follen and sailed with him from Le Havre in 1824.

Once established at Round Hill, Beck immediately built an indoor gymnasium, actually the first in the United States.[5] Beck's success at Round Hill was soon recognized, and in 1832 he was called to Harvard

3. Lieber had been recommended by Jahn for the directorship of the Boston Gymnasium when the latter refused to come himself. The *American Journal of Education* of Boston printed this announcement in 1826: "Proposals of Dr. Francis Lieber to found a Gymnasium in America"—That if 1,000 dollars be given in the first year, Dr. Lieber will take Mr. A. Baur, student of theology, with him to America, to assist in teaching, which will be very advantageous to the pupils, as Mr. Baur presided over the Gymnasium at Tübingen; and was several years under Dr. Jahn in the central institution at Berlin. Dr. Lieber thinks that Mr. Baur would accompany him to America if there were for future time any prospect of employment as teacher of gymnastics or as a protestant minister" (*1, 700*).

4. For further information on Lieber see T. S. Perry, *The Life and Letters of Francis Lieber* (Boston, Osgood, 1882).

5. See Faust, *The German Element in the United States*, pp. 214–15.

as professor of Latin, in which capacity he served with eminent success for eighteen years. Just as Follen had introduced the little known works of German literature, so Beck lectured to American students on the great progress which German scholars had made in classical philology.[6]

With Beck at Harvard was Hermann Bokum who left the University of Pennsylvania for Harvard when Follen resigned in 1835. Even before this date Bokum's name and work were well known among New England scholars. In 1832 he published a German text book, *An Introduction to the Study of the German Language,* similar to Follen's but limited to prose, purposely simplified by interlinear translations.[7] Upon his arrival in Boston Bokum delivered a series of public lectures on the German language and literature.[8] In the first lecture he stressed a defense of the German language, and by reading aloud the "Erlkönig," he tried to demonstrate the beauty of German poetry. He also discussed the superiority of German scholarship, and announced that in other lectures of the series he would present a survey of German literature from the middle of the eighteenth century until his own time.[9]

During the winter of 1835–36 Bokum wrote *The Stranger's Gift,* a commentary on the German immigrants and their customs. The *Christian Examiner* of March, 1836, said of him in reviewing this work:

> This little work is the production of one of that small but honored company of German scholars, who have made their home amongst us. They have sought under our institutions a sphere more congenial, than those of the old monarchies of Europe, to the temper of liberal minds, sympathizing with their race, and loving a free activity. They bring with them the goodly leaven of German thoroughness and industry, that zeal for learning for learning's sake, which we of this country need more of to rectify the popular superficialness to which we are all too prone. . . . They adorn our letters, and within the scope of their influence do much to promote elementary education, and to animate and guide our young men in the pursuit of liberal studies. With remarkable readiness and facility they adopt our manners, language, sympathies, and enter into the spirit of our institutions. They are both *with* us and *of* us. They are more than welcome.[1]

6. Goebel goes even further and says, "Seitdem haben die Amerikanischen Studenten keinen griechischen oder römischen Schriftsteller gelesen, dessen Text und Anmerkungen nicht auf der Vorarbeit deutscher Gelehrten beruhte." p. 49.

7. Bokum contended that the German material previously published had not been on an elementary level.

8. This was in the spring of 1836.

9. So far as we know, only his first lecture was published. See Perry, p. 36.

1. *20, 47.*

It is evident, therefore, that in the previous decade a small but decidedly brilliant group of Germans had made their mark in New England as teachers and scholars. Although we are not concerned here with the later careers of these men, it must be remembered that they all contributed to the American way of life. We shall always be indebted to Beck, who made the teaching of the classics come alive; to Lieber, whose encyclopedia and numerous writings on political ethics and the law cannot be overestimated; and to Follen—most important of the group—who, before he died in 1840, was to prove his worth as a teacher, lecturer, Unitarian minister, and agitator against slavery. These were men of large views endowed with high public spirit, who in turn influenced ambitious young American scholars, among them a number of the Transcendentalists, to develop an attitude of inquiry and tolerance.

PART II

German Scholarship Among the Transcendentalists

I

Chronological Survey (1813-45)

A BRIEF chronological survey of the growing popularity of German culture within the Transcendental circle should precede any assessment of German literary influences on its individual members. Perhaps the first book dealing with German thought which had profound significance for the Transcendentalists was Madame de Staël's *De l'Allemagne,* printed in London in 1813.[1] To this translation and its New York reprint (1814) one can attribute the earliest contacts of several of the Transcendentalists with German literature. Almost all the important literary magazines reviewed the book or copied the comments of the *Edinburgh Review* and the *Quarterly Review.*[2] William Ellery Channing, William Emerson, Edward Everett, George Bancroft, Ralph Waldo Emerson,[3] Margaret Fuller, and James Freeman Clarke all acknowledged their debt to Madame de Staël.[4] The flow of American students to German universities before 1820 may be partly attributed to the enthusiasm which her book aroused.[5] They could not help being curious about Madame de Staël's statement that all the north of Germany was filled with the most learned universities in Europe and that in no country, not even in England, did the people have so many

1. This book, written in 1810, introduced German philosophy into France, although it received small notice there until Cousin incorporated parts of it into his philosophy.
2. See also the *Analectic Magazine, 3* (April, 1814), 284ff., and the *Quarterly Review* reprinted in New York, *10* (January, 1814), 355ff.
3. The earliest recorded date that Emerson withdrew *De l'Allemagne* from the Boston Library Society was March 21, 1822, but he may have seen it earlier, since many of his acquaintances owned it. He mentioned the book in his journals in 1821 and again in 1825, 1826, 1827, and 1829.
4. Julius Goebel, the German commentator on German culture in America, reiterated the importance of Madame de Staël's work: "Da erschien im Jahre 1813 ein französisches Buch, das in der europäischen Welt ausserhalb Deutschlands geradezu revolutionär wirkte. Ich meine das Buch der geistreichen Französin Madame de Staël *Über Deutschland* [*De l'Allemagne*], das für die damalige Kulturmenschheit die Entdeckung einer ganz neuen Welt bedeutete. ... Es ist uns bezeugt, dass kein Buch am Anfang des 19. Jahrhunderts so tief und weithin wirkte in Amerika, als Madame de Staëls Schrift *Über Deutschland.*" See *Der Kampf um deutsche Kultur in Amerika* (Leipzig, 1914), p. 85.
5. Goebel agrees with this statement in his essay "Das Deutschtum in den Vereinigten Staaten von Nord Amerika." Ticknor also said that the reading of *De l'Allemagne* first gave him the desire to study at a German university. See Ticknor, *Life, Letters, and Journals, I,* 11.

63

means of instructing themselves, and of bringing their faculties to perfection.[6]

For the Transcendentalists Madame de Staël's work also offered one of the few accurate interpretations of German character. At that time the German language was probably less familiar to Americans than, let us say, Swedish is to the average person today, and aside from contacts with a handful of immigrants in 1814, the German people themselves were unknown. We must remember that during the previous twenty-five years a virtual embargo had been in effect. When Madame de Staël praised the Germans as a conscientious, faithful, and reliable race, with a tremendous capacity for work and a marked intellectual ability, here was tangible evidence on which to re-evaluate German character. She spoke of their independence of thought, a trait which probably appealed to the Transcendentalists, who prided themselves on their individualism and disapproved of Americans who copied opinions of Englishmen. They could also be pleased with her statement that Germany, unlike France, had escaped the immorality and atheism of the Regency, for along with a Luther the Germans could now boast of a Kant who had saved religion from the doubters by uniting it with science.

Of even greater importance is the fact that one can trace partly to her work a new evaluation of German literary figures. Instead of Gessner, Goethe assumed first rank; instead of Kotzebue, Schiller; and to complete her triumvirate, she stressed Jean Paul Richter, highly admired by all the Transcendentalists. Even her adverse criticism of Goethe took hold, and in spite of the later and more persistent influence of Carlyle's writings, what she said of the creator of *Faust* was repeated by all the Transcendentalists with the possible exception of Margaret Fuller.[7]

With the return of American scholars from Göttingen, young men studying at Harvard, such as Emerson and Ripley, found a new and daring source of inspiration. Emerson in 1821 attended the lectures of Ticknor and almost idolized Edward Everett, who, he said, opened up "a new morning" to his students by the introduction of the wealth of German criticism.[8] Theodore Parker, later referring to this period, called it a veritable German epidemic which affected all classes and caused undue alarm and worry. In 1817 Everett brought back his German library from Göttingen, and the following year Harvard College

6. Madame de Staël, *Germany* (London, 1814), *1*, 171.
7. Madame de Staël disapproved of his moral offenses and his aloofness from everyday life, his lack of patriotism and his little sympathy with the creatures of his own imagination. In contrast, she portrayed Schiller as a man of perfect sincerity and a lover of truth. "His muse was Conscience," she said, "and no consideration, drawn either from success, from the prevailing fashion, from prejudice, or from any thing, in short, that proceeds from others, could ever have prevailed on him to alter his writings." *Ibid.*, p. 274.
8. Emerson, *Works, 10*, 330.

not only purchased the Thorndike collection but received Goethe's works as a gift. Only one Transcendentalist, however, had already begun to study the German language. He was Frederic Henry Hedge, who went to Germany under Bancroft's care, and with the possible exception of Parker, became the most learned Transcendentalist in German philosophy and literature.

During this same period another important fountainhead of German idealism for the English-speaking world, and particularly for the New England Transcendentalists, was found in the writings of Thomas Carlyle and Samuel Taylor Coleridge. In 1824 Carlyle's translation of *Wilhelm Meisters Lehrjahre* appeared to become perhaps the most censured and the most highly praised book of its time.[9] From 1827 to 1832 Carlyle's great essays on German literature, especially on Goethe, appeared in the leading magazines. Carlyle's main aim in the essays was to correct the misconception of Goethe and to teach the ethical value of his writings. "Close thy Byron, open thy Goethe," he cried, for in Goethe he found a "true Hero," the Hero as Literary Man. After Carlyle's articles had been published, Goethe was no longer a mere name.[1] Editions of his works were accessible in the libraries of Harvard College, in the Athenaeum, and in the private collections of such men as Hedge, Emerson, and Ripley.[2]

Just as New Englanders found in Carlyle an introduction to Romantic literature, so they found in Coleridge an introduction to Romantic philosophy.[3] In 1829 Coleridge's *Aids to Reflection* was published with an introduction by James Marsh, who proposed Kant, Jacobi, the English Platonists, and Coleridge as a substitute for the current philosophy. Frederic Henry Hedge wrote a review of this book and immediately brought the work of Coleridge to a focus.[4] Mainly through the efforts of Coleridge the philosophy of German Romanticism, especially the metaphysical speculations of Fichte and Schelling, first became popular in New England.

During this same period, 1825 to 1835, Professor Charles Follen was also reaping a fruitful harvest at Harvard. We have already spoken

9. The very copy from which Carlyle translated Goethe's *Wilhelm Meister* can now be found in the Speck Collection.
1. Although we have no evidence that Emerson read much of Carlyle before 1828, he had already dipped into translations of the Schlegels (whether August or Friedrich we do not know) and Grimm's *Correspondence Litteraire*. William Emerson had meanwhile visited Goethe, and in November, 1824, Emerson asked his brother whether he thought it advisable for him to study German. See Emerson, *Letters, 1,* 154–5.
2. Emerson, terming the essays "the most original and profound essays of the day," collected them and brought about their publication in 1838–9.
3. As late as 1877 Bronson Alcott wrote to a friend: "I think Coleridge is always most stimulating and profitable reading." See MS letter dated February 12, 1877, Yale Collection of American Literature, Yale University.
4. *Christian Examiner, 14* (March, 1833), 109ff.

of his influence on the individual Transcendentalists.[5] Few of his students could resist his fiery enthusiasm for the writers of his native country. Emerson wrote to Carlyle in 1835: "We know enough here of Goethe and Schiller to have some interest in German literature. A respectable German here, Dr. Follen, has given lectures to a good class upon Schiller. I am quite sure that Goethe's name would now stimulate the curiosity of scores of persons." [6]

In the 1820's, however, Emerson hesitated to fall in line. When Frederic Henry Hedge tried to interest him in German literature, the Concord bulwark of self-reliance laughingly said that as he was entirely ignorant of the subject, he should assume that it was not worth knowing.[7] Yet he could not resist the trend of the time for long. In 1828 Emerson withdrew *Wilhelm Meisters Lehrjahre* from the Harvard College Library, perhaps as a text with which he might begin the study of the German language.

By 1829 even William Ellery Channing was secretly pleased with the spread of German metaphysics. Writing to Lucy Aikin he said: "Passing from old times to new times, I have two pieces of intelligence for you, that German metaphysics (in the train of which German theology may follow) have got into Cambridge, where youths are puzzling their brains with Kantianism; and that it is whispered—monstrum horrendum!—that Unitarianism is infecting some of the most enlightened of the clergy of Oxford." [8] Emerson also yielded. Comments on German literature in his journals were no longer limited to Carlyle's translations of *Wilhelm Meister*. By 1832 he was familiar with the names of Lessing, Schiller, Fichte, Novalis, Hegel, and Jung-Stilling as well as Goethe, and from the Boston Library Society and the Boston Athenaeum he withdrew volumes of Herder, Humboldt, and Mueller. Nor was he unique in his growing interest. Parker had already become an ardent enthusiast of Follen's teachings, and Margaret Fuller, then twenty-two years old, had also heard the wild bugle call of Thomas Carlyle in his articles on Richter, Schiller, and Goethe.

The seeds of the Transcendental groups were being sown, for these people now had a common interest which drew them together. They would often visit each other for the sole purpose of discussing Goethe, Carlyle, and German literature. In fact during the following year, 1833, James Clarke and Margaret Fuller saw each other every day so that they could read German together. Even Bronson Alcott was aroused to an interest in German, and read in these early years several volumes of

5. See p. 57.
6. *Emerson-Carlyle Correspondence, I,* 55.
7. J. E. Cabot, *A Memoir of Ralph Waldo Emerson* (Boston, Houghton Mifflin, 1887), *I,* 139.
8. *Correspondence of William Ellery Channing, D.D., and Lucy Aikin,* ed. A. L. Breton (Boston, Roberts, 1874), pp. 41, 42.

criticism on Kant's philosophy. Emerson too labored at his German, and in his pocket notebook [9] he listed to be read at this time the following books and articles:

> German Romance   4 vols.
> Life of Schiller
> Translation of Wilhelm Meister 3 vols.
> In the Edinburgh Review No. 92 Article—German Literature
> + Vol   Novalis
> Foreign Review   No. 1   Goethe's Helene—Werner
> 2   Art. Goethe
> 8   Germ Lit in 14 & 15 Centuries
> 10   Goethes Works
> 3 134   Schiller

Even during his first European trip (1832–33) he used Goethe's *Italienische Reise* as a guide book and at odd moments glanced into *Wilhelm Meister*.

Scholars outside the Transcendental circle were beginning to notice and criticize this state of affairs. They resented a foreign influence which probed into the meaning of life and upset the orthodox way of thinking. Andrews Norton in 1833 wrote in the *Select Journal of Foreign Periodical Literature* an exceedingly hostile criticism of Goethe, his works, and his admirers,[1] but the Transcendentalists were not slow to answer. Ripley retaliated with a series of articles in the *Christian Examiner* protesting against the indiscriminate charge of mysticism, obscurity, and irreligion brought against German philosophy.

Hedge, in his review of Coleridge's work, published an ardent defense of the German Transcendental philosophers. He explained their point of view as follows:

> There is only one point from which we can clearly understand and decide upon the speculations of Kant and his followers; that point is the interior consciousness, distinguished from the common consciousness, by its being an active and not a passive state. In the language of the school, it is a free intuition, and can only be attained by a vigorous effort of the will. . . .
>
> The pre-eminence of Germany among the nations of our day in respect of intellectual culture, is universally acknowledged; and we do fully believe that whatever excellence that nation has attained in science, in history, or poetry is mainly owing to the influence of her philosophy, to the faculty which that philosophy has imparted of seizing on the spirit of every question, and determining at once the

9. The list is copied from the original manuscript in the Houghton Library.
1. *Select Journal of Foreign Periodical Literature, 1* (April, 1833), 250–92.

point of view from which each subject should be regarded,—in one word, to the transcendental method. . . . A philosophy which has given such an impulse to mental culture and scientific research, which has done so much to establish and to extend the spiritual in man, and the ideal in nature, needs no apology; it commends itself by its fruits, it lives in its fruits, and must ever live, though the name of its founder be forgotten, and not one of its doctrines survive.[2]

In the fall after his return from England when Emerson read Hedge's review of Coleridge's work, he was elated. He also found "good things" in Schleiermacher and Schelling, but for Goethe in 1834 he felt only "a qualified admiration."[3] He was annoyed by the "velvet life" Goethe led, and the puritan in him could accept "no apology for bad morals in such as *he.*" Carlyle, however, was not dismayed by this remark. On the contrary, he urged Emerson now more than ever to study the German language itself so that he might discover what was the only healthy mind in Europe—namely Goethe's.[4]

The other Transcendentalists, meanwhile, were far ahead of Emerson. Alcott was finding new food for thought in Goethe, Schiller, and Richter, and Thoreau was studying the German language with Orestes Brownson. Margaret Fuller not only began to work on her life of Goethe but also completed a metrical translation of *Torquato Tasso.* Although the translation failed to find a publisher, her many acquaintances who were not proficient in German read it, Emerson among them. Carlyle's work on the Germans was enthusiastically received as soon as it reached these shores. The *Christian Examiner* and the *North American Review* evaluated his *Life of Schiller* in July, 1834, and would have praised it unanimously except for the fact that Schiller used stimulants and wrote drama—"a department of art surely destined to decay."[5]

Ripley's articles on Herder in 1835 did much to dispel the idea that German philosophy, theology, and literature were irreligious and immoral.[6] In discussing Marsh's translation of Herder's *The Spirit of Hebrew Poetry,* Ripley commented on the attention that German books were beginning to receive in our country. "Within a few years past," he said, "they have been rescued from the hands of incompetent translators and anonymous critics, who seem to have been impelled to their literary undertakings by no other motive than that of hunger, and made the subject of profound and generous study."[7] On the other hand, he

---

2. *Christian Examiner, 14* (March, 1833), 119, 126-7.
3. *Emerson-Carlyle Correspondence, 1,* 29.
4. *Ibid., 1,* 29ff., 39ff.
5. *Christian Examiner, 16* (July, 1834), 367.
6. *Christian Examiner, 18* (May, 1835), 167ff. and *19* (November, 1835), 172ff.
7. *Ibid., 18* (May, 1835), 167.

pointed out that the study of German theology had not progressed so much.

> It is rather singular, that, in our own country, where a zeal for religion and a love of speculation, form a part of our birthright, we should have given so little attention to the labors of others, who have explored every part of the field on which we are employed ourselves. . . . We are by no means so enthusiastic as to suppose, that a knowledge of German theology would settle any controversies now pending, but we think it very possible, that a sober examination of its achievements might present some facts or points of view, which would be of service to us in our inquiries, although they had escaped our notice in the course of our own personal studies.[8]

Ripley was not referring in this criticism to the Transcendentalists. They were absorbed even in the most radical of German theological writers. One must not forget that in this year Strauss's *Das Leben Jesu* was published. On his return to America the Reverend Henry A. Walker brought a copy with him and lent it to Theodore Parker, who, after reviewing it for the *Christian Examiner,* broke from the Unitarian Society.[9]

The *Western Messenger,* then a young organ of Transcendental ideas, also took up the cudgel for German theology with these words:

> There is a great deal of folly in this world, no doubt; many foolish things are done, many more uttered; but we think of all subjects, the one which has elicited of late years the most nonsensical remark, is that of German Theology, or Neology (the two words seem to be used as synonymous).
>
> . . . One professor Sears (professor of what, or whereabout professing, we cannot inform the curious reader) is, it appears, inditing a series of communications with respect to the heathenish darkness of this unfortunate land of the reformation—land of Luther and Melancthon, and in later days of Klopstock, Herder and a thousand others whose piety is world-renowned. But what says professor Sears? "The great majority of the Germans who are occupied with these subjects (sacred philology) are decidedly hostile to the spiritual nature of the gospel. It is a curious spectacle to see a nation of infidels expounding the Bible.
>
> So we should think. But these wholesale assertions smack too much of the style of the Trollope and Fidler school of travellers to win implicit credence. The German people has always been distin-

8. *Ibid.,* pp. 167–8.
9. J. Weiss, *Life and Correspondence of Theodore Parker* (London, 1863), *1*, 122.

guished by its deep sentiments of piety and by its patient investigation after truth.[1]

The fact that as early as 1835 the *Western Messenger* devoted many of its pages to the works of German writers gives it a unique place among the Transcendental periodicals. It is also to be observed that in criticism and translation of German literature, it can be favorably compared with the *Dial,* which did not begin publication until 1840. In 1836, the editor, James Freeman Clarke, began to print in the *Western Messenger* his translations of De Wette,[2] which were later included in Ripley's *Specimens;* from time to time, throughout subsequent issues, he brought out portions of the works of Goethe,[3] Schiller,[4] Richter, Herder, and Uhland. By the end of 1836, Clarke could say: "Five years ago the name of Goethe was hardly known in England and America, except as the author of a silly book, Merther [*sic*]—an incomprehensible play, Faust—and a tedious novel, Wilhelm Meister. So at least our critics called them. But now a revolution has taken place. Hardly a review or magazine appears that has not something in it about Goethe, and people begin to find with amazement that a genius as original as Shakespeare, and as widely influential as Voltaire, has been amongst us." [5]

On September 19, 1836, the first meeting of the Transcendental Club was called at the house of George Ripley in Boston. Ripley, Emerson, Hedge, Clarke, and Alcott were among those present, and invitations were also sent to William Henry Channing, Jonathan Phillips, John Dwight, James Walker, Cyrus Bartol, and Nathaniel Frothingham. By the following year Theodore Parker, Margaret Fuller, and Elizabeth Peabody were added to the list of membership.[6] In 1836 Emerson's *Nature* was also published, as well as the first American edition of Carlyle's *Sartor Resartus.*

The Transcendentalists had declared themselves. In writing to Carlyle Emerson said that the newspaper writers were warning people against him and against Transcendentalism, Goethe, and Carlyle.[7] Orestes Brownson in the *Boston Quarterly Review* also defended the Transcendentalists from a new attack which had appeared in the *Christian Examiner,* November, 1837:

Who these Transcendentalists are, what is their number, and what are their principal tenets, the writer does not inform us. Nor does he

1. *Western Messenger, 1* (June, 1835), 43-4.
2. *Ibid., 1* (February, 1836), 531-3.
3. *Ibid., 1* (January, 1836), 457-9.
4. *Ibid., 2* (November, 1836), 231-2.
5. *Ibid., 2* (August, 1836), 60-1.
6. For details see *American Literature, 3* (March, 1931), 14-21.
7. *Emerson-Carlyle Correspondence, 1,* 183.

tell us precisely the dangers we have to apprehend from their labors; but so far as we can collect his meaning, it would seem that these dangers consist in the fact that the Transcendentalists encourage the study of German literature and philosophy, and are introducing the habit of writing bad English. He may be right in this. It is a matter we do not feel ourselves competent to decide. So far, however, as our knowledge extends, there is no overweening fondness for German literature and philosophy. We know not of a single man in this country, who avows himself a disciple of what is properly called the Transcendental Philosophy.[8]

The year 1838 was even a fuller year for the Transcendentalists. The *Western Messenger* printed a long study by Margaret Fuller on Karl Theodor Körner, the German patriotic poet who had been praised so highly at an earlier date by Professor Follen. Clarke also paid tribute in this periodical to the German contribution of Carlyle. Carlyle, he said, had done a great deal by his writings to make Americans acquainted with the modern literature of Germany. When he began to write, eight or ten years before, they knew little more of German literature than Wieland's *Oberon,* Klopstock's *Messiah,* Kotzebue's plays, Schiller's *Die Räuber,* Goethe's *Werther,* a dim notion of his *Faust,* and what they could learn from Madame de Staël's *De l'Allemagne.* Of the philosophy which Kant had founded they had only to say "mystical or Transcendental and having pronounced these two pregnant words," they judged themselves excused from all further examination. Yet, at this very time, there existed a literature unsurpassed in the history of the world for genius, variety, and extent. Of all this they knew little. Much praise then was due Carlyle for having introduced them to this fair circle of gifted minds.[9]

Of even greater importance in 1838 was the publication of a series of volumes called *Specimens of Foreign Standard Literature* under the editorship of George Ripley.[1] Monumental in making the German and French writers familiar to American readers, it included the writings of Cousin, Jouffroy, Constant, Goethe, Schiller, Eckermann, Menzel, De Wette, and the German lyric poets. Ten of the fourteen volumes were devoted entirely to German writings, and the most learned German scholars among the Transcendentalists collaborated on the work. Ripley himself undertook the first two volumes, *Philosophical Miscel-*

---

8. *Boston Quarterly Review, 1* (January, 1838), 86.
9. *Western Messenger, 4* (February, 1838), 422–3.
1. The series was published in Boston by Hilliard, Gray and Company from 1838 to 1842. Ripley had first planned to include in the series a much larger number of works. His prospectus listed the names of Fichte, Richter, Herder, Schelling, Schleiermacher, Lessing, Jacobi, and Novalis, but these volumes never materialized because of financial difficulties.

lanies, which were given over to the French interpreters of German philosophy, Cousin, Constant, and Jouffroy. William Henry Channing translated Jouffroy's *Introduction to Ethics* in two volumes, and Professor Cornelius C. Felton translated Menzel's *German Literature* in three volumes.[2] James Freeman Clarke contributed De Wette's *Theodore, or the Skeptic's Conversion,* and Samuel Osgood translated De Wette's *Human Life, or Practical Ethics.* Brooks's and Dwight's best volumes of German lyrics also appeared in this series.[3]

In 1839 Margaret Fuller's translation of *Eckermann's Conversations with Goethe* came out as the fourth volume of Ripley's series.[4] The *New York Review,* although not usually enthusiastic about German literature, had only good to say of Miss Fuller's contributions, especially of the admirable preface which she added to the translation. In the *Quarterly Review* Sarah Whitman stated that this volume furnished another valuable link in the extensive, yet fragmentary chain of memorials which the public already possessed in relation to Goethe, and one which perhaps assisted them toward the better interpretation of character not yet fully understood. In Miss Fuller's preface to this volume she found much just and comprehensive thought expressed in few words. "Here is neither affected humility," she said, "nor arrogant dictation. She tells us distinctly and simply, what Goethe has been to her own mind, and she does this with so fine an insight into his modes of thinking, so true a sympathy with his character and genius, that we look forward with increased interest to the more complete delineation of them which we have been led to expect from her." [5]

2. Emerson, Margaret Fuller, and Parker censured this work in the *Dial.* See pp. 124–25, 138–39.

3. The *Boston Quarterly Review* spoke in glowing terms of Dwight's translations, as well as of those contributed to the volume by Frothingham, Bancroft, Clarke, Channing, Hedge, Cranch, and Margaret Fuller. The *Christian Examiner* gave credit to Dwight but still preferred Goethe to Schiller. On the other hand, the *North American Review,* the *New York Review,* and the *Western Messenger* had only praise for the work.

4. In regard to Margaret Fuller's translation, John Oxenford wrote in his unabridged translation of the same work: "I feel bound to state that, while translating the First Book, I had had before me the translation by Mrs. Fuller, published in America. The great merit of this version I willingly acknowledge, though the frequent omissions render it almost an abridgement." See *Conversations with Eckermann and Soret* (London, 1909), p. vi.

Emerson evaluated Margaret Fuller's translation from a more personal point of view. "I am so much in your debt by the Eckermann book," he wrote to her, "that I must at least acknowledge the gift. The translating this book seems to me a beneficent action for which America will long thank you. The book might be called—Short way to Goethe's character—so effectually does it scatter all the popular nonsense about him, & show the breadth of common sense which he had in common with every majestic poet, & which enabled him to be the interpreter between the real & the apparent worlds. The Preface is a brilliant statement—with which I have no quarrel, but great contentment & thanks instead. I like it for itself, & for its promise. That you can write on Goethe, seems very certain in all this decision and intelligence ; and moreover, you will give us the comfort of good English, as the whole book declares." See Emerson, *Letters, 2,* 201–3.

5. *Boston Quarterly Review, 3* (January, 1840), 21.

All was not smooth sailing, however. In 1839 two crushing articles written by J. W. Alexander and Albert B. Dod appeared in the *Princeton Review*. Since these men opposed the Transcendental philosophy on account of its pantheistic tendencies and had brought charges of atheism against De Wette, Spinoza, and Schleiermacher, Andrews Norton republished the articles at Cambridge under the title "The Latest Form of Infidelity." Ripley refuted the charge in a spirited rejoinder, "The Latest Form of Infidelity Examined; a letter to Andrews Norton," and the next year he resigned his pastorate. Clarke in the *Western Messenger* also spoke up. "Most English and American writers," he said, "seem perfectly paralyzed with terror, when they undertake to look into German Theology. . . . If German Theology be rank infidelity, as many in their simplicity suppose, is it not better to know something of it and be able to meet it and confute it?" [6] Of course, the Reverend William Ware shielded Norton in the pages of the *Christian Examiner* and castigated the Transcendentalists for their radical beliefs. Emerson, in particular, was subjected to criticism.

> The Princeton Reviewers express alarm at what they understand to be the progress of such [Transcendental] doctrines among the Unitarians of Boston and its neighborhood. . . . We can assure these gentlemen, that they who even "affect to embrace" this creed are very few. We know of but a single individual whom the public has any sufficient ground for regarding as a believer of it. From the published writings of Mr. Emerson, quoted by the Reviewers, and their accordance with the language quoted from the German philosophers, it may with great apparent certainty be inferred that he is of their school; and beside him there are a few others, who, if not to be termed followers, yet hold generally with him. But it is by no means a safe conclusion, the Reviewers must understand, that because Mr. Emerson was admired as a lecturer, he was therefore received as a master or authority in either philosophy or religion; for we suppose it true that not an individual out of his crowd of hearers at the close of his lectures could have stated with any confidence what his religious or philosophical system was; whether he himself was theist, pantheist, or atheist. . . .[7]

The opposition was losing ground, however, as we can see by a review of the dispute in the *Boston Quarterly Review*. It pointed out that it was unfair to lump all the Transcendentalists together and that no single term could describe them. With regard to the charge of being of a foreign origin, the writer went on to say:

6. *Western Messenger, 6* (November, 1838), 57-8.
7. *Christian Examiner, 28* (July, 1840), 388.

Truth transcends both time and space, and . . . it matters little whether its first discoverer be a Frenchman, a Dutchman, or a Yankee. But in point of fact the charge is unfounded. . . . The movement is really of American origin, and the prominent actors in it were carried away by it before ever they formed any acquaintance with French or German metaphysics; and their attachment to the literatures of France and Germany is the effect of their connexion with the movement, not the cause.

Moreover, there are no members of the movement party, who would adopt entirely the views of any one of the distinguished foreigners named. We are inquiring for ourselves, and following out the direction of our own minds, but willing to receive aid, let it come from what quarter it may. . . . We have nothing to do with Hegel, or Schelling, or Kant, or Cousin, any further than our own inquiries lead us to approve their speculations. We are aiming at truth, and believe that here, where thought is free, and the philosopher may tell his whole thought without any circumlocution or reticence, we may attain to a purer philosophy than can be found in either France or Germany.[8]

Reviews and occasional defenses such as this were not enough to appease the Transcendentalists. By this time they realized that they needed their own periodical to express the ideas which had engaged their attention during the past two decades. In 1840, therefore, the *Dial: a Magazine for Literature, Philosophy and Religion* was published for the first time under the editorship of Margaret Fuller. In the sixteen volumes which appeared four times a year between July, 1840, and April, 1844, are found some of the most significant comments on German literature made by the Transcendentalists. In this chronological survey it would not be fitting to analyze these articles in detail, but a list of the major contributions to the *Dial* on German subjects might be useful.[9]

July, 1840
    M. Fuller, Richter
October, 1840
    R. W. Emerson, Thoughts on Modern Literature
    C. Tappan, From Goethe
January, 1840
    T. Parker, German Literature
    M. Fuller, Menzel's View of Goethe
July, 1841

8. *Boston Quarterly Review, 3* (July, 1840), 270–2.
9. This list contains only complete articles and poems dealing with German literature and thought. Many incidental references and passages pertaining to German culture, however, appeared in almost every article of the *Dial.*

M. Fuller, Goethe
C. Tappan, Bettina
M. Fuller, Goethe's Faust
October, 1841
 M. Fuller, Lives of the Great Composers
 M. Fuller, Festus
January, 1842
 M. Fuller, Bettine [*sic*] Brentano and her Friend Günderode
 M. Fuller, Epilogue to the Tragedy of Essex, from the German of Goethe
 R. W. Emerson, Transcendentalism
 M. Fuller, Goethe's Egmont
April, 1842
 C. A. Dana, Herzliebste
 T. Parker, Harwood's "German Anti-Supernaturalism"
July, 1842
 F. H. Hedge, Uhland, The Castle by the Sea
 R. W. Emerson, Schelling in Berlin
October, 1842
 M. Fuller, Romaic and Rhine Ballads
January, 1843
 R. W. Emerson, Lectures on the Times III. The Transcendentalist
 T. Parker, The Life and Character of Dr. Follen
 C. S. Wheeler [Letters from Heidelberg]
 F. H. Hedge, Schelling's Introductory Lecture in Berlin
 R. W. Emerson (?) Letters of Schiller
 R. W. Emerson (?) Life of Jean Paul Richter
 R. W. Emerson (?) Fables of La Fontaine
 R. W. Emerson (?) Goethe and Swedenborg
 C. Lane, An Essay on Transcendentalism
April, 1843
 R. W. Emerson, Europe and European Books
 C. Wheeler, Letter from Heidelberg
October, 1843
 W. E. Channing, William Tell's Song
January, 1844
 R. W. Emerson (?) Deutsche Schnellpost
April, 1844
 C. T. Brooks, Freiligrath, The Emigrants
 C. T. Brooks, Freiligrath, The Moorish Prince

Of the articles in this list the most important was Theodore Parker's championship of German literature. Beginning as a review of Menzel's

German Literature, which had violently attacked Goethe, Parker developed it into a full-fledged encomium of German literature, thought, and achievement.[1] Not all prejudice was overcome. The *Dial* contributors themselves were at times among their own sternest critics, but at least their own opinions hereafter were more liberal in tone. Nor did the Transcendentalists always agree among themselves. Emerson's essay in the *Dial,* "Thoughts on Modern Literature," was not altogether complimentary to Goethe, and Margaret Fuller did not hesitate to reprove him for some of his comments.[2] In a letter to Emerson on July 19, 1840, she wrote: "I am very glad I am to own these remarks about the Meister. As to the genius of Goethe, the statement, though so much better than others, is too imperfect to be true. He requires to be minutely painted in his own style of hard finish. As he never gave his soul in a glance, so he cannot be painted at a glance." [3]

No more was there any doubt about the Transcendentalists' point of view. They were not asking merely for toleration of German culture but for its acceptance on an equal footing with anything the English-speaking world could offer. All their activities from this time forth reflected this trend of thought. At Brook Farm, for example, German literature assumed an important role. Charles A. Dana, an enthusiastic linguist fresh from Harvard, collected a class of seven students to study German at the Farm. Georgiana Kirby wrote in her book *Years of Experience:* "What a royal time we had! The whole progress from Follen's *Reader* to Schiller's *Song of the Bell, Pegasus,* Goethe's *Hermann and Dorothea,* and *Faust,* was a delight." [4] Evening classes were formed where Immanuel Kant could be studied.[5] Kant also formed the staple of conversation at the dinner table.[6] Mr. Ripley spent Sunday afternoons expounding Kant's philosophy to those who wished to hear him,[7] and among Brownson's papers are preserved his analysis of Kant's *Kritik der reinen Vernunft,* showing how elaborate were his preparations for the discussion of the matter. Father Hecker, kneading at the dough-trough, fastened Kant's *Kritik* upon the wall before him, and when Hecker completed that, he turned to Fichte and Hegel.[8]

1. Dr. W. T. Harris wrote in March, 1889: "Theodore Parker's article in the *Dial,* January, 1841, was the cause of much study of German literature and of my own study of it among the rest." See *Report of the Commissioner of Education for the Year 1897–1898, 1,* 613.

2. Nevertheless, Emerson's remarks on Goethe and German literature in this essay are more revealing in an estimate of his ideas than his later essay on Goethe in *Representative Men.*

3. See G. W. Cooke, *Introduction to the Dial, 1,* 74.

4. *Years of Experience* (New York, 1887), pp. 97–8. See also A. E. Russell, *Home Life of the Brook Farm Association* (Boston, 1900), p. 62.

5. J. T. Codman, *Brook Farm, Historic and Personal Memoirs* (Boston, 1894), p. 45.

6. H. F. Brownson, *Orestes A. Brownson's Early Life* (Detroit, 1898), *1,* 413.

7. The *Century Magazine, 45* (November, 1892), 146.

8. W. Elliott, *The Life of Father Hecker* (New York, Columbus Press, 1894), p. 31.

In the *Harbinger,* a periodical published by the Brook Farm Association, almost every phase of German literature was canvassed.[9] In fact, German literature in America had come to stay and the increase in publications of German works inside and outside the Transcendental circle received a tremendous impetus. A few of the important contributions in the 1840's were Clarke's translation of De Wette's *Theodore; or the Skeptic's Conversion* (1841), Brooks's second collection of *German Lyric Poetry* (1842), Parker's translation of De Wette's *Einleitung in das alte Testament* (1843), Brooks's *Life of Jean Paul Richter* (1845), Samuel Gray Ward's publication of Goethe's *Essays on Art* (1845), Hedge's *Prose Writers of Germany* (1847), and Emerson's essay on Goethe in *Representative Men* (1850).

What a contrast from the early years! In 1800 hardly a German book could be unearthed in Boston. By the time of the *Dial* and Brook Farm there were few educated people in Boston who could not speak fluently about some phase of German philosophy, German literature, or German music, and the Transcendentalists deserve much of the credit for this change. Theodore Parker might have been speaking for all his acquaint-

9. Typical articles dealing with German literature in the *Harbinger* are the following:

June 14, 1845: Review of Goethe's *Essays on Art.*
June 21, 1845: Review of *Correspondence between Schiller and Goethe from 1794 to 1805.*
July 12, 1845: Translations of German poems by J. S. Dwight.
July 19, 1845: Translation of Novalis' *Hymn to the Night.*
 Article on "Social Movements in Germany."
Aug 9, 1845: Review of *Tales from the German* by Zschokke.
Aug 23, 1845: Review of *Flower, Fruit and Thorn Pieces* by Jean Paul Richter.
 Translation of Uhland's "The Minstrel's Curse" by C. P. Cranch.
Aug 30, 1845: Translation of Rückert's "The Beauty of the Earth."
Sept 13, 1845: Translation of Heine's "Mutual Longing."
Sept 27, 1845: Review of Goethe's *Essays on Art* edited by Samuel Gray Ward.
Oct 4, 1845: Poem "Example" by Goethe.
Oct 18, 1845: Poem "Thought and Action" translated from the German.
 Poem "To the Moon" by Hölty.
 Poem "Hymn to Joy" by Schiller.
Dec 13, 1845: *Gems of German Song* reviewed.
Jan 3, 1846: *From the Deutsche Schnellpost*—brief on Heine.
Jan 24, 1846: Poem "The Last Poet" translated by Frothingham.
 Review of Parke Godwin's translation of Goethe's *Autobiography.*
Feb 28, 1846: "The Religious Movement in Germany."
Mar 28, 1846: Note on Heine in Column from the *Schnellpost.*
Apr 18, 1846: Review of *Memoir of Johann Gottlieb Fichte.*
 Poem "The Question" translated from Heine.
July 4, 1846: Poem "A Cradle Song" translated from Rückert.
Aug 22, 1846: Note on Freiligrath.
Aug 29, 1846: Translation of poem "Via Crucis Via Lucis."
Nov 21, 1846: Translation of German poem by Goethe.
Dec 26, 1846: Translation of German poem by Goethe.
Jan 2, 1847: Poem "Stille Liebe."
Feb 27, 1847: "The Artists" from Schiller's Ode.
Mar 20, 1847: Poem "Wanderer's Night Song" by Goethe.
Mar 27, 1847: Poem "Proverbial" by Goethe.

ances when in 1847 he wrote to a friend in Germany: "I feel so much indebted to your country for the efforts so often made for the freedom of mankind, that I rejoice at the thought of paying back to any one a small part of the debt which I owe to the great souls which have risen up in Germany. German literature is well known in this country, and is sowing the land with fruitful seed." [1]

Apr 10, 1847: Poem "Uhland" by W. A. Butler.
Apr 24, 1847: Poem "Dithyrambic" by Goethe.
May 8, 1847: Poem "Metamorphosis of Plants" from Goethe.
July 10, 1847: Review of Parke Godwin's translation of Goethe's *Autobiographiy,* Parts 3 and 4.
July 17, 1847: Poem "Mohamet's Song" by Goethe.
   Poem "Longings" by Goethe.
Oct 2, 1847: Note on Bettina von Arnim.
   1. Weiss, *1,* 269.

2

The Transcendentalists

A. THE MEN OF LETTERS
EMERSON AND HIS CONCORD FRIENDS

IN THE peaceful village of Concord, Massachusetts, almost a century and a half ago, little, as said, was known of German literature. The philosophy and thought of England, especially in regard to religious and moral teachings, had been enough for these people. A few hardy souls dared to scan the writings of the French philosophers, but no one as yet had the courage to carry the search any further. Rumors were adrift from Harvard that John Quincy Adams, the Everett brothers, and a few other young radicals had exhumed a new body of literature in Germany, but one could hardly expect it to be a source of orthodox, Christian thought. Besides, New Englanders had already sampled German literature. Scandalous, sentimental, and immoral works like *Die Räuber* and *Werther* were well known in the vicinity of Boston. Even if it were true that more serious thinkers had arisen, particularly a man by the name of Immanuel Kant, no one could be bothered to learn their barbarous language.

Such was the opinion in Concord of German culture, but during the first four decades of the nineteenth century a quiet revolution in traditional thought took place in this village. Within the environs of Concord itself a new group of writers and thinkers arose who may have adopted their name, Transcendentalist, from the teachings of Kant. Actually in the early decades they knew little of this man's writings. Their information came not so much from German philosophy as from German literature, which they read with boundless enthusiasm. They were still shocked by its franchised thought and its unorthodox approach to traditional moral concepts, but they no longer hesitated to import German books, attend lectures and courses on German culture, and even send their sons to study the new doctrines at the universities of Göttingen, Berlin, Heidelberg, and Bonn.

Of the Transcendentalists the Concord men of letters were by no means the most learned in the field of German literature. If one were to list them according to the thoroughness of their German background, people like Emerson, Alcott, Thoreau, and Hawthorne could not compare with Hedge, Parker, Ripley, Dwight, Clarke, or Margaret Fuller. In fact, in the early years the Concord writers played down their interest in German thought. Even Emerson, on his first journey to Europe in 1833, made no effort to visit Germany. Nor did he become acquainted with any famous German writer until late in life and then only with one, Hermann Grimm. Alcott never learned the German language, and Thoreau did not enjoy acknowledging any foreign influences on his ideas except perhaps the Greek and Latin classics. He wrote in *A Week on the Concord and Merrimack Rivers:* "Scholars are wont to sell their birthright for a mess of learning. But is it necessary to know what the speculator prints, or the thoughtless study, or the idle read, the literature of the Russians and the Chinese, or even the French philosophy and much of German criticism?" [1] This statement, however, was not his last word. In a remarkably short time he came to admire the new learning almost as much as did any other member of the Transcendental circle.

If the Concord writers were not great students of German literature, one may ask why they should be considered ahead of their more learned associates in the Transcendental group. Three reasons may be advanced. In the first place, although many of the other Transcendentalists were more competent critics and scholars of the German language and literature, they often turned to the Concord group for inspiration. Secondly, although the Concord writers were more tepid about German literature than some of their friends, they read the works of German authors intermittently over a period of sixty years. Finally, by studying their divers strictures on German literature, one is able to form a more accurate picture of the ideas, aims, and accomplishments of all the Transcendentalists.

Emerson did the spade work for the Concord group in the study of the German language. Perhaps when he withdrew *Wilhelm Meisters Lehrjahre* from the Harvard College Library on December 5, 1828, he had that idea in mind. Yet as far as we know he took no formal lessons in the language before 1836. At that time Hermann Bokum, then teaching German at Harvard, proposed to give him private instruction. Bokum recommended Elizabeth Hoar as a competent teacher, but ultimately Margaret Fuller undertook the task of teaching him German pronunciation. Emerson in his journal thus recorded his struggle to learn the language: "Margaret Fuller left us yesterday morning. Among many things that make her visit valuable and memorable, this is not the least, that she gave me five or six lessons in German pronunciation, never by my offer and rather against my will each time, so that now, spite of myself, I shall always have to thank her for a great convenience

1. *The Writings of Henry David Thoreau* (Boston, Houghton Mifflin, 1906), *1*, 98.

—which she foresaw." [2] He never entirely mastered German pronunciation.[3] Emerson used the language for reading only, and when he was
able to obtain a good translation, he did not refuse it. "I should as soon
think of swimming across Charles River when I wish to go to Boston,"
he once said, "as of reading all my books in originals when I have them
rendered for me in my mother tongue." [4] In spite of this statement, he
read his favorite German authors, especially Goethe, in the original.[5]

Emerson was still far more at home in the German language than his
other Concord friends. Thoreau did not take his first lessons in German
until 1835, when he spent the winter with Orestes Brownson at Canton,
Massachusetts.[6] Brownson, who was then interested in Transcendentalism, undertook to teach him the language, but Thoreau never learned
it well enough to read German literature in the original. So far as we
know, his reading of translations also did not begin before 1836. In
September and again in October of that year Thoreau borrowed from
the Harvard College Library Schlegel's *Lectures on the History of
Literature*.[7] He also may have read at this time Zimmermann's *Thoughts
on the Influence of Solitude on the Heart,* a book which might have
had an effect on his plans for the Walden experiment.[8] Another German romanticist who appealed to Thoreau was Friedrich von Harden-
berg, better known as Novalis. This writer was recommended in the
Dial [9] as well as in an essay by Carlyle, and the *Hymns to the Night*
[*Hymnen an die Nacht*] made some impression on Thoreau. At least
with Novalis he shared a liking for the night.

2. Emerson, *Journals, 4, 225.*

3. Emerson said to Grimm in 1861, "I read German with some ease, and always better,
yet I never shall speak it." See *Emerson-Grimm Correspondence,* p. 60. In 1871 he admitted to Edward Waldo Emerson that he wished he could write German, were it only
to correspond with Hermann Grimm. See Emerson, *Letters, 6, 188.*

4. Emerson, *Works, 7, 204.*

5. James B. Thayer tells this anecdote, which is only one of many illustrations proving
Emerson's lifelong reading of Goethe in the original: "As we crossed Illinois, in the long,
delightful leisure of our first day in the *Huron,* Mr. Emerson began by pulling out of his
satchel a little German dictionary and a small volume that Mr. George Bancroft had sent
him as a New Year's present, Goethe's *Sprüche in Prosa.* . . . He found it an excellent time to study his German, in the cars." See *A Western Journey with Mr. Emerson*
(Boston, Little, Brown, 1884), pp. 16–17.

6. Thoreau also studied German with Mrs. Sarah Ripley in Concord and attended some
of Longfellow's classes. Henry Canby described the latter experience as follows: "In the
spring of his senior year, he took the informal round table course in German, in which
the young dandy, Longfellow, just back from Europe, translated ballads and talked of
German literature. It was Longfellow's first actual course, and may have proved too informal for the serious young man of Concord to whom German as the tongue of the
philosophers already meant so much." See *Thoreau* (Boston, Houghton Mifflin, 1939),
p. 43.

7. See K. W. Cameron, *Emerson the Essayist* (Raleigh, N.C., Thistle Press, 1945), *2,*
193.

8. Zimmermann, often called the German Rousseau, gained popularity in America by
means of this book. Between the years 1793 and 1825 the book passed through ten editions.

9. See *9* (July, 1842), 132.

Since Bronson Alcott never studied the German language, it is often erroneously assumed that he had no particular interest in German culture. Other critics grudgingly concede that he was led by Emerson to glance at a few German translations. These assumptions are not correct. On the contrary, one may almost say that Alcott interested Emerson in German philosophy. We find our best evidence of Alcott's reading in his numerous diaries and published works, such as *Concord Days*. On April 22, 1834, he wrote in his diary that the literature of England had been a great drawback to his spiritual and intellectual growth. Ignorant until shortly before this time of the wealth of German literature and the ancient classics, he found himself plodding his way "shrouded in the darkened atmosphere of self-ignorance" and feeding his yearning spirit "with the godless nutriment of a literature spawned from the heart of moral disease." [1] Three weeks later he again complained that English literature was remarkably barren in all that relates to pure morality or deep metaphysical analysis. He found only "commonplace sentiment" and "superficial philosophy" in them. The French and particularly the Germans excelled the English in these subjects, but, he added, "little reaches us from these quarters." [2]

Although Alcott had begun to read German literature in the 1820's, Carlyle's *Sartor Resartus*, which appeared in *Fraser's Magazine* beginning in February, 1833, first made him aware that in German literature he might find a guide to the philosophy he was looking for. He also enjoyed Carlyle's *Life of Friedrich Schiller* and the translation of *Wilhelm Meister*. Two other English interpreters of German thought took high rank in Alcott's estimation. In the writings of Samuel Taylor Coleridge, Alcott, like many of his contemporaries, found his first opportunity to become acquainted with the idealistic philosophy of Schelling. He did not limit his German reading, however, to the philosophers. Since the English writers could no longer supply the deeper wants of his nature, he soon made the acquaintance of such writers as Herder, Lessing, Goethe, Richter, and the Schlegels. He found their work teeming with the spirit of man and far removed from "the dust of the earth," of "the plodding business of sublunary life." In their writings, he said, imagination and reason blended in one whole, and the human spirit was led onward by their mutual aid. [3]

Alcott depended entirely upon translations, although at times his household hummed with the study of the German language. German books were even added to his small but choice library. In England he

1. *The Journals of Bronson Alcott,* ed. Odell Shepard (Boston, 1938), p. 38.
2. *Ibid.,* p. 43.
3. Odell Shepard, *Pedlar's Progress: the Life of Bronson Alcott* (Boston, Little, Brown, 1937), p. 160.

acquired Fichte's *Vernunft* and *Bestimmung,* Schelling's *Bruno,* and Novalis' *Schriften.*[4] He stocked his library at Fruitlands with Jacob Böhme's *Works,* Spinoza's *Works* and *Epistles,* and Homberg's *Mythologie der Griechen und Römer.*[5] In a catalogue of his library which appeared in the *Dial,* April, 1843, other German works are also mentioned, including *Selections in German* by Madame Guion and Krummacher's *Parabeln.*[6]

When Alcott had difficulty understanding these Germans, he sought out his friends for aid. On August 3, 1839, he recorded in his journal that he had ridden to Jamaica Plain to see Margaret Fuller. Finding her absent, he spent the afternoon discussing theological subjects with Theodore Parker. Evidently German scholarship in theology made the subject of conversation, since Alcott added: "Parker is a student of German theology and sympathizes with the new views. He has made translations of several German works, which he intends to publish." [7]

Other residents of Concord also learned the language with varying degrees of success. Sarah Ripley, who lived at the Old Manse, studied German along with her Latin, Greek, French, and Italian. Although she found it "an abominable language" in which she thought she had made little progress, she soon mastered its strange grammar, vocabulary, and sentence structure.[8] Before long she choked the Manse with German books. The minister's study, the upstairs hall, even the attic alcoves spilled over with the works of the German theologians, philosophers, dramatists, and poets. It was here that Nathaniel Hawthorne, already exposed to German culture by the Peabody family, first found the stories of Tieck, for Mrs. Ripley owned Tieck's complete works.[9] On March 21, 1838, Hawthorne wrote to Longfellow from Salem: "I am going to study German. What dictionary had I better get? Perhaps you can procure me a second-hand one without trouble—which, as perhaps it is a large and costly work, would be quite a considerable favor. But it is no great matter; for I am somewhat doubtful of the stability of my resolution to pursue the study." [1] His enthusiasm, as he predicted, did not survive the summer heat. By midsummer Sophia Pea-

---

4. *Ibid.,* pp. 340–1.

5. C. E. Sears, *Bronson Alcott's Fruitlands* (Boston, Houghton Mifflin, 1915), pp. 177–85.

6. The *Dial, 12* (April, 1843), 545–8.

7. *The Journals of Bronson Alcott,* p. 134.

8. G. Bradford, *Portraits of American Women* (Boston, Houghton Mifflin, 1919), p. 30.

9. The volumes of Tieck which Hawthorne used still stand in the Manse on the open shelves along with the amazing collection of other German works which Mrs. Ripley gathered together.

1. See Nathaniel Hawthorne, *The American Notebooks,* ed. Randall Stewart (New Haven, Yale University Press, 1932), 320ff.

body told her sister Elizabeth that Mary had invited Hawthorne and his sister to come and read German, but that he did not wish to take the trouble.[2] In 1843 he resumed his study of German, principally to continue the reading of Tieck, but the interest was again short lived.[3] On April 11 just when he was "on the point of choking with a huge German word," the maid announced Mr. Thoreau, and Hawthorne never again mentioned his study of the German language.[4] Like his acquaintances, he took the easy way out and read available translations.[5]

If the Concord writers did not know the German language in the early decades of the nineteenth century, they did know German literature. Emerson, as early as February, 1817, withdrew from the Boston Library Society Klopstock's *Messiah,* translated by Joseph Collyer. During his studies at Harvard he had only praise for Ticknor's lectures on foreign literature, and his enthusiasm for Everett's knowledge of the German classical scholars suggests the possibility that he read works recommended by them.[6] By 1822 he had already become initiated into the works of the Schlegels;[7] he also withdrew Madame de Staël's *De l'Allemagne* from the library. In 1823 Emerson conveyed his delight to a friend at Andover over the fact that German and Hebrew were being taught, and to his brother William studying in Germany he wrote in November, 1824: "If you think it every way advisable, indisputably, absolutely important that I shd do as you have done & go to C—— & you can easily decide—why say it distinctly & I will make the sacrifice of time & take the risk of expense, immediately. So of studying German. . . . Say particularly if German & Hebrew be worth reading for tho' I hate to study them cordially I yet will the moment I can count my gains."[8] In spite of his brother's enthusiasm, Emerson decided against the idea. As late as 1828 he even denied to Frederic Henry Hedge that he had any knowledge of German literature.[9] One cannot, however,

2. See Julian Hawthorne, *Nathaniel Hawthorne and his Wife* (Boston, Houghton Mifflin, 1884), *1*, 185, 192.

3. Lowell in *A Fable for the Critics* called Hawthorne "a Puritan Tieck." The resemblances between the German and American writer are, for the most part, superficial.

4. *The Amercian Notebooks,* pp. 333–43.

5. At Brook Farm Hawthorne again showed no special interest in the general enthusiasm for the German language. He even ridiculed the practice among the Transcendentalists in his story "The Celestial Railroad."

6. Most scholars contend that Emerson was first introduced to German literature by Carlyle. That is far from the truth. Carlyle no doubt intensified his study of German, especially the language itself and the writings of Goethe, but Emerson was by no means ignorant of the German writers at least from 1821 on.

7. Whether it was August Schlegel's *A Course of Lectures on Dramatic Art and Literature* or Friedrich Schlegel's *Lectures on the History of Literature* is uncertain. He again read Schlegel in 1824. Thoreau also read Friedrich Schlegel's work in September and October, 1836.

8. Emerson, *Letters, 1*, 154–5.

9. See J. E. Cabot, *A Memoir of Ralph Waldo Emerson, 1*, 139.

take this statement too seriously. By that time he had already been introduced to Goethe's writings,[1] and had read Carlyle's series of essays on German literature published in the *Edinburgh Review, Fraser's Magazine,* and the *Foreign Quarterly Review.* He also purchased two volumes of Eichhorn, the German Biblical scholar who had been William's teacher at Göttingen.[2] On a trip to New Hampshire he took along a German book, although he did not read a line of it.[3]

Emerson's knowledge of the Orient, over which much ink has been spilled, also depended on his knowledge of German. Even Arthur Christy, author of *The Orient in American Transcendentalism,* admits that Emerson knew no Oriental languages but modeled his lines on the German of von Hammer-Purgstall rather than directly on the Persians.[4] In Emerson's personal copy of von Hammer-Purgstall's rendering of Hafiz, Mr. Christy found a small sheet on which was written a passage from the German and then two renderings into English. One finds these translations interesting not only as an example of the type of Persian poetry which Emerson preferred, but as evidence of his proficiency in German and the freedom of his translation. Emerson's friend Sanborn said of these translations from the German: "I had a great pleasure, a week or two since, in hearing Emerson read some of his unprinted poems, among them some translations from the Eastern poets, Hafiz, Saadi, and others, which he knows through the German of Von Hammer." [5] Emerson had also read Goethe's translations of Hafiz, and perhaps first encountered the Persian poet in works like the *West-oestlicher Divan.*[6]

Likewise the knowledge of science influencing Emerson's Transcendental ideas was rooted in German. Between 1830 and 1840 he had been reading such books by Goethe as *The Introduction to Morphology* and *The Metamorphosis of Plants,*[7] which, as he said himself, "laid the philosophic foundations of comparative anatomy in both vegetable and animal worlds." [8] Again in the essay "Poetry and Imagination" he wrote: "Science does not know its debt to imagination. Goethe did not

1. He withdrew *Memoirs of Goethe* [*Dichtung und Wahrheit*] from the Boston Library Society, April 3, 1828.
2. Emerson, *Letters, 1,* 250.
3. Probably the book was a volume of Goethe, which Emerson had drawn from the College library a few days before.
4. See also F. I. Carpenter, *Emerson and Asia* (Cambridge, Harvard University Press, 1930), pp. 190–1 and 203.
5. F. B. Sanborn, *Ralph Waldo Emerson* (Boston, Small, Maynard, 1901), p. 101. Emerson's custom was first to turn the rhythmical German into prose and then to versify it. *Ibid.,* p. 116.
6. Emerson's knowledge of Neoplatonism also had part of its origin in German sources. In 1837 he copied into his journals a long passage from Plotinus which he had found quoted in Goethe.
7. *Versuch die Metamorphose der Pflanzen* and *Die Morphologie.*
8. See Emerson, *Journals, 3,* 293–5 for discussion of Goethe's ideas on plants.

believe that a great naturalist could exist without this faculty. He was himself conscious of its help, which made him a prophet among the doctors. From this vision he gave brave hints to the zoölogist, the botanist and the optician." [9]

Before the publication of *Nature* Emerson read for the first time or reread, excluding Goethe's works, the writings of Novalis,[1] the Schlegels, Karl Müller, Jung-Stilling's *Autobiography,* Mendelssohn's *Phaedo,* Herder's *Outlines of the History of Man,* Heeren, Fichte, Tieck, Lessing, Schleiermacher, Schelling,[2] Richter, Wieland (whose letters to Merck he found charming), Boerne, Winckelmann, Zelter's *Correspondence with Goethe,* Schiller's *Correspondence with Goethe,* Friedrich Wolf, Camper, and Tischbein. By 1838 he added to his reading list the names of Spinoza, Niebuhr, Herschel, and Bettina von Arnim.[3]

Certain writers in this list fixed his attention more than others. Although Schiller never became one of his heroes, Emerson read at one time or another almost all his important writings. Emerson's opinion of the individual works was not particularly flattering. *Die Räuber* he considered the crude fruit of a yet immature mind, the *Aesthetics* a struggle with Kantian metaphysics, and Schiller's poetry and history mere intellectual experiments.[4] *Das Lied von der Glocke* he did not read in German, at least not before 1850, when he told William Henry Furness that he did not like it very well, fancying that it owed its popularity to the illustrations of Retsch and to the musical accompaniment.[5] *Die Geschichte des dreissig jährigen Kriegs* he thought could not compare with the description of the Battle of Lützen in the Harleian Miscellany.[6] In spite of such adverse criticism of Schiller as writer, Emerson

9. Emerson, *Works, 8,* 10–11. Emerson's son wrote of his father that Goethe's scientific studies were "a bridge to the reading and understanding of the work of the leading scientists of the time." See E. W. Emerson, *Emerson in Concord* (Boston, Houghton Mifflin, 1889), p. 65.

1. The whole Transcendental group found Novalis' writings of profound interest. He was recommended in the *Dial* (July, 1842) and his works were to be found in the personal libraries of Emerson, Alcott, Clarke, Parker, Ripley, Hedge, and Margaret Fuller.

2. Coleridge's *Aids to Reflection* was his first source of Schelling's philosophy. Alcott was also impressed by this book.

3. To supplement this list gathered from the published reading lists plus his journals and letters, I found in the unpublished manuscripts prior to 1836 the following information. As early as 1830 in one of his blotting books he copied numerous long quotations, not only from Goethe's works such as *Wilhelm Meister, Dichtung und Wahrheit,* and *Die Wahlverwandtschaften,* but also from Fichte and Novalis. From 1830 to 1833 he was also reading Schiller's works as translated in the *New Monthly Magazine* and in the *Foreign Quarterly Review.*

4. Emerson, *Journals, 2,* 525–6.

5. See *Records of a Lifelong Friendship, 1807–1882; Ralph Waldo Emerson and William Henry Furness,* edited by H. H. Furness (Boston, Houghton Mifflin, 1910), p. 73.

6. Emerson read this work of Schiller as early as 1829.

called Schiller the man pure gold.[7] His opinion of Schiller's personality, no doubt, was colored by Carlyle's *Life of Schiller,* which, gaining great popularity in this country, materially aided the spread of German literature among American scholars.

Jean Paul Richter's works were also well known in Concord. Emerson, however, did not care for him, occasioning some surprise from his friend Furness, who questioned him about it. He wrote to Emerson: "You told me I recollect, that you did not & do not take to Richter. How is it? Is he not full of the purest humor? And is it not a curious fact in literature, in life, the twin-like resemblance between him & Carlyle? Carlyle is no imitator & yet he is, in his fancy & his fun J. Paul over again." [8] Thoreau also noticed this resemblance between Carlyle and Richter. In fact, he regretted that Carlyle had not cultivated the style of Goethe more and that of Richter less.[9] Emerson, however, remained bland in his enthusiasm, although he did purchase a number of Richter's works and lent them to his friends, the Alcotts.[1]

One German author who captured the hearts of all the Concord Transcendentalists was, strangely enough, Bettina von Arnim. When in 1838 Emerson was introduced to her writings for the first time, he immediately began to make a series of laudatory comments about her. He wrote to Margaret Fuller that Bettina's book had won his admiration, that nothing could be richer and nobler than her nature, and that if he went to Germany he should desire to see only her.[2] He wondered why Margaret Fuller did not write to her, since she was worth all the Jamesons and Müllers on earth. Moreover, she was the only formidable test that had ever been applied to Goethe's genius, since her genius was purer than his own.[3] In his journal on July 7, 1839, he spoke of her only in superlatives: "Wonderful Bettina!" he cried. "The rich inventive genius of the painter must all be smothered and lost for want of the power of drawing." [4] Although his enthusiasm did not remain in this high key, as late as 1858 he confessed to Fräulein Gisela von Arnim, afterwards the wife of his friend Hermann Grimm, that he had been for fifteen years an admirer of her mother's genius. He owned all her works, he believed, and he sent his respects to the Frau von Arnim,

7. Emerson, *Journals, 2,* 526.
8. *Records of a Lifelong Friendship,* p. 64.
9. Not that Goethe's style was the kind of utterance most to be prized by mankind, Thoreau said, but it could serve for a model of the best that had been successfully cultivated. See Thoreau, *Writings, 4,* 332.
1. After Louisa May Alcott read one of them, she decided to write a novel with two characters in it like Jean Paul Richter and Goethe, but the plan was never carried out. See E. D. Cheney, *Louisa May Alcott, her Life, Letters and Journals* (Boston, Roberts, 1889), p. 162.
2. For Margaret Fuller's opinions of Bettina see p. 141n.
3. Emerson, *Letters, 2,* 210.
4. Emerson, *Journals, 5,* 237–8.

thanking her for the many happy hours she had formerly given to friends of his and to himself through her writings.[5] Bettina's death was a profound blow to Emerson. He regretted that he had not established his alliance with her circle earlier so that he might have told her how much he and his friends owed her. Emerson circulated Bettina's *Correspondence with Goethe* among his friends; he also lent to Bixby his copy, from which the American edition was printed. In a letter to Heath in Germany he said that Bettina had written a most remarkable book, and that she was "a finer genius than George Sand or Madame de Staël, more real than either, more witty, as profound, and greatly more readable." [6] "Who had such mother wit? such sallies? such portraits? such suppression of commonplace?" he wrote to Grimm.[7] Even when Aunt Mary damned the book, he did not swerve from his opinion. From Emerson's praise the popularity of Bettina radiated throughout Concord. It even had its humorous side. After Louisa May Alcott read Emerson's copy, which she had found while browsing in his library, she was fired with the ambition to be a second Bettina. Louisa decided to make Emerson her Goethe and she wrote letters to him, but never sent them. She even left wild flowers on the doorstep of her "master," and sang Mignon's song under his window in very bad German, but whether Emerson was aware of his little friend's devotion we are not sure.[8]

One might consider the interest in Bettina among the Concord writers as merely a sidelight of the much greater interest in Goethe. For Emerson, Alcott, and Thoreau Goethe always remained the most important of the Germans.[9] Before he met Carlyle on his first journey to Europe in December, 1832, Emerson had already read Goethe's most important works. A letter to Aunt Mary, August 19, 1832, speaks of this new interest: "I am entering into acquaintance with Goethe who has just died. . . . If I go into the country to books, I shall know him well, & you will come & board with Mother & me, & we will try him whether he deserves his niche. . . . In the Wilhelm Meister he leads a child of Nature up from the period of 'Apprenticeship' to that of 'Self production' & leaves him, Schiller says, assured on the way to infinite per-

5. *Emerson-Grimm Correspondence*, pp. 27–8.
6. Emerson, *Letters, 3*, 77.
7. *Emerson-Grimm Correspondence*, pp. 42–4.
8. When Louisa made a list of the most important books to read, she included along with Goethe's and Schiller's works Bettina also. See Cheney, pp. 57, 68.
9. Alcott even used as a means of metaphor in his speech the names of Goethe's works and characters. In his diary he wrote: "Life is but a Werther's Sorrows to many, with an end as tragical; nor can it be otherwise till we come forth from our woes to speak peace to the wailers." The date of this entry is uncertain. See *The Life and Genius of Goethe* (Lectures at the Concord School of Philosophy edited by F. B. Sanborn, Boston, Ticknor, 1886), p. 172.

fection. But the *form* of the book is for us so foreign that it long repels, —full of theatricals, green room etc." [1]

During his travels in Italy Emerson pocketed Goethe's *Italienische Reise* as a handbook.[2] He wrote to George Adams Sampson at this time: "Then so inveterate is my habit of depending upon my books that I do not feel as if my day had substance in it, if I have read nothing. So I labor at German & Italian a little." [3] Emerson later admitted that he would have visited Germany if Goethe had been still living,[4] but with Goethe gone, Emerson turned to the one person, Thomas Carlyle, who could tell him what he wanted to know about this German.

Spurred on by Carlyle, Emerson made tremendous strides in his knowledge of Goethe. A great deal has been written concerning this influence of Carlyle on Emerson. William S. Vance, for example, goes too far in his thesis when he contends that the complete German influence on the Transcendentalists can be traced to the Scotsman.[5] The influence, therefore, was not German at all, but Carlylean. I cannot accept these assumptions. Some of the Transcendentalists, including Emerson, read Carlyle's translations and essays in the *Edinburgh Review,* not because they were Carlyle's writings, but because in the 1820's and early 1830's they still lacked the ability to read the German writers in the original, and few other translations were available. It was not even always known that Carlyle was the author of these works. His *Life of Schiller,* for instance, was published in this country without his name on the title page, and the reviewers of the work did not mention Carlyle by name. Carlyle, like Coleridge or Madame de Staël, merely served as a vehicle for the newly-aroused interest in German literature. His opinions were read with interest but often refuted even by his greatest admirers. One has merely to examine the Emerson-Carlyle correspondence to be convinced of this fact. In November, 1834, Emerson first wrote to Carlyle of German literature, and disagreed with him on the merits of Goethe:

> Far, far better seems to me the unpopularity of this Philosophical Poem (shall I call it?) [*Sartor Resartus*] than the adulation that followed your eminent friend Goethe. With him I am becoming better acquainted, but mine must be a qualified admiration. It is a singular piece of good-nature in you to apotheosize him. I cannot but regard it as his misfortune, with conspicuous bad influence on his

1. Emerson, *Letters, 1,* 354.
2. *Ibid.,* p. 373.
3. *Ibid.,* p. 377.
4. Emerson, *Works, 5,* 4.
5. "Carlyle and the American Transcendentalists," unpublished dissertation, University of Chicago, 1941.

genius,—that velvet life he led. What incongruity for genius, whose fit ornaments and reliefs are poverty and hatred, to repose fifty years on chairs of state! and what pity that his Duke did not cut off his head to save him from the mean end (forgive) of retiring from the municiple incense "to arrange tastefully his gifts and medals"! Then the Puritan in me accepts no apology for bad morals in such as *he*.[6]

Carlyle attempted to change Emerson's opinion by urging him to study the German language with a view toward reading Goethe's works. His was the only healthy mind, of any extent, that had been discovered in Europe for long generations, he wrote to Emerson. Furthermore, he suspected that as yet Emerson knew only Goethe the Heathen, but when he would learn to know Goethe the Christian, he would like that one far better.[7] In a large measure, Carlyle's prophecy came true. On September 17, 1836, Emerson mentioned the fact that he was reading Goethe "with a great interest." By April 22, 1840, the time when Emerson's interest in German literature had reached its peak, he answered a letter of Carlyle, saying: "You asked me if I read German, and I forget if I have answered. I have contrived to read almost every volume of Goethe, and I have 55, but I have read nothing else. . . . There is no great need that I should discourse to you on books, least of all on *his* books; but in a lecture on Literature in my course last winter, I blurted all my nonsense on that subject, and who knows but Margaret Fuller may be glad to print it and send it to you? I know not." [8] Whatever his judgments of Goethe were, they remained independent of Carlyle's opinion. Throughout his life Emerson used his own standards of measurement, not only for Goethe, but for all literature.

By 1836 Emerson had read most of his fifty-five volume set of Goethe's works printed at Stuttgart and Tübingen, and in spite of adverse criticisms of Goethe, he conceded in his journal that every one of his own writings had been taken from the whole of nature, and bore the name of Goethe.[9] Emerson was one of the few in New England at so early a date to possess a complete set of Goethe's works. We are not certain just when he acquired them; it is more than likely that he made the purchase during his first trip to Europe. While at Rome in April, 1833, he may have quoted from volume twenty-nine in a letter to his brother Charles. This set was not the only edition of Goethe in his private

6. *Emerson-Carlyle Correspondence, 1*, 29–30. Although Emerson grew more appreciative of Goethe's merits as the years went by, we find a similar statement as late as the essay on Goethe in *Representative Men*, published in 1850.

7. *Emerson-Carlyle Correspondence, 1*, 39–40.

8. I am quoting from the original MS letter in the Speck Collection of Goetheana at Yale University, since the printed letter in the *Emerson-Carlyle Correspondence* (*1*, 285) is not accurate. In this letter Emerson was referring to the lecture "Thoughts on Modern Literature," which was printed in the *Dial, 2* (October, 1840), 137–58.

9. Emerson, *Journals, 2*, 349.

library.[1] One finds editions published as late as 1877, and many trans-lations of Goethe as well as the originals are still scattered among his heterogeneous collection in Concord.[2]

In August, 1836, he said to his brother: "Goethe is a wonderful man. I read little else than his books lately. Nor yet have weighed him enough to have entirely settled & defined my idea of him."[3] A month later he confessed that he considered Goethe the high priest of the age and the truest of all writers, for his books were all records of what had been lived, and his sentences and words seemed to see.[4] For Emerson Goethe was always the great conveyor of wisdom. In one stanza of the poem "Solution" he exalted this sagacity above all other qualities:

> In newer days of war and trade,
> Romance forgot and faith decayed,
> When Science armed and guided war,
> And clerks the Janus-gates unbar,
> When France, where poet never grew,
> 'Halved and dealt the glove anew,
> Goethe, raised o'er joy and strife,
> Drew the firm lines of Fate and Life,
> And brought Olympian wisdom down
> To court and mart, to gown and town;
> Stooping, his finger wrote in clay
> The open secret of to-day.[5]

From 1837 on, an undercurrent of comment on the works of Goethe ran through the journals and letters of Emerson, Thoreau, and Alcott. Some of these statements merit examination since they clarify ideas later to be expressed in the *Dial* and elsewhere.[6] In his journals, for in-stance, Thoreau copied translations from Goethe's *Torquato Tasso* and *Die Italienische Reise*.[7] On December 8, 1837, he commented on the

1. For a complete list of the German books in Emerson's library, including the Goethe material, see appendix B.
2. That Emerson was generous in lending his German books is proved in his cor-respondence with his friends. Margaret Fuller was one of the greatest borrowers and lenders of German books, especially Goethe's works. She wrote to Emerson, April 11, 1837: "I take the liberty to send Merck and the two first vols of Zelter. Do not trouble yourself to send them back" (Boston Public Library, Fuller MS, No. 64). Again on May 30 she wrote from Groton: "I have now of yours two vols. of Milton, one of Jonson, one of Plutarch's Morals, two of Degerando, with the 7th and 8th of Goethe's nachgelassene Werke. These I should like to keep this summer, if you do not want them, but if you do, please say so." *Ibid.*, No. 65.
3. In the same letter he told how he purchased fifteen volumes of Goethe's *Nachgelas-sene Werke* published in 1832-33. See Emerson, *Letters, 2*, 32-3.
4. Emerson, *Journals, 4*, 94.
5. Emerson, *Works, 9*, 223.
6. Whole passages about Goethe in Emerson's journals appeared in his later essays.
7. Thoreau, *Writings, 7*, 3-11.

latter work: "He [Goethe] is generally satisfied with giving an exact description of objects as they appear to him, and his genius is exhibited in the points he seizes upon and illustrates. His description of Venice and her environs as seen from the Marcusthurm is that of an unconcerned spectator, whose object is faithfully to describe what he sees, and that, too, for the most part, in the order in which he saw it. It is this trait which is chiefly to be prized in the book; even the reflections of the author do not interfere with his descriptions." [8] One of Goethe's chief hallmarks as a writer, he believed, was his ability to render an exact description of things as they appeared to him, and to gauge their effect upon him. "Most travelers," Thoreau said, "have not self-respect enough to do this simply, and make objects and events stand around them as the centre, but still imagine more favorable positions and relations than the actual ones, and so we get no valuable report from them at all." Goethe, on the other hand, traveled in Italy at a snail's pace, and was always mindful of the earth beneath him and the heavens above him. "Above all he possessed a hearty good-will to all men, and never wrote a cross or even careless word." [9]

For Emerson at this time the most important volume of Goethe was the *Conversations with Eckermann*.[1] "Wise mellow adequate talk, on all topics indifferently, always up to the mark," he wrote of this work, and then he added about Goethe: "He is among the Germans what Webster *was* among the lawyers, as easily superior to the great as to the small." [2] Again on April 11, 1837, he praised *Eckermann* in his journal: "I wrote George Bradford that *Eckermann* was full of fine things and helps one much in the study of Goethe. Always the man of genius dwells alone and, like the mountain, pays the tax of snows and silence for elevation. It would seem as if he hunted out this poor Dutch Boswell for a thing to talk to, that his thoughts might not pass in smother. His thinking, as far as I read him, is of great altitude and *all level*. . . . But he is a pledge that the antique force of nature is not spent, and 'tis gay to think what men shall be." [3]

8. *Ibid.,* p. 15.
9. *Ibid., 1,* 347.
1. Emerson urged Margaret Fuller to undertake the translation of this work.
2. Furness, pp. 81-2. To a group of Negro students at Howard University Emerson recommended as important reading Goethe's *Conversations with Eckermann* and Goethe's *Autobiography*. See F. P. Stearns, *Sketches from Concord and Appledore* (New York, Putnam, 1895), pp. 107-8.
3. Emerson, *Journals, 4,* 201-2. Other works of Goethe which interested Emerson included the *Tag und Jahres Hefte*. He mentioned it in his journal as early as 1834, although not without censuring Goethe's so-called immorality. In general, he found it a book unparalleled in America, and an account of all events, persons, studies, taken from one point of view. It proved to him that Goethe "was a person who hated words that did not stand for things," and since he had a sympathy with everything that existed, he never wrote without saying something. See *ibid., 3,* 313-15. Emerson also liked the *Essays on Art* translated by Samuel Gray Ward. In a letter dated May 28, 1845, Emer-

Toward other works of Goethe he was less charitable. *Iphigenie auf Tauris* (a work which should have appealed to Emerson, since the main character is a heroine of the ideal rather than of the actual) he found nothing more than "a pleasing, moving, even heroic work, yet with the great deduction of being an imitation of the antique." [4] Thoreau also must have been familiar with *Iphigenie auf Tauris*, since he commented on December 18, 1847 : "He required that his heroine, Iphigenia, should say nothing which might not be uttered by the holy Agathe, whose picture he contemplated." [5]

Of all Goethe's works, however, the one most misunderstood and abused by the Concord writers was *Die Wahlverwandtschaften*, or *Elective Affinities*. This novel in which Goethe had actually defended the institution of marriage and had preferred moral restraint on the part of the individual for the sake of the greater good, Emerson glossed as the most menacing and unsound of all his works. A few American critics, such as Hedge and Margaret Fuller, had sought its deeper meaning; the majority of the Transcendentalists like Emerson dismissed it as merely the depraved work of an immoral mind.

Emerson, Thoreau, and Alcott made many significant observations on *Wilhelm Meister* and *Faust* in their letters and journals. Emerson pronounced Carlyle's translation of *Wilhelm Meister* "goodly to see, good to read,—indeed quite irresistible." The *Apprenticeship* [*Die Lehrjahre*] he raced through immediately, promising Carlyle to "dispatch the *Travels* [*Die Wanderjahre*] on the earliest holiday." [6] He counseled Charles Woodbury that *Wilhelm Meister* had to be read thoroughly, for it contained an analysis of life. [7] Emerson's essay on Goethe in the *Dial*, however, aimed its main shaft at the immoral tendency in *Wilhelm Meister*, a factor which Thoreau ignored in *A Week on the Concord and Merrimack Rivers*. Thoreau preferred to take issue with the pettiness or exaggeration of trifles, "a magnifying of the theatre till life itself is turned into a stage." He lamented Goethe's lack of idealism, stress of worldly attainments, and lack of primitive virtues, but, unlike Emerson, said not a word of Goethe's moral laxity. [8]

---

son called the *Essays* "good on all grounds, a strong sensible wise book that one can bear to read & to keep, and then also with the agreeable addition that the book is not cabalistic, but can lie in the college libraries & public reading rooms, & go to remove that local *prestige* [sic] against Goethe, by vindicating his claim to the largest share of good sense possessed by his contemporaries." See Emerson, *Letters, 3,* 285-6.

4. Emerson, *Journals, 4,* 34.

5. Thoreau, *Journals, 1,* 19.

6. Emerson, *Journals, 2,* 349.

7. In a letter to Christopher Gore Ripley (see Emerson, *Letters, 2,* 426), Emerson commended Goethe's critique on *Hamlet* in *Wilhelm Meister*.

8. Goethe's autobiography, *Dichtung und Wahrheit,* Thoreau believed, contained similar flaws. The fault of Goethe's education was its merely artistic completeness. "Nature is hindered, though she prevails at last in making an unusually catholic impression on

Concord read Goethe's masterwork, *Faust,* with heightened interest, although its praise was not unanimous. Emerson never could endure *Faust, Part I.*[9] As early as 1830, when he read excerpts from the work by Gower and Shelley, Emerson found it a bold, varied, grotesque creation, but out of nature and wide of Shakespeare.[1] For the *Helena* episode, however—the only version of *Faust, Part II* which he seems to have read thoroughly—he created a special category. In fact, a re-reading of the *Helena* made him recant his former criticism of Goethe.[2] This more gallant opinion becomes obvious in his essay "Nominalist and Realist":

> If you criticise a fine genius, the odds are that you were out of your reckoning, and instead of the poet, are censuring your own caricature of him. For there is somewhat spheral and infinite in every man, especially in every genius, which, if you can come very near him, sports with all your limitations. For rightly every man is a channel through which heaven floweth, and whilst I fancied I was criticising him, I was censuring or rather terminating my own soul. After taxing Goethe as a courtier, artificial, unbelieving, worldly,—I took up this book of Helena and found him an Indian of the wilderness, a piece of pure nature like an apple or an oak, large as morning or night, and virtuous as a briar-rose.[3]

Alcott also read *Faust* and, unlike Emerson, he found it much more praiseworthy. Alcott believed that Goethe had treated the striving of the worst for the best, in nature, more cunningly than either Moses or the author of the Book of Job. Moreover, Goethe, with his eye for subtleties, was better equipped for this old-world fable than any other person of his time. "The demons sat to him," Alcott said, "and we have

---

the boy. It is the life of a city boy, whose toys are pictures and works of art, whose wonders are the theatre and kingly processions and crownings. As the youth studied minutely the òrder and the degrees in the imperial procession, and suffered none of its effect to be lost on him, so the man aimed to secure a rank in society which would satisfy his notion of fitness and respectability." See Thoreau, *Writings 1,* 349. The *Autobiography,* nevertheless, made a lasting impression upon Thoreau. As late as 1857 he recommended the book to B. B. Wiley, along with the biographies of Gibbon, Haydon, and Franklin. *Ibid., 6,* 301.

9. Emerson once said that he thought *Faust* lacked the eternal spirit. See Stearns, pp. 107-8. See also C. J. Woodbury, *Talks with Ralph Waldo Emerson* (New York, Macmillan, 1890), p. 54.

1. Emerson, *Letters, 1,* 305.

2. The same withdrawal of censure appeared in his journals whenever he examined the *Helena.* He wrote in 1843: "In Goethe is that sincerity which makes the value of literature and is that one voice or one writer who wrote all the good books. In *Helena,* Faust is sincere and represents actual, cultivated, strong-natured Man; the book would be farrago without the sincerity of Faust. I think the second part of *Faust* the grandest enterprise of literature that has been attempted since the *Paradise Lost.* It is a philosophy of history set in Poetry." Emerson, *Journals, 6,* 466.

3. Emerson, *Works, 3,* 241-2.

before us the world he knew so well and also the one in which almost all are conversant." [4]

In 1851 when Alcott turned to another version of *Faust* by Anna Swanwick, he found himself ushered more intimately than by Hayward's or Austin's version "into the subtleties of the modern Satan, the world-spirit of the nineteenth century." [5] Goethe's portrait of the devil especially excited him, and he only regretted that Goethe could not have met Daniel Webster, whose "head, shoulders, all" should have gone into the picture. Then he rewarmed in almost identical words the usual hand-me-down opinions of Goethe from the Transcendentalists. He granted that Goethe was the most remarkable instance in literature of "an intellect holding its eye coincident with the plane of things," and that he was endowed with "an aptitude to seize at the niche of time every aspect of the demonic forces as these emerged from their hiding places in Nature." Yet he regretted that Goethe, who lived aloof from life and from the spirit of permanence, was unable to identify himself with the heart and whole of things, the soul of souls. He concluded his criticism with this statement:

> Goethe was cunning, but he was never wisely wise. Too noble for mere prudence, he was coeval with fate; but never magnanimous and Fate's victor; and as the Fates made, so they slew him too, but by incantations soft, siren-like, and prolonged, melodizing his muse, and intimating (almost persuading us the while) his claim to a perpetuity of genius which was not theirs to give. All he was his Faust has taken and celebrates. Faust is admitted to heaven as Goethe to mortality, without the fee of a divinity which alone opens honestly the gates. [6]

For Alcott Goethe stood out as the prime example of reverent faith in nature and the tenderness of treatment that becomes her students and devotees. [7] In spite of Goethe's shortcomings, Alcott defined him as a world teacher, who would remain so for some time to come. He had embodied the spirit and movement of an age in his books, and one could read, with a growing reverence at every perusal, the mind that saw and so well portrayed the world-spirit.

In addition to *Faust*, Alcott read Goethe's *Werther, Zur Farbenlehre,*

4. *The Life and Genius of Goethe,* ed. F. B. Sanborn, pp. 74-5.
5. *Ibid.,* p. 173.
6. *Ibid.,* p. 175. In his book *Concord Days* Alcott reemphasized many of these statements about Goethe. Here we find perhaps the real reason why Goethe appealed to him. "Most edifying," Alcott said, "is the author who suggests, and leaves to his reader the pleasure and profit of following his thought into its various relations with the whole of things, thus stimulating him to explore matters to their issues. The great masters have observed this fine law, and of modern scholars especially Goethe." See *Concord Days,* p. 158.
7. *Ibid.*

Wilhelm Meister, the *Essays on Art*,[8] *Helena* or *Faust, Part II*, the *Correspondence with Bettina*, and *Dichtung und Wahrheit*. Goethe's *Orphic Sayings* [*Urworte. Orphisch*], translated by James Freeman Clarke in the *Western Messenger*, stimulated him to write a similar group of orphic sayings in the *Dial*.[9] Although it may be true that they were "an amazement to the uninitiated and an amusement to the profane," [1] they betray a deep appreciation for the German writer.[2] That these aphorisms were known in Germany we can assume from an interesting anecdote told by Frederick Willis in the book *Alcott Memoirs:*

> During the second summer that I lived with them at Concord an elaborately bound volume addressed to Mr. Alcott arrived by post from Germany. I do not remember the name of the author or the title of the book save that it was written by a then famous German Philosopher. Imprinted upon the cover was a bust of Mr. Alcott and beneath it, in letters of gold, one of his "Orphic Sayings." I have never forgotten the ecstatic expression that came upon Mrs. Alcott's face as she looked upon it, realizing it was something more than a mere compliment. To her it was a token of recognition from a high authority of her husband's fitness to rank among the famous thinkers of the day.[3]

Opinions of Goethe expressed by the Concord writers did not radically differ from each other. Although Thoreau and Alcott may not always have emphasized the same aspects of Goethe's character and talent, for the most part, they followed Emerson's line of reasoning, perhaps because it was obvious to them that he knew far more about Goethe than they. If one were to look for a joint opinion from these men on the subject of Goethe's writings, one could perhaps turn to Emerson's two essays on Goethe, the first which appeared in the *Dial*, October, 1840, and the second in the volume *Representative Men*. Although the essay in the *Dial*, entitled "Thoughts on Modern Literature," was supposed to have dealt with literature in general, the greater part of it was devoted to Goethe—an indication of the importance that this German writer was assuming in the minds of the Transcendentalists. Emerson acknowledged Goethe as the poet, naturalist, and philosopher who of all men had united in himself the tendencies of the era, for "he learned as

8. Samuel Gray Ward's translation of various essays by Goethe.

9. The *Dial*, *1* (July, 1840), 85. One of them called "Vocation" sounds as if Goethe himself had written it: "Engage in nothing that cripples or degrades you. Your first duty is self-culture, self-exaltation; you may not violate this high trust."

1. O. B. Frothingham, *Transcendentalism in New England* (New York, Putnam, 1876), p. 133.

2. A fine example of one of these orphic sayings is to be found in an Alcott MS at the Boston Public Library. The MS is called "Spiritualism."

3. Frederick L. Willis, *Alcott Memoirs* (Boston, Badger, 1915), pp. 52–3.

readily as other men breathe." He praised Goethe for not being afraid
to live, for his bravery, his freedom from narrowness, his perfect
propriety and taste, his sagacity, his industry of observation, and finally
his rejection of all conventions and traditions. He marveled at Goethe's
sharp eye for form and color, for botany, engraving, medals, persons,
and manners. He lauded Goethe's ability to pierce through to the purpose of a thing and to reconcile that purpose with his own being. "To
read his record is a frugality of time," he said, for in it was no word that
did not stand for a thing.

On the other hand, Goethe's "Olympian self-complacency" and the
patronizing air which he adopted toward the performances of other
mortals nettled Emerson. Although this subtle element of egotism in
Goethe did not cripple his compositions, Emerson believed that it dimin-
ished the moral influence of the man. Since Goethe kept himself apart
from his fellow human beings and aimed always at astonishment, no
man could call him brother.[4] While Goethe loved truth sincerely, one
could not overlook the absence of moral sentiment and the equiv-
alence of good and evil action in his writings. Although he may have
truly painted the actual, the ideal remains truer than the actual. To
Emerson, therefore, *Wilhelm Meister* seemed an abject failure. It may
have reproduced a society with painstaking fidelity, but it was nothing
more than that. The limits of artificial society were never quite out of
sight; one was never lifted above oneself. Goethe, then, had to be set
down as "the poet of the Actual not of the Ideal; the poet of limitation,
not of possibility; of this world, and not of religion and hope; in short
. . . the poet of prose, and not of poetry." Because Goethe's moral
perception was flawed, he failed, in the high sense, to be a creator. Humanity eventually would have to let him pass by and continue to wait
patiently for its physician at the side of the road. Emerson thus ended
the discussion elegiacally, feeling that a man so dowered as Goethe
should not have left the world as he had found it. Being so much, he
could not forgive him for not being more.[5]

4. In his *Life of Goethe* Peter Hume Brown, who took issue with this statement by
Emerson, commented: "The implication of the remark is that there was some grave
defect both in his head and in his heart. As for Goethe's heart, it has to be said that
those who knew him best in life were most attracted to him. . . . Jung-Stilling, whom
he knew in his youth and to whom he did many kind offices, said that his heart was as
great as his intellect, and others bore the same witness in almost the same words. . . .
The bond between him and Schiller was primarily intellectual, but his memories of
Schiller were of the heart as well as of the mind. Knebel, who was his friend for over
fifty years, described him as the best of men, the most lovable of mankind. . . . In his
youth and in his old age children delighted in him and he in them—the most evident
proof that he could have been neither cold-hearted nor a pedant." See *Life of Goethe*
(New York, Henry Holt, 1920), *2*, 787.

5. Emerson's contributions to the *Dial* in the field of German literature were not
limited to his interest in Goethe. George Willis Cooke attributed to Emerson a series
of book reviews which no other writer ever claimed and which were printed during the

In the final analysis, Emerson's fundamental theories of life parted company from Goethe's. Goethe, who was not especially steeped in metaphysical speculation, who thought not so much of what might be, as what is, set life down as he had found it. His goal, however, was truth, not art alone, as Emerson seemed to imply. To be sure, Goethe, as the poet of the actual, portrayed man as he knew him. Goethe's universal tolerance barred him from a complete indictment of human nature. His heroes—Tasso, Werther, Orestes, Eduard, Faust, and Wilhelm Meister—were, therefore, never perfect, nor great, nor manly, nor ideal by the standards of Ralph Waldo Emerson. Since all these characters were the personifications of Goethe's own longings, strivings, and hopes, it was impossible for them to achieve the heroic dimensions of Emersonianism.

Yet it was but natural that Emerson should have charged Goethe with worldliness, since as realist Goethe was absorbed in the man of this life, and the man who reached greatness in this world. He wished man, by never losing touch with worldly reality, to find happiness among his fellow beings. He did not expect him to perform great, heroic, and ideal actions, since man was prone to err; but as long as he lived and strove, he would not lose his morality. Goethe believed that God had placed man on this earth to help his fellow man, and in so doing, to develop himself. Man's reward thus lay in social endeavor, an idea which became the leitmotiv of Faust's salvation. Emerson was not completely aware of Goethe's subordination of self-culture to altruism. He insisted that Goethe wished only to develop himself, no matter what happened to the rest of society. This error is the fatal flaw of Emerson's criticism. Emerson also subscribed to the belief that man's duty to serve the ideal God ranked higher in importance than his duty to serve his fellow man. He refuted the theory that only man's deeds measure his character, for he was interested in the man himself. The doctrine of works thus clashed with the doctrine of faith. Goethe, who perhaps became almost Catholic at the end of *Faust,* came to blows with Emerson the Calvinist.

In the winter of 1845–46 Emerson delivered a series of lectures devoted to a number of men whom he considered the leading thinkers of their age. Five years later he published these lectures under the title *Representative Men.* The sixth and last was a lecture on Goethe. Although it is a decisive statement, it adds little to his former comments,

---

time that Emerson was in charge of the *Dial.* They were never included in the various editions of Emerson's works. How much trust we can put into this assumption of authorship is, therefore, doubtful. The articles include a review of a life of Jean Paul Richter, *11* (January, 1843), 404; a review of J. L. Weiss's translations of *Letters of Schiller, 11* (January, 1843), 411; a short commentary on Goethe and Swedenborg, *11* (January, 1843), 416; a comment on *Wilhelm Meister, 12* (April, 1843), 524; a laudatory passage on Bettina and a rare comment on Hölderlin, *14* (October, 1843), 265–70; and finally a recommendation of the *Deutsche Schnellpost, 15* (January, 1844), 408.

and is by no means superior to the other essays in the volume.[6] Yet the essay offers less harsh criticism of Goethe, and demonstrates the gradually ascending opinion which Emerson developed for Goethe even though he never accepted him whole-heartedly.

That Emerson hesitated to include Goethe among his selection of representative men becomes obvious in the following letter to Carlyle in September, 1845: "I am to read to a society in Boston presently some lectures,—on Plato, or the Philosopher; Swedenborg, or the Mystic; Montaigne, or the Sceptic; Shakespeare, or the Poet; Napoleon, or the Man of the World;—if I dare, and much lecturing makes us incorrigibly rash. Perhaps, before I end it, my list will be longer, and the measure of presumption overflowed. I may take names less reverend than some of these,—but six lectures I have promised." [7] The sixth lecture not listed by title in this letter was given over to Goethe. He was also mentioned in the other essays of the series. Plato, for instance, Emerson called "the eldest Goethe." Goethe and Plato he classed with Shakespeare and Swedenborg as the greatest thinkers and observers. Coleridge and Goethe, he said, were the only critics who had expressed our convictions concerning Shakespeare with any adequacy.

In the sixth essay Emerson considered Goethe as the representative poet not of all time but of his own century, for his was "a manly mind, unembarrassed by the variety of coats of convention with which life had got encrusted." He drew his strength from his full communion with nature, and "amid littleness and detail, he detected the Genius of life." He wrote in the plainest and lowest tone, omitting a great deal more than he wrote, always putting a thing for a word. He defined the scope and laws of the arts. He said the best things about nature that were ever said, and no matter what topic he wrote upon, he gravitated toward truth.

Emerson once again praised the *Helena,* or the second part of *Faust,* calling it "a philosophy of literature set in poetry, the work of one who found himself the master of histories, mythologies, philosophies, sciences, and national literatures." In this book he found Goethe a "poet of a prouder laurel than any contemporary," a poet who "strikes the harp with a hero's strength and grace." The wonder of the work, Emerson said, was its superior intelligence. Whole new mythologies seemed to ferment in Goethe's head. His Mephistopheles in particular was the first organic figure to be added to the pantheon of humanity and would remain there as long as the Prometheus.

Emerson also had more to say of *Wilhelm Meister.* He called it a

6. Oliver Wendell Holmes said of the essay: "It flows rather languidly, toys with side issues as a stream loiters round a nook in its margin, and finds an excuse for play in every pebble." See *Ralph Waldo Emerson* (Boston, 1886), p. 208.

7. *Emerson-Carlyle Correspondence, 2,* 98.

novel in every sense, the first of its kind. No book of the century could equal it in stimulating the mind and gratifying it with solid thoughts, just insights into life, manners, and characters. Although it contained excellent directives for the conduct of life, no rhetoric or dullness marred it. Yet he found it an unsatisfactory book; it would suit neither lovers of light reading out for romance nor readers who expect to find a history of genius. In spite of its faults, however, the book was so crammed with wisdom, with knowledge of the world, the persons so truly and subtly drawn, that he decided to let it go its way, and take from it what was good.

Goethe himself, Emerson said, shared with his nation a habitual reference to interior truth. Goethe was very wise, though his talent often veiled his wisdom. "The old Eternal Genius who built the world has confided himself more to this man than to any other." Yet there were nobler strains in poetry than any he had sounded. Goethe could never be dear to men, for he was not devoted to pure truth, but to truth for the sake of culture. If he was a lawgiver of art, he was not an artist, maybe because he knew too much. His sight was so microscopic that it interfered with the just perspective, the seeing of the whole.

Such statements as these were less derogatory than Emerson's previous criticisms, but they were still limited in their appreciation of Goethe. Save in moments of enthusiasm, Emerson accepted Goethe with only half a heart. He never could avoid the barriers which he himself had erected because of the differences in his own tastes and those of the German writer. No one will deny that Emerson admired Goethe in many respects. He never hesitated to praise him for his talent, ingenuity, and resourcefulness. Among all his contemporaries, Emerson said some of the finest things about Goethe, but he also did not hesitate to censure him in the strongest terms. Goethe may have deserved part of this censure, although most of Emerson's adverse criticism can be attributed to the following facts.

In the first place, Emerson, in spite of his arguments for freedom from convention, was the inheritor of the prejudice which his Puritan Calvinistic elders held. A preacher and idealist himself, Emerson misconstrued Goethe's moral perception, which, he felt, was not proportionate to his other powers. Emerson saw all things as tending to a moral end. This point of view precluded a true evaluation of Goethe's achievements. Emerson erred in believing that Goethe had no moral sentiment and that good and evil action made no difference to him. If this were so, *Werther, Die Wahlverwandtschaften,* and other works of Goethe might have ended quite differently.

Secondly, Emerson could not help being conditioned by the climate of opinion which prevailed in New England. From the time that his works were first introduced into America, Goethe had been classified as a godless philosopher who was partial to atheistic thinking. Goethe had also been brought up in the silver-spoon traditions of a leisure class. As an American, Emerson could not stamp that with approval. Inculcated with the spirit of independence, Emerson disliked to see a man of Goethe's intellect stoop to what he thought was the "velvet life" of a courtier.[8] Goethe also did not concern himself with the great political problems of the day. Here again Emerson thought him out of tune.

Thirdly, Emerson lacked what has been called "emotional energy," and therefore underestimated the importance of the human passions.[9] He often wore blinders to the joys of the flesh, unconsciously classifying this part of life with ugliness and evil rather than with goodness and beauty.[1] Goethe, on the other hand, was not afraid to show man's emotions and passions in all their aspects. Emerson, who was primarily a thinker, emphasized the intellect to the exclusion of the emotions, and therefore misunderstood a worldly personality such as Goethe.

His leading objection to Goethe always rested upon ethical foundations. The charge was based on the false premise that immorality described artistically could produce only an immoral effect. Therefore, no matter how perfect the artistic beauty or the mastery of style of a work might be, a religious conscience could not sanction it. All his life Emerson found the German writer a paradox, and once spoke of him as "our wise but sensual, loved and hated Goethe." [2] He never could make himself approve of Goethe the man, but he recognized him as "a leader of the mind of a generation." [3] He taxed him as a courtier, artificial, unbelieving, and worldly; [4] but he admitted that the old Eternal Genius

8. Emerson wrote in his journal on January 23, 1834: "I cannot read of the jubilee of Goethe, and of such a velvet life, without a sense of incongruity. Genius is out of place when it reposes fifty years on chairs of state, and inhales a continual incense of adulation. Its proper ornaments and relief are poverty and reproach and danger, and if the grand-duke had cut Goethe's head off, it would have been much better for his fame than his retiring to his rooms, after dismissing obsequious crowds, to arrange tastefully and contemplate their gifts and honorary inscriptions." See Emerson, *Journals,* 3, 251–3.

9. "He passed at one step from the life of the senses to the life of the spirit, virtually omitting that vast intervening realm of the human emotions which is the main content of ordinary life and of literature. This is the central deficiency in Emerson, and explains most of his more specific deficiencies. . . . This is the reason why, unlike Carlyle, he gave little more than a formal recognition to the genius of Goethe." See Norman Foerster, *American Criticism* (Boston, Houghton Mifflin, 1928), p. 104.

1. Emerson wrote in his journal on May 11, 1833: "I ought not to forget the ballet between the acts. Goethe laughs at those who force every work of art into the narrow circle of their own prejudices and cannot admire a picture as a picture, and a tune as a tune. So I was willing to look at this as a ballet, and to see that it was admirable, but I could not help feeling the while that it were better for mankind if there were no such dancers. I have since learned God's decision on the same, in the fact that all the *bal-lerine* are nearly idiotic." See Emerson, *Journals, 3,* 113.

2. Emerson, *Journals, 4,* 29.

3. Emerson, *Works, 10,* 297.

4. *Ibid., 3,* 242.

who built the world had confided himself more to this man than to any other. In 1836 he felt that time would play havoc with Goethe's reputation,[5] but thirteen years later he classed his works with Shakespeare's of which "every word is a poem." [6] Emerson was able to appreciate Goethe, the genius, with his great knowledge, achievements, tolerance, love of truth, and poetic ability; but he failed to understand Goethe, the man, with his lovable, human qualities. In his old age Emerson found himself closer to Goethe, the sage. He loved the wisdom of the German and preferred his *Sprüche* to all his other works. His views of Goethe grew increasingly mild. At its worst, his censure turned into a kind of autumnal regret comparable to tolerance. He wrote to Hermann Grimm on June 27, 1861:

> I believe I sympathize with all your admirations. Goethe and Michael A. [Michelangelo] deserve your fine speeches, and are not perilous, for a long time. One may absorb great amounts of these, with impunity; but we must watch the face of our proper Guardian, and if his eye dims a little, drop our trusted companions as profane. I have a fancy that talent, which is so imperative in the passing hour, is deleterious to duration; what a pity we cannot have genius without talent. Even in Goethe, the culture and varied, busy talent mar the simple grandeur of the impression, and he called himself a layman beside Beethoven.[7]

In these later years Emerson spent many hours with Alcott discussing the value of Goethe, Schiller, and Richter, and of his debt to them and to Carlyle. Alcott once described an evening visit made by Emerson, who asked him to read aloud some sketches from his book of Men and Opinions. Since Emerson preferred the moderns, Alcott chose Goethe and Carlyle.[8] On January 5, 1871, Emerson expressed to Grimm this final tribute to Goethe: "I duly received from you the brochure on Schleiermacher, and read with interest, though his was never one of my high names. For Goethe I think I have an always ascending regard." [9]

5. Emerson, *Journals, 4*, 30.
6. *Ibid., 8*, 52.
7. *Emerson-Grimm Correspondence*, p. 59.
8. *The Journals of Bronson Alcott*, p. 337. Alcott never published a book under this title, but much of the material is to be found in *Tablets* and *Concord Days*.
9. *Emerson-Grimm Correspondence*, p. 85. There are also a number of interesting anecdotes which show the increasing importance of Goethe's name in the Emerson household. F. P. Stearns relates that during the last year of Emerson's life, when he could hardly remember names and people, Emerson said to a visitor: "I have lately been reading a most interesting book about—" he hesitated a moment, "the greatest man that has lived for more than two centuries." Then he walked across the room and pointed to a shelf of books. It was his set of Goethe's works. See *Sketches from Concord*, p. 104.
   Moncure Conway tells a less serious but highly delightful story of the Goethe cult in the Emerson household. One of the children had the fancy to name her cat "Goethe,"

Since Emerson took such a deep interest in Goethe's writings, we next ask ourselves whether Goethe had any particular influence on Emerson's doctrines. Critics show little agreement on this subject. I side with those persons who believe that much in Emerson's thought and philosophy which may appear German is merely Yankee. That Emerson's statements on Goethe had a marked influence upon the American public, as Mr. Wahr asserts, I cannot accept.[1] Emerson's journals and letters were not available to the public at large, and the two criticisms of Goethe which he published in the years 1840 and 1850 came too late to affect the general opinion of Goethe. At the most, these writings may have substantiated old commendations as well as old prejudices, but they hardly originated them.

Although Emerson read Goethe before the publication of *Nature,* he found in the writings of this German not so many new ideas as the confirmation of those already long established in his mind. Of course we can find interesting parallels. Goethe said, for instance, "The works of nature are ever a freshly uttered word of God." [2] In the chapter on Spirit in *Nature* Emerson wrote: "The noblest ministry of nature is to stand as the apparition of God. It is the organ through which the universal spirit speaks to the individual, and strives to lead back the individual." Again Emerson quoted Goethe in his journal: "The smallest production of nature has the circle of its completeness within itself, and I have only need of eyes to see with, in order to discover the relative proportions. I am perfectly sure that within this circle, however narrow, an entirely genuine existence is enclosed." [3] In *Nature* he wrote, "A leaf, a drop, a crystal, a moment of time is related to the whole, and partakes of the perfection of the whole. Each particle is a microcosm, and faithfully renders the likeness of the world." [4] Professor Cameron believes that a few other passages in *Nature* came from Goethe. One of them dealing with his theory of art was taken from the *Zweiter Römischer Aufenthalt.* Emerson translated the passage in February, 1836, and may have drawn upon it for his chapter on Beauty in *Nature.* Later he used it for the revision of "Michael Angelo" which he published in the *North American Review,* January, 1837.[5] Five months before *Nature* was published, however, Emerson made this note: "Only last evening I found the following sentence in Goethe, a comment and consent

---

and Emerson did not object to the idea. Once when the cat was in the library and scratched itself, he opened the door and politely said, "Goethe, you must retire, I don't like your manners." See *Autobiography, Memories and Experiences of Moncure Daniel Conway* (Boston, Houghton Mifflin, 1904), p. 147.
1. See F. B. Wahr, *Emerson and Goethe* (Ann Arbor, Mich., 1915), p. 10.
2. Emerson, *Journals, 2,* 350.
3. *Ibid., 2,* 349–50.
4. Emerson, *Works, 1,* 43.
5. K. W. Cameron, *Emerson the Essayist* (Raleigh, North Carolina, 1945), *1,* 321.

to my speculations on the All in Each in Nature this last week." [6] Even though such passages had no serious effect on *Nature* as a whole, at least they are evidence of Emerson's growing proficiency in the German language and the increasing importance which Goethe's works were assuming in his studies.

It is easier to establish the fact that Emerson read such German literary figures as Goethe than it is to prove his reading of the German philosophers; the line of influence becomes more nebulous here. This much we know: Emerson did not belong to the group of disciples who easily accept the teachings of any one master. He allowed himself to be affected by all great men, to test their teachings, value their individual contributions, and then add his own independent views.

Emerson's friends almost unanimously denied that he had found his ideas in the theories of the German philosophers.[7] Christopher P. Cranch wrote in a letter to his father, July 11, 1840: "Mr. Emerson has been said to have imported his doctrine from Germany. But the fact is, that no man stands more independently of other minds than he does. He seems to me very far from Kant or Fichte." [8] Emerson's friend Octavius B. Frothingham backed up this statement. In his analysis of Transcendentalism he denied that Emerson was a disciple of Kant, Jacobi, Fichte, or Schelling; Emerson called no man master and received no teaching on authority.[9] Edward Everett Hale in his life of Emerson was just as dogmatic: "I have satisfied my own conscience by saying that he did not borrow from any Hegel or Fichte or other German idealist or metaphysician. I might satisfy myself by saying that his thought, as his utterance, is purely of New England growth. Indeed, if we are to speak of evolution, his prophecy is clearly a direct outgrowth and result of William Ellery Channing's ministry and prophecy." [1] The best modern scholars, and even some of the Germans, tend to agree with these statements.[2] Paul Elmer More insisted that the whole cast of

6. Emerson often found such confirmations in Goethe's writings. On April 12, 1834, he wrote in his journal: "I had observed long since that, to give the thought a just and full expression, I must not prematurely utter it. Better not talk of the matter you are writing out. It was as if you had let the spring snap too soon. I was glad to find Goethe say to the same point, that 'he who seeks a hidden treasure must not speak.'" See Emerson, *Journals, 3,* 273.

7. An outstanding exception is to be found in Henry A. Brann's article, "Hegel and his New England Echo." He credits Emerson with a reading of Hegel long before Emerson was introduced to Hegel's works. See the *Catholic World, 41,* 58. Emerson did not mention Hegel in his letters until 1845, after his most important works had been written.

8. L. C. Scott, *The Life and Letters of Christopher Pearse Cranch* (Boston, Houghton Mifflin, 1917), p. 51.

9. Frothingham, p. 226.

1. E. E. Hale, *Ralph Waldo Emerson* (Boston, Brown, 1899), p. 33.

2. Although some of their compatriots were not so frank, two German scholars, Hedi Hildebrand and Friedrich Linz, also admitted this fact. I quote from their works as follows:

Emerson's mind had been set before German and Oriental speculation were open to him, and although they often colored his language, they scarcely altered his views.[3]

That the term Transcendentalism came from Kant one cannot deny. Emerson himself made the assertion in his lecture "The Transcendentalist," [4] but there is no proof that Emerson or the other Concord writers read Kant or most of the other philosophers until long after their doctrines had been formulated. It is true that as early as 1833 Alcott read *Elements of Kant's Philosophy* by Anthony Wellick, as well as *A View of Professor Kant's Principles* by F. A. Nitsch, a former pupil and associate of Kant. From Nitsch's work Alcott copied no less than fifty-seven pages. It is evident, therefore, that he was by no means dependent upon the French and English interpreters of the German Transcendentalists. Alcott also read carefully James Hutchison Stirling's treatise on Hegel's philosophy. In *Concord Days* he commented: "Stirling's fervor and strength in advocating Hegel's ideas command the highest respect. Having had Schelling's expositor in Coleridge, we now have Hegel's in Stirling. . . . Nothing profound or absolute can be expected from minds of the type of Mill, Herbert Spencer, and the rest,— if not hostile, at least indifferent to and incapable of idealism; naturalists rather than metaphysicians." [5] No doubt Emerson and Alcott discussed

"Was er diesen Deutschen verdankt, kam ihm meist aus zweiter Hand zu. Gedanken von Deutschen wie Eckhart, Böhme, Schelling, Kant, Hegel finden wir gelegentlich in ähnlicher Form in Emersons Werken wieder, aber von einem bestimmten, direkten Einfluss kann man hier nicht sprechen, da Emerson wieder diese Philosophen gründlich studierte, nach ihnen einen originellen Wert beimass. . . . In seinem ganzen Tagebuch, das für uns eine sichere Kontrolle für Emersons Lektüre und Geisteserträge ist, fanden wir keinen Hinweis auf ein direktes Studium Hegels aus erster Quelle." See Hedi Hildebrand, *Die Amerikanische Stellung zur Geschichte und zu Europa in Emersons Gedenkensystem* (Bonn, 1936), p. 94.

"Das Emerson das Kantische, Fichtesche und Schellingsche System, wenigstens im Umriss, gekannt hat, geht aus seinen Schriften unzweideutig hervor. Wir wissen auch, dass es vornehmlich die Werke Coleridges auf der einen und der Einfluss Carlyles auf der andern Seite gewesen sind, die ihm die Bekanntschaft des deutschen Idealismus vermittelt haben. Es ist aber Grund zu dem Zweifel, ob er die Werke der genannten Philosophen selbst gelesen hat. Jedenfalls weisen keine Spuren auf eine Detailkenntniss, die nur aus den Werken selbst geschöpft sein könnte. . . . Für Emersons naturphilosophische Entwickelung kommt Kant kaum in Betracht. Um so grösser ist indes der Einfluss Fichtes und Schellings." See *Emerson als Religionsphilosoph* (Barmen, 1911), p. 48.

3. P. E. More, *A New England Group and Others* (Shelburne Essays, eleventh series, Boston, 1921), p. 81.

4. He said in the essay: "It is well known to most of my audience that the Idealism of the present day acquired the name Transcendentalism from the use of the term by Immanuel Kant, of Königsberg, who replied to the skeptical philosophy of Locke, which insisted that there was nothing in the intellect which was not previously in the experience of the senses, by showing that there was a very important class of ideas or imperative forms, which did not come by experience; but through which experience was acquired; that there were intuitions of the mind itself; and he denominated them *Transcendental* forms." See Emerson, *Works, 1,* 339–40.

5. *Concord Days,* pp. 144–5.

the German philosophers with their friends, Hedge,[6] Parker, and Brownson among the Transcendentalists, and with Follen, Ticknor, and Bancroft at Harvard. They also read about the philosophers in the writings of Madame de Staël, Coleridge, and Carlyle. Yet one cannot consider such sources as primary material.

David Maulsby contends that Emerson showed some familiarity with Kant when he said, "Science has come to treat space and time as simply forms of thought," and again when he credited its author with his famous rule for moral conduct: "Act always so that the immediate motive of thy will may become a universal rule for all intelligent beings." [7] There may also be something more than accident in the similarity of emphasis which Kant placed upon the absolute good that resides in a being of good will and a being who does his duty, and Emerson's assertion at the close of "Compensation" that the good man alone enjoys the absolute good. But even Maulsby admits that Emerson never read Kant in the original nor mastered the outlines of his philosophy as a whole.[8] Later in his life Emerson, like Alcott, relied upon Stirling's book *Secret of Hegel,* and Edward Caird's *A Critical Account of the Philosophy of Kant.* Since these books were not published until 1865 and 1877 respectively, they bore little on Emerson's ideas in spite of the fact that they reposed in his library.

German thought, therefore, may have strengthened the Transcendentalists' revolt against the arid rationalism of the eighteenth century as well as against the utilitarianism of the nineteenth century, but it was no systematic study of the German metaphysicians which caused the revolt. The Concord men of letters were not profound students of any language, philosophy, or science. Although at times they used the names of the German philosophers rather freely and accepted their terms, their references, certainly before the publication of Emerson's *Nature,* were based on second-hand information. Moreover, they were apt to trust their intuition much more than their reason, and they looked upon life more as seers than as philosophers. For this reason they preferred Böhme, Schelling, and Goethe to Kant and Hegel.

What has led scholars to look for a direct influence is the fact that a bond of sympathy and a parallel trend of thought linked the Concord writers with the German philosophers without an intimate knowledge

6. After his return from England Emerson read enthusiastically Frederic Henry Hedge's review of Coleridge's work, together with a synopsis of German metaphysics which appeared in the *Christian Examiner,* March, 1833.

7. D. Maulsby, *The Contributions of Emerson to Literature* (Tufts College, Mass., 1911), p. 44. Quotations are from Emerson's *Works, 6,* 320 and *7, 27.*

8. I have examined in Emerson's library an anonymous translation of *The Critique of Pure Reason* published in 1838, and it shows some markings as well as an index with entries such as "Locke and Hume," "Immortality," and "Oblate Sphericity." Emerson also accepted Cabot's paper on Kant for the *Dial,* and in 1870 he wrote to Harris that Cabot was reading lectures on Kant at Harvard.

of their works. Emerson, Alcott, and Thoreau also clamored for freedom from traditional authority, and contemned sham and compromise. Just as the Germans had demanded a new humanism for decaying Europe, so these New Englanders in the fields of religion, political science, and education developed similar ideas for the benefit of their young nation. Like the early German mystics they were in accord with the doctrines of self-renunciation and dependence upon God, and like the later German writers they believed in the doctrines of individuality and self-reliance. The intuitive man whom these Germans treated as the ideal man appealed to them, and the idea of seeing God (often expressed by Goethe as well as other Germans from Lessing to Novalis), had their full sympathy.

The Concord writers themselves denied that they had much in common with the German thinkers. Alcott wrote in his journal as late as 1883: "I confess to less interest in the philosophic methods of German thinkers than in the more familiar English methods of treatment. With difficulty I follow even Harris in his interpretations of Hegel, Fichte, Schelling and others." [9] Similar comments abound in Emerson's writings. John Burroughs quoted him as saying in his Journals in 1837: "I do not draw from them great influence. The heroic, the holy, I lack. They are contemptuous. They fail in sympathy with humanity. The voice of nature they bring me to hear is not divine, but ghastly, hard, and ironical. They do not illuminate me: they do not edify me." [1] In the parts of the journals published by Cabot, Emerson referred prior to 1836 only once to Kant, twice to Schelling and Hegel, and three times to Fichte. [2] From Fichte he copied a few extracts without as yet knowing the original language. In the unpublished journals one finds a few more references to Schelling, but this knowledge of Schelling came, for the most part, through Coleridge, whose works he had been reading at that time. Of the post-Kantians the Concord writers had more in common with Schelling than with anyone else. Although it is not probable that they were to any great extent directly affected by Schelling, much of what they taught can be found in the writings of this philosopher.

One must also distinguish between their first-hand knowledge of the German philosophers before and after 1840. There are many indications that they read them after their own doctrines had been formulated and used them to substantiate what they had originally stated. For instance, Emerson's comments on the philosophers are fairly numerous in his later letters, journals, and conversations. Sometimes they are only *obiter dicta*,

9. *The Journals of Bronson Alcott*, pp. 373, 536.
1. See *The Last Harvest* (Boston, Houghton Mifflin, 1922), p. 3.
2. In the *Essays, First* and *Second Series*, we also find only a few passing references to the German philosophers and thinkers. In "Intellect" Emerson referred to Kant, Spinoza, and Schelling; in "Character" to Schiller, Stilling, Hegel, Tischbein, Herder, and Meyer.

such as his comment to Woodbury that Fichte would use any weapon to convert a hearer, that he would "trepan a person, if so he could pass his own edacious conceptions into the bared brain." [3] On other occasions he would attempt to crystalize a more definite opinion. Of Schelling he wrote to James Cabot in September, 1845: "This admirable Schelling, which I have never fairly engaged with until the last week, demands the 'lamp' & the 'lonely tower' and a lustrum of silence. I delight in his steady inevitable eye, and the breadth of his march including & disposing of so many objects of mark." [4] To Carlyle he said that Schelling continued to interest him, but he found himself so poor a reader of subtle dialectics, that he let them lie a long while near him as if in hope of an atmospheric influence when the understanding refuses his task.[5]

Thus a quiet revolution had taken place in little Concord, so imperceptible at times that the Transcendentalists were often unaware of it. What once had been to them an unexplored and even dangerous field of knowledge had now seeped into their veins, becoming part of their very essence. German thought, literature, music, indeed all aspects of German culture, had enriched their lives, and they, in turn, passed on this inspiration to their followers.

B. THE THEOLOGIANS

CHANNING, RIPLEY, HEDGE, AND PARKER

Although Emerson, Thoreau, and Alcott were aroused at times to great enthusiasm by their reading of German literature, they could by no means compare with other members of the Transcendental group in the field of German scholarship. The Concord men of letters, who read little German philosophy and theology in the original texts, were also less familiar with the best of German poetry and fiction.

With the exception of Emerson, Thoreau, and Alcott, one can roughly divide the Transcendentalists into three categories: theologians, critics, and translators. Of them all, the theologians were the most numerous.[1]

---

3. *Talks with Ralph Waldo Emerson* (New York, Baker and Taylor, 1890), p. 54.

4. Emerson, *Letters, 3,* 298.

5. *Ibid.,* p. 304. In the *Dial, 9* (July, 1842), 136, Emerson wrote a short article describing a lecture which Schelling, then almost seventy years old, gave at the request of the King of Prussia. Emerson and Alcott also read in later years the writings of the German mystics, especially Jacob Böhme. In 1844 Emerson expressed the opinion in his journals that Böhme was a great man but could not rank with the masters of the world. His value, rather, was chiefly for rhetoric (Emerson, *Journals, 6,* 518). Elizabeth Peabody, however, said that Emerson's favorite book was Böhme's *The Way to Christ,* which she borrowed as late as 1860. When Emerson lent it to her, he remarked, "This is my *vade mecum.*" See A. Ireland, *Ralph Waldo Emerson* (London, 1882), pp. 20-1.

1. It is dangerous, however, to pigeonhole them in this fashion, since the lines often crossed. Parker, Ripley, and Clarke fit all three categories, Hedge and Margaret Fuller at least two, not to mention the ability that they all had in creative writing.

In fact, since the number of ordained ministers among the New England Transcendentalists was amazingly high,[2] one should consider to what extent German philosophy and theology impinged upon their ideas. This study does not aim, however, to analyze the philosophical and theological doctrines emanating from Germany, whether of Kant, Fichte, and Hegel, or of Schelling, Schleiermacher, and De Wette, but rather to establish the sources of information about these German thinkers, the number of their works read, and the defense of that reading prevalent among the Transcendentalists.

Earliest of the theologians and one of the founders of the Transcendental movement, William Ellery Channing was weakest of the group in the knowledge of German, but his seniority in years and his premature interest at least a decade before the others placed him in a unique position. Channing was first introduced to German literature when he read Madame de Staël's *De l'Allemagne* shortly after its appearance in 1813. He was also among those who were attracted to Carlyle's articles in the *Edinburgh Review*,[3] as well as to the writings of Coleridge. Channing's knowledge of Transcendental philosophy, in fact, came, for the most part, from Coleridge rather than directly from the German thinkers. Although he was not indebted to Kant and to the other German philosophers for his ideas, he recognized them as the fountainheads of Transcendental doctrine, and found his own views buttressed in their teachings. In his correspondence with Lucy Aikin we observe that he secretly rejoiced when Kant's teachings began to make inroads at the English universities of Cambridge and Oxford. He wrote on December 31, 1829: "As to Kantism, I shall be glad to hear of an irruption of it into any university or any part of your country. I want to see the English mind waked up on the great subject of intellectual philosophy." [4]

Channing himself gladly responded "to Schelling's sublime intimations of the Divine Life everywhere manifested through nature and humanity," and the heroic stoicism of Fichte charmed him by its full assertion of the grandeur of the human will.[5] "You must have discovered in me a touch of that malady called mysticism," he wrote to Lucy Aikin, "and will therefore wonder the less at my German leanings." [6]

No reader of German himself, Channing, as early as 1823, advocated

2. The most important for our purposes are Channing, Parker, Ripley, Hedge, and Clarke.

3. A decade later in 1838 Channing wrote to Lucy Aikin that Carlyle was a prophet without honor in his own country. He also mentioned the fact that Carlyle had many ardent admirers in America, and he added as an afterthought, "So had German philosophy and German literature." See *Correspondence of William Ellery Channing and Lucy Aikin*, p. 304.

4. *Ibid.*, p. 43.

5. G. W. Cooke, *Introduction to the Dial, I*, 42.

6. *Correspondence of William Ellery Channing and Lucy Aikin*, p. 375.

the study of French and German authors in order to emancipate American literature from its dependence on England.[7] Yet he still somewhat suspected the ultimate influence of German literature. George Ripley related that Channing guardedly advised William Emerson in 1823 to study at Harvard rather than Göttingen because he believed that a New England minister might find greater moral influence and religious feeling in New England.[8] In 1825, however, Professor Follen came to Harvard, and the friendship which sprang up between him and Channing convinced the Unitarian minister of the great benefits to be derived from a knowledge of German. At the age of forty-eight he finally embarked on a study of German, to secure a deeper understanding of German thought.

Of the German writers exclusive of the philosophers, Channing gained a superficial knowledge, but mainly through translations.[9] He felt especially at home with Richter,[1] Goethe, and Schiller, like most of his friends, preferring Schiller to Goethe. Elizabeth Peabody in her *Reminiscences of Channing* described those winter evenings at Channing's home when they would sit and read German books like *Wilhelm Meister* until he would become bored and say, "That is enough for tonight; let us have something a little more enlivening." Then he would turn to Miss Mitford's sketches or something else as light.[2]

Channing may have preferred Schiller to Goethe, but his criticism of Goethe was not so stringent as we might expect. Miss Peabody quoted him as saying that the greatest lesson Goethe taught the human race was the insufficiency of genius without the sovereign moral sense, to read aright the riddle of the Sphinx. He thought that while his natural temperament was extraordinarily tender, Goethe lacked depth of heart. He took issue with Goethe for making frivolity his highest conception of life and for being a stranger "to the heroic nobleness of patriotism." Channing blamed these faults on a lack of moral power in the German writer, and Channing conceived of moral power as the most important

7. W. E. Channing, *Works* (Boston, American Unitarian Association, 1869), *1, 277.*
8. O. B. Frothingham, *George Ripley* (Boston, Houghton Mifflin, 1886), 20f.
9. One of his biographers, John Chadwick, said, "Where the translators failed him, he stopped short." See *William Ellery Channing, Minister of Religion* (Boston, Houghton Mifflin, 1903), p. 207.
1. Channing wrote to Lucy Aikin, April 1, 1837: "Yesterday I was reading a story of Richter (Jean Paul), and was a little struck with finding there at full the thoughts which I had expressed in my last letter to you, on the power of a *great idea.* Perhaps one reason of my interest in German books is, that I meet so much of my own mind in them. I well remember when I read Madame de Staël's Germany, on its first appearance, how amazed and delighted I was to find it overflowing with thoughts which had been struggling and forming in my own breast, some half-formed, some matured." See *Correspondence of William Ellery Channing and Lucy Aikin,* p. 289.
2. E. Peabody, *Reminiscences of Rev. Wm. Ellery Channing* (Boston, Roberts, 1880), pp. 336–7.

principle in human nature. In his essay "Self Culture" he expatiated as follows:

> This disinterested principle in human nature we call sometimes reason, sometimes conscience, sometimes the moral sense or faculty. But, be its name what it may, it is a real principle in each of us, and it is the supreme power within us, to be cultivated above all others, for on its culture the right development of all others depends. The passions indeed may be stronger than the conscience, may lift up a louder voice; but their clamor differs wholly from the tone of command in which the conscience speaks. They are not clothed with its authority, its binding power. In their very triumphs they are rebuked by the moral principle, and often cower before its still, deep, menacing voice.[3]

This same obsession with moral values is to be found in the second of the theologians, George Ripley, who never studied in Germany, but who, nevertheless, stood in the forefront of German scholars in the Transcendental circle. As a student and later as a Unitarian minister, Ripley amassed a remarkably fine library, including the writings of the German philosophers and theologians, Kant,[4] Schleiermacher, Herder, De Wette, Hegel, and Schopenhauer, the latest works on Biblical criticism by Paulus, Bauer, Tholuck, Lücke, Bertholdt, Winer, Bretschneider, Ammon, Reinhard, Ritter, Fichte, and Eichhorn, as well as the works of Goethe, Schiller, Wieland, Heine, and the German romanticists.[5]

Having become familiar with German Transcendentalism, Ripley was the logical person to spread its doctrines among his friends.[6] His most important contribution came as a series of articles and reviews printed in periodicals like the *Christian Examiner*.[7] The best appeared in May, 1835, in a review of James Marsh's translation of Herder's *The Spirit of Hebrew Poetry*. Ripley did not like the translation itself, since Herder suffered much in the hands of Marsh; but in the same article he analyzed the growth in the vogue of German literature in the English-speaking world. Ripley bemoaned the fact that German theology was not so well known as German poetry, and he found it rather singular that in this

---

3. W. E. Channing, *Works, 2*, 358.
4. Ripley expressed no great sympathy for Kant in the *Christian Examiner, 18* (May, 1835), 209.
5. Like many of the other Transcendentalists, Ripley had come into contact with the Göttingen men at Harvard, especially with Edward Everett. See E. G. Jaeck, *Madame de Staël and the Spread of German Literature*, p. 229.
6. At his house in 1836 the members of the newly formed Transcendental Club held their first meeting.
7. Between 1830 and 1837 he wrote ten articles for this periodical alone. He also contributed such articles on German literature as a paper on Heine to *Putnam's Magazine, 8* (1856), 517–26.

country, where zeal for religion and a love of speculation had always been a part of our birthright, we should have given so little attention to the labors of others who explored every part of the field on which we were employed ourselves. Ripley contended that it was wrong for us to be ignorant of a nation of thinkers who came from the same good old Saxon stock with ourselves. "If any fear evil to our faith or morals from such knowledge," he said, "they will perhaps be quieted with the assurance that the 'antidote' flows from the same fountain with the 'bane,'—that if startling errors have been maintained by German theologians, it is also by German theologians that these errors have been assailed and put down." [8] That German literature was obscure, full of mysticism, and irreligion, he denied completely.

Herder remained for Ripley one of the great names of literature. His theological works in particular he deemed "a treasure of learning, refined from the dross and base admixtures of the mine, and wrought up into the most beautiful and winning forms." For a later issue Ripley wrote a short biography of Herder with a description of his works.[9] To the *Dial* (October, 1840) he contributed the article "Letter to a Theological Student," in which he recommended Herder's *Letters on the Study of Theology*. Ripley found them a seminal source of noble and glorious thoughts, and he never read them without feeling his heart elevated and made better, even though they did not impart much positive and exact instruction. If one did not read German, he added, the perusal of that book alone would be payment enough for the six months' study of leisure hours, which it would cost to acquire the language.

In March, 1836, Ripley wrote an article on Schleiermacher, who, he believed, was without a counterpart in our theological progress. Yet he deserved to be placed at the head of all the theologians of the present day.[1] Ripley blamed this condition on the fact that the tendency of the English mind, even among our most highly educated men, moved but little in the direction of profound speculation: "The German mind, on the other hand, is so absorbed in the investigation of fundamental principles, in inquiries which serve, not merely to accumulate opulent stores of exact knowledge, but to settle the relative validity and true foundation of every kind of knowledge, that the outward forms of expression are often neglected, and the most original and fruitful ideas clothed in difficult and forbidding language." [2]

Ripley's articles on Pestalozzi in the *Examiner* make manifest his

8. *Christian Examiner, 18* (May, 1835), 168.
9. *Ibid.*, pp. 174–221.
1. In 1852 Ripley wrote to Theodore Parker: "I regard Schleiermacher as the greatest thinker who ever undertook to fathom the philosophy of religion." See O. B. Frothingham, *George Ripley*, p. 229.
2. *Christian Examiner, 20* (March, 1836), 2.

interest in German educational experiments.[3] He was convinced that the manner of teaching adopted by Pestalozzi was a return to the dictates of nature and good sense. Pestalozzi was no charlatan advocating devices to obtain knowledge without paying the price. His aim, rather, "was to make the pupil something more than a learned parrot—to make him a man, a thinking, well-principled, self-directing, independent man." [4]

Ripley's knowledge of the German theologians and philosophers qualified him to refute the attacks of Andrews Norton, whose article "The Latest Form of Infidelity" condemned the writings of De Wette, Spinoza, and Schleiermacher, and the Transcendental philosophy. He cleared them of the charges of atheism and irreligion in his answer, "The Latest Form of Infidelity Examined."

More important was Ripley's editorship of a series of fourteen volumes known as *Specimens of Foreign Standard Literature.* Although Ripley did not contribute to the German translations of this series, he was a thorough student of the German language and criticized the translations of his friends. In a letter dated April 6, 1838, and addressed to John S. Dwight, he wrote as follows: "Your translation, I think is very successful; and if you always do as well you need no crutch of another's opinion, but may go along without fear of fall. There is only one word that I could pronounce incorrect; that is in the 11th line, 1st page of your MS. . . . With this exception, your translation is singularly accurate, as far as I can judge, especially for one so free and flowing." [5]

The wealth of German literature which appeared in the *Specimens* has already been discussed,[6] but a fact not so well known is that Ripley had a direct hand in founding the *Dial.* When Andrews Norton first denounced the Transcendentalists, Channing suggested to Ripley that a new periodical should be started.[7] The *Dial* was born of this discussion. Ripley assisted Margaret Fuller and Emerson in the editorship until he became involved in the Brook Farm experiment.

Just as crucial to the Transcendental circle in spreading German literary influence, although less well known, is the third of these theo-

3. Alcott also was interested in the psychology of education and pedagogical methods. His ideas of teaching were totally different from those of the old tradition. Having read of the experiments of Pestalozzi, Alcott attempted much the same thing. He abandoned the use of corporal punishment, and advocated greater freedom for the pupils. Instead of forcing them to learn a series of facts, he wished to make the children utilize their own intelligence by means of the conversational method. These innovations, however, found little favor with the majority of the parents, and he was finally forced to give up the experiment.

4. *11* (January, 1832), 372.

5. The person to whom the letter is addressed is not indicated in the MS letter at the New York Public Library, but the date coincides with the publication of Dwight's *Select Minor Poems of Goethe and Schiller.*

6. See pp. 71-2.

7. E. Peabody, *Reminiscences of Wm. E. Channing,* p. 371.

logians, Frederic Henry Hedge. In fact, of all the persons connected with the Transcendental movement, he was the only one who received his first knowledge of the German language and literature in Germany itself. When George Bancroft visited that country in 1818, Professor Levi Hedge of Harvard decided to entrust his son, then only thirteen years old, to Bancroft's care so that the boy might have the opportunity to gain a more thorough foundation in German scholarship.[8] Upon his return from Germany Hedge embarked on the study of theology at the Harvard Divinity School, and in 1829 he was ordained as a Unitarian minister. Today we think of him less as a religious leader than as a teacher who devoted his life work to the diffusion of German literature and philosophy in America.

Hedge was especially fortunate in the gift of two mother tongues. Since from the time of his boyhood English and German were equally familiar to him, his feeling for things German was neither mechanical nor artificial. Hedge confirmed this fact when he told Caroline Dall that the only substantial benefit he had derived from his years in Germany was a thorough knowledge of the language, some acquaintance with its literature, and an early initiation into the realm of German idealism.[9]

Hedge's connection with the Transcendentalists is most significant in relation to the question of German influence, an influence which was not always realized. When O. B. Frothingham published in 1877 his *Transcendentalism in New England,* he completely glossed over Hedge's relation to the group, much to the dismay of the surviving band. Caroline Dall said it was like the play of *Hamlet* with the part of Hamlet left out. Hot with indignation, she addressed a letter to Dr. Hedge, who was still living, asking him to describe his relations with the Transcendental movement. Since his answer is of utmost importance, it deserves to be reprinted:

Cambridge, February 1, 1877

My dear Mrs. Dall,—You ask me to give you a statement of my connection with the Transcendental movement. It has no importance, except in so far as I was the first in this country, to the best of my knowledge, to move in that direction. In the "Christian Examiner" for March, 1833, in an article on Coleridge I attempted a vindication of German metaphysics, with a brief account of some of the leading positions of the early writers of the school of Kant. . . . German metaphysics had been characterized as wild, visionary mysticism, unworthy the attention of sober minds. I am not so vain as to suppose that the words of one so young and so unknown as I then was could have had any power to remove this prejudice. Still, it was significant that

8. For five years Hedge attended German schools in Saxony and elsewhere. He was one of the first Americans to complete his education at a German Gymnasium.
9. See C. Dall, *Transcendentalism in New England* (Boston, Roberts, 1897), p. 13.

the "Christian Examiner," an influential organ of the Unitarian body, should admit, and by admitting seem to endorse, my words. Already there were here and there receptive and inquiring minds, whom the writings of Coleridge and of Carlyle . . . had predisposed to the rejection of the old sensualistic ideas.

Prominent among these were George Ripley and Waldo Emerson. German metaphysics, I think, had been studied *in the original* by no American except myself. . . . When Carlyle sent three copies of "Sartor Resartus"—then unpublished in America—to Emerson, bidding him keep one for himself and give the others to persons most in sympathy with the author, he gave one to me and one to Mrs. Samuel Ripley.

In September, 1836, George Ripley, Waldo Emerson, and myself called the first meeting of what was named in derision "The Transcendental Club." There was no club in any strict sense,—only occasional meetings of like-minded men and women. No line was drawn between those who were members and those who were not, except that as a matter of course certain persons were always notified. Emerson, Alcott, Thoreau, Stetson, George Ripley and his wife, Mrs. Samuel Ripley, Margaret Fuller, John S. Dwight, Elizabeth Peabody, Theodore Parker, Jones Very, Robert Bartlett, John Weiss, Dr. Francis, Dr. Bartol, and myself were expected. Orestes Brownson met with us once or twice, but became unbearable, and was not afterward invited. George Bradford, Samuel Osgood, and Ephraim Peabody were sometimes present. Dr. George Putnam came to one of the first meetings, —in fact, was one with Ripley, Emerson, and myself to start them; but they took a turn unexpected to him, and after the first meeting at Emerson's he ceased to come.

My coming from Bangor, where I then resided, was always the signal for a meeting.

When "The Dial," the natural outcome of our movement, was started in 1840, I was asked to be one of its editors. This I declined for want of time; and I feel some compunction now in thinking how little I did for it. Some verses of mine printed in it, and written about 1834, Emerson thought fit to preserve in his "Parnassus." They were called "Questionings," have a Transcendental character, and indicate the problems with which my mind was then laboring. . . .[1]

In my "Prose Writers of Germany," the introductory notices of Boehme, Kant, Fichte, Hegel, and Schelling contain in the shortest space condensed statements of the characteristic positions of those philosophers, which, brief as they are, will give proof of my first-hand

[1]. As early as 1835 Hedge wished to establish a periodical, but his removal to Bangor delayed the project, and no periodical fully representing the Transcendental movement appeared until the *Dial* in 1840.

acquaintance with their writings. Of Schelling's second system I have said nothing, for it was not published at the time of my writings. . . .

Faithfully your friend

Frederic Henry Hedge [2]

That Hedge has often been overlooked is due to a number of factors. In the first place, his was not the aggressive nature which craved prominence. Secondly, Hedge moved away from the center of activity in 1835, and took up his residence in Bangor, Maine. His removal did not cut him off from the Transcendentalists; he still corresponded with many of them, including Emerson, Ripley, Clarke, and Margaret Fuller.[3]

His connections with these Transcendentalists are noteworthy. Emerson recorded in his journal in 1834 that Hedge read to him "good things out of Schleiermacher." [4] Bronson Alcott also said that Hedge probably had read even more German literature than Theodore Parker, and was more deeply versed in German philosophy and theology than any other mind in the Transcendental group. In fact, Alcott considered Hedge as being truly German in his faculties and habits.[5] Margaret Fuller, who had met Hedge at Harvard, continually borrowed his books. James Freeman Clarke said that Margaret found Hedge's conversations full of interest and excitement. Out of their discussions of German literature germinated a volume of selections which Hedge finally published under the title *Prose Writers of Modern Germany* (1848). The résumé of Goethe's life and works in this collection was grounded largely on Margaret Fuller's article in the *Dial;* Hedge acknowledged his debt to her in a footnote. George Ripley also read Hedge's article on Coleridge and the German philosophers in the *Christian Examiner,* March, 1833.[6]

In this article Hedge used Coleridge's philosophical achievements merely as a peg on which to hang a discussion of the German Transcendental philosophers, and defended them by attempting to state a brief but concise idea of their doctrines. He pointed out the pre-eminence of Germany among the nations in intellectual culture, and believed that whatever excellence that nation had attained in science, history, and poetry was mainly owing to the influence of her philosophy. The article also demonstrates how much he underlined the doctrines of the German philosophers in developing American Transcendentalism. He was especially impressed by what Kant and his followers did to advance the hu-

---

2. Dall, pp. 14–17.

3. In the *Report of the Commissioner of Education for the Year 1897–1898* we also find the statement that Hedge was a scholar thoroughly equipped and fully possessed of the German spirit. The report goes so far as to call him the German fountain among the Transcendentalists (*1,* 614).

4. Emerson, *Journals, 3,* 393.

5. *American Literature, 3* (March, 1931), 24–5.

6. Mrs. Ripley praised the article in the *Register,* and no doubt influenced her husband's mind. See O. B. Frothingham, *George Ripley,* pp. 96–7.

man intellect: the strongly marked distinctions of subject and object, reason and understanding, phenomena and noumena; the moral liberty proclaimed by Kant as it had never been proclaimed by any before; the authority and evidence of law and duty set forth by Fichte; and the universal harmony illustrated by Schelling. Nor were these the only accomplishments of that philosophy in science, history, and poetry. Hedge believed that all theologians owed it a debt for that dauntless spirit of inquiry and for that amazing erudition which investigated and illustrated every corner of Biblical lore. A philosophy, Hedge concluded, which had given such an impulse to mental culture and scientific research and which had done so much to establish and to extend the spiritual in man, and the ideal in nature needed no apology. "It commends itself by its fruits, it lives in its fruits, and must ever live, though the name of its founder be forgotten, and not one of its doctrines survive." [7]

In 1834 Hedge reviewed favorably Carlyle's *Life of Friedrich Schiller,* although he did not hesitate to point out the weaknesses of Schiller's works. He had little respect for *Die Räuber,* considering it puerile and lacking in depth when compared to the work of Goethe and others. He praised Schiller's qualities as an artist and paid special tribute to the beauty of his poems and ballads. Hedge translated a number of the poems to back up his point of view. He also reviewed for the *Christian Examiner* Brooks's translation of *Faust,*[8] and contributed numerous articles to the *North American Review* and the *Atlantic Monthly,* including critiques of Leibnitz, Schopenhauer, and Kant.[9]

While Hedge's first volume, *Prose Writers of Germany,* was not published until 1848, selections of it were read many years before by all the Transcendentalists.[1] He made a number of contributions to the *Dial,* but they were not of profound importance. One article called "The Art of Life—the Scholar's Calling" contained the following quotation from Goethe: "I respect the man who knows distinctly what he wishes. The greater part of all the mischief in the world arises from the fact, that men do not sufficiently understand their own aims. They have undertaken to build a tower, and spend no more labor on the foundation

7. *Christian Examiner, 14* (March, 1833), 127.
8. *63* (July, 1857), 1–18.
9. G. W. Cooke, *Introduction to the Dial, 2,* 71–2.
1. It included twenty-eight German authors ranging from Martin Luther to Adelbert von Chamisso. He did not make all the translations by himself, but borrowed freely from the work of Thomas Carlyle, J. Elliot Cabot, John Weiss, Charles Brooks, George Bradford, George Ripley, Margaret Fuller, and Sarah Austin. The effect of the collection on the American public was similar to the effect of Carlyle's translations from the German twenty-five years earlier. Edward Waldo Emerson stated that the book not only established Hedge's reputation as a scholar, but led many years later to his appointment as Professor of German at Harvard. See *The Early Years of the Saturday Club* (Boston, Houghton Mifflin, 1918), p. 279.

than would be necessary to erect a hut." [2] Then he added: "Is not this
an exact description of most men's strivings? Every man undertakes
to build his tower and no one counts the cost." In July, 1842, he translated for the *Dial* Uhland's poem "The Castle by the Sea," and in January, 1843, he translated Schelling's introductory lecture in Berlin.

During the 1830's and 1840's Hedge, therefore, helped to make the
Transcendentalists familiar with at least a smattering of German philosophy, especially the theories of Kant, Fichte, and Schelling [3] as well
as the more popular literary works.[4] One may wonder, then, what
Hedge's position in the Transcendental constellation might have been
if he had remained in the vicinity of Concord and Cambridge. Miss Peabody contended that if Hedge had not gone to Bangor he might have
introduced Transcendentalism without the extreme individualism which
became associated with it in America.[5] Be that as it may, his influence
in the study of German cannot be overestimated.

Indeed, only one other theologian, Theodore Parker, held a more
prominent position. He was without any doubt the most learned in
German literature and philosophy, even if he did not know the language
so well as Hedge. It has already been mentioned that Parker was first

2. The *Dial, 1* (October, 1840), 175.
3. Ronald V. Wells in his book *Three Christian Transcendentalists* (New York,
Columbia University Press, 1943) contends that Hedge knew more of Kant than James
Marsh, and based his own writings largely upon the conclusions of Kant's critiques
(p. 123).
4. With the publication of his German anthologies, Hedge began to be recognized as
an authority on German literature. The German population of Boston invited him in
1859 to give an oration for the Schiller centennial. What he said there reflects the
growing interest in German culture in New England. Hedge recalled the time when
the name of Schiller was nothing but an empty sound, suggesting at the most a questionable stage play, *Die Räuber,* which together with Goethe's *Werther,* represented
the genius of Germany to American minds. Scarcely a dozen people in Boston could
then read German, and the most common belief about the Germans was based on mis-
conceptions taught by the English.
In 1863 he wrote a criticism of Henrich Heine (see H. B. Sachs, *Heine in America,*
Philadelphia, Americana Germanica Press, 1916, p. 35). Hedge's translations of Heine
did not appear until 1886, when the volume *Hours with the German Classics* was published. This latter work grew out of his lectures as Harvard professor of German, and
followed a pattern similar to his earlier work *Prose Writers of Germany.* Since it was
meant for popular reading, Hedge made little attempt to delve very deeply into the
various aspects of German thought. Although he covered the important German literary
works from the earliest beginnings until his own day, he dwelt mainly on the authors
with whom he himself was sympathetic. To Goethe he devoted ninety pages, over a
sixth of the book, and to Schiller fifty pages. Two years later Hedge published a third
collection of German literature under the title *Martin Luther and Other Essays,* and
finally in 1889 he issued a translation of Chamisso's *Peter Schlemihl,* one of the most
popular tales of German romantic literature.
5. Elizabeth Peabody, *Reminiscences of Wm. E. Channing,* p. 371. See also Harold
C. Goddard, *Studies in New England Transcendentalism,* who says of Hedge: "He
would have played—had he lived nearer to Boston, and had his nature been a little more
aggressive—a far more prominent part than he did in the movement. As it is, he must
be reckoned one of the earliest and most influential of transcendentalists." See p. 33.

introduced to German literature during his student days at Harvard under the direction of Professor Follen. He soon increased his knowledge of German through his associations with George Ripley, who made available his personal library of German literature.[6] In a short time he read the poets Klopstock, Lessing, Schiller, Goethe, and Herder. He was also one of the few Transcendentalists who really understood such German philosophers as Kant, Fichte, Hegel, and Schelling, and theologians like Baur, Schleiermacher, Eichhorn, De Wette,[7] Jacobi, and Spinoza. Henry Commager, therefore, does not exaggerate when he says of Parker: "It was surprising enough to find an American who read a German book, but this young man carried the whole of the Theologische Jahrbücher in his head." [8] At West Roxbury he continued this reading in a most systematic way.[9]

Goethe's life and works, for instance, he explored with punctilious care. He began by reading the whole edition of Goethe's writings, including supplementary volumes, then the correspondence with Jacobi and Nicolai, and finally the biographies of Goethe by Döring, Schäfer, and others. At first Parker was not especially enthusiastic about Goethe. He wrote in his journal that he found no indications of greatness, nothing, in short, but commonplace morality, and an exceedingly graceful use of language.[1] He soon changed his opinion enough to register this praise:

> There must be a period in the life of a great and thoughtful man, when he passes from the fiery madness of youth, from the deep enthusiasm for particular good things, and a determination towards one special object, to a more passive state, when the enthusiasm has become reverence for the good, and true, and lovely, and will has given place to resignation. We see this change well marked in most great characters, in Coleridge and Goethe. It is less marked in Schiller, because his was so eminently an ethical genius. Jean Paul never passed through the change, so he gains with the million, but loses with the cool admirers of real greatness. Emerson and Channing have passed this period.
>
> Goethe is a beautiful instance of a man reaching this state. To

6. Parker later purchased Ripley's library, and used it as a foundation for his own German collection, which became one of the most important of its kind among private collections in the country.

7. In 1837 Parker translated De Wette's *Einleitung in das Alte Testament*. This translation, John Chadwick said, with his additions, notes, and comments, proved to be the most important study of his life. See *Life of Theodore Parker* (Boston, Houghton Mifflin, 1901), p. 51.

8. H. S. Commager, *Theodore Parker* (Boston, Little, Brown, 1936), p. 95.

9. The Reverend Convers Francis, Unitarian pastor in Watertown, also lent him German books.

1. John Weiss, *Life and Correspondence of Theodore Parker* (New York, D. Appleton, 1864), *2*, 20.

many who themselves scarce dream there is such a condition, he seems indifferent, fish-blooded, feeding the world on snow-broth; but not so to the wise. The self-renunciation and intense diligence of Goethe are the secret of his success, of his long life, and permanent creativeness. Such were some of the great men of antiquity, Aeschylus, Sophocles, and Cicero, and all the sages, Plato, Socrates, Aristotle, Anaxagoras, Pythagoras.[2]

Later he added this comment: "My admiration of the man rises more and more; but he was a selfish rogue." Perhaps if Goethe had had to struggle for his education or even for his livelihood as Herder, Schiller, Jean Paul, and Heine had done, Parker would have found him nobler. He felt that excess of good fortune had undone Goethe. Yet he could not help admiring Goethe's untiring industry, which had made him the great man he was. Nothing was beneath his notice, Parker said, and no labor too great for him to undertake.[3]

Surprising as it may seem, Parker preferred *Hermann und Dorothea* to the more serious works of Goethe. His choice among Goethe's dramas also differed from that of his contemporaries. In *Egmont* Parker was especially attracted by the character of Clärchen, and like Margaret Fuller he had special praise for Goethe's understanding of women. Yet not all of Goethe's women pleased him. Philina in *Wilhelm Meister* he condemned because she had "not a fig-leaf of modesty." Mignon he called a "creature of passion from crown to heel," and he objected to them on the grounds that they caused an immoral effect.

Parker compared Goethe with Voltaire and found the German not such a scoffer but less of a man. He thought Goethe less earnest, less humane, less intellectual, and with less large influence on man. Neither person, he believed, afforded much help to lofty men in their lofty works, for both were destitute of a religious poise of character, so essential to real greatness in literature.[4]

Parker's ultimate lack of appreciation for Goethe was due to the same factors which made Emerson accept him only with frigid reservations. Both of these New Englanders ranked the religious and ethical evaluations of a writer far higher than the aesthetic qualities. Goethe, therefore, seemed flawed to their eyes. Parker inevitably accented the moral deficiencies of Goethe's personal life more than they should have been. He pitied such a person as Frederike Brion, whom he said "the cold-blooded genius plucked . . . as a flower from the garden, wore her on his bosom, then threw her away."[5]

2. *Ibid.*, pp. 20–1.
3. *Ibid.*, p. 21.
4. *Ibid.*, p. 22.
5. *Ibid.*

Yet surprisingly Parker liked Schiller even less than Goethe.[6] In commenting on the *Correspondence of Schiller and Goethe* he said frankly that he disliked Schiller heartily and always did. He found him "proud, inflated, stiff, diseasedly self-conscious." He missed in him "the great gushing genius of Goethe," and he condemned the oratorical pedantry of Schiller's poetry. He wrote of Schiller's *Aesthetic Letters:* "Hardly worth the oil, it seems to me. I have, when a boy, sometimes climbed up a high fence, and looked over, expecting tulips and violets at the least, and found—toadstools. So in books; after climbing over a palisade of tall words, I have found a great space covered with—nothing!"[7] So ran the strictures of an independent mind who was not satisfied to award Schiller the palm, merely because he had led a highly moral life. This was the opinion of a man who could respect even such a radical as Henrich Heine. Parker's writings are rich in references and quotations from Heine's poetry. He also translated a number of Heine's poems, such as "Vorrede zur dritten Auflage," "Die Lorelei," "Und wüssten's die Blumen, die kleinen," "Du hast Diamanten und Perlen," "Die Linde blühte, die Nachtigall sang," "Du bist wie eine Blume," and "Mein Kind, wir waren Kinder."[8] Years later, in 1857, Parker wrote to Mrs. Apthorp:

> Heine has a deal of the Devil in him, mixed with a deal of genius. Nobody could write so well as he—surely none since Göthe; that Hebrew nature has a world of sensuous and devotional emotion in it, and immense power of language also. But this genius is lyric, not dramatic, not epic; no Muse rises so high as the Hebrew, but it cannot keep long on the wing. The Psalms and Prophets of the Old Testament teach us this; Oriental sensuousness attained their finest expression in the Song of Solomon and in Heine's *Lieder.* . . . Much in Heine I hate—much, likewise, I admire and love.[9]

On his travels in Germany Parker met Bettina von Arnim, whose correspondence with Goethe had attracted him earlier and whom he continued to respect. According to an entry in his journal on May 23, 1844, he discussed religion with her, and transcribed the following interesting conversation:

6. In this opinion he differed sharply from most of his contemporaries.

7. Weiss, *2*, 23. Parker gave this opinion about a volume of selections from Schiller translated by John Weiss under the title *The Aesthetic Letters, Essays, and Philosophical Letters of Schiller* (Boston, 1843).

8. These translations have musical quality. Parker also translated specimens of Paul Gerhardt's *Hymns of the Mystics,* selections from Arnim and Brentano's famous anthology *Des Knaben Wunderhorn,* and from the works of Rückert, Körner, and Geibel. For as deep and serious a thinker as Parker, it seems strange that almost invariably he chose simple didactic verse or folk ballads as his favorites among German poetry.

9. Weiss, *1*, 307–8.

I told her that, if the men lack courage she had enough; that she had the courage of a Jewish prophet and the inspiration of a Christian apostle. She said she was not Christian, but heathen,—she prayed to Jupiter. I told her that was nothing; there was but one God, whose name was neither Jupiter nor Jehovah, and he took each *true* prayer. Then she said again she was no Christian. I asked, "Have you no respect for Christ?" "None for the *person,* for he had done more harm to the world than any other man." I found, however, that for the man Jesus of Nazareth, and for all the great doctrines of religion, she had the profoundest respect. I told her there was, to my thinking, but one religion,—that was *being good and doing good.*[1]

Religion and theology were always in the mainstream of Parker's interest. In the *Dial,* April, 1842, he wrote a short but interesting article called "Thoughts on Theology." It did not so much defend as explain the progress of German theology. Parker first pointed out that Germany was the only country where theology was studied for its own sake much as poetry, eloquence, or mathematics; he read the German theological writers as earnestly as did any of the Transcendental circle.[2]

A theological work which we know had a great influence on Parker, as it had on thinkers throughout the old and new continent, was Friedrich Strauss's *Das Leben Jesu,* published in 1835. Parker first examined it in 1837 when the Reverend Henry A. Walker brought back a copy from Europe. To prepare a review of this book for the *Christian Examiner,* July, 1840, Parker read not only the original text of 1,600 pages, but all the arguments pro and con and all the defenses and attacks which had appeared in England, Germany, and America. To this he added his tremendous fund of knowledge culled from the other German theologians and philosophers.

Of all the Transcendentalists Parker was one of the few who read Kant in the original and—what is more important—he understood him. He wrote in his journal of what he owed to Kant: "The brilliant mosaic, which Cousin set before the world, was of great service, but not satisfactory. I found most help in the works of Immanuel Kant, one of the profoundest thinkers in the world, though one of the worst writers, even of Germany; if he did not always furnish conclusions I could rest in, he yet gave me the true method, and put me on the right road." [3] In the *Dial* Parker spoke of Kant as an influence on Christology that would never pass away, because by acknowledging an absolute spiritual power, Kant found the common ground on which to reconcile philosophy and

1. Chadwick, pp. 136–7.
2. Alcott once said of Parker: "He was a voracious reader, an eater of books, and had the power of absorbing what he read. Probably his views were very largely influenced by the German philosophy." See *American Literature, 3* (March, 1931), 24.
3. Weiss, *2,* 454.

Christianity.[4] Chadwick believed that Parker cared little for philosophy except as the handmaid of religion.[5] Whether he cared for German philosophy or not is not so important as to determine how much he knew of it. Considering the discussions devoted to the philosophers in his journals, it is almost certain that he was familiar with the whole group.[6]

In 1840 when Emerson was looking for a suitable scholar to defend German literature in the *Dial,* he turned at once to Parker. This article, "German Literature," [7] one of the most memorable, most learned, and yet wittiest discussions in the periodical, had a decided effect on contemporary scholars. Parker's friend Convers Francis wrote to him after its publication:

> Thanks, a hundred thanks, to you for your article in the last *Dial,*—an article which has learning enough to make the fortune of a stout octavo, but in which the learning is far outdone by the riches of profoundly significant thought, and the beauties of exquisitely happy expression. Such pieces as this (but how few such can be expected) are just what is wanted to make *The Dial* not only better than any other American journal (for this is not saying much), but equal to the best in Europe; it has that grasp of elaborate thought which takes up a subject with the easy power of a strong man: the whole mind moved to the composition of it. A friend said to me: "If that article had appeared in the first number, it would at the outset have placed *The Dial* triumphantly high, above all cavil." I think so, too; and if the editors can in future furnish much such matter, they need not fear for their work that any *Daily Advertiser* (which means a whole genus) can touch a hair of its head. The humor at the beginning is capital; and the noble defence of German literature which follows must strike our foolish babblers dumb, and enlighten the wisest.[8]

In a letter which Dr. William T. Harris wrote as late as March, 1889, he expressed the opinion that Parker's article in the *Dial* caused much study of German literature, his own among the rest.[9] Professor Goodnight goes even further to say that the legitimacy of the study of German literature,—always excepting Goethe—was probably not often called in question after the appearance of this article.[1]

4. See the *Dial, 8* (April, 1842), 520.
5. Chadwick, p. 176.
6. Hedge said in a letter to Caroline Dall that Parker asked him to recommend a course of reading in German philosophy. Hedge was then living at Bangor, Maine. The exact date is unknown. See Dall, p. 17. Edna Cheney in her *Reminiscences* also expressed the opinion that German philosophy and theology influenced Parker. See p. 188. In Weiss's biography of Parker we find long excerpts from the journals dealing with all the major German philosophers. See *1,* 243ff.
7. See the *Dial, 3* (January, 1841), 315.
8. G. W. Cooke, *Introduction to the Dial, 2,* 31-2.
9. *Report of the Commissioner of Education for the Year 1897-1898, 1,* 613.
1. Goodnight, p. 52.

Parker was supposed to review Menzel's *German Literature,* which Professor Felton of Harvard had just published in Boston, but the review soon rallied to defend German literature in general. Parker set out by quoting the current rumors that New England was infected with a German mania. Whatever was German New Englanders admired, especially the immoral and irreligious writings, which, it was supposed, the Germans were chiefly engaged in writing to corrupt the youth of the world and restore the worship of Pan or the Pope. This epidemic was supposed to extend from the girls' boarding schools to the universities, and had even attacked clergymen. The remedy, Parker said, was simple. Merely replace this reading with a strong infusion of dullness. For his part, however, Parker denied that he had met any of these dangerous people. Most people with whom he was familiar read German literature like any other literature for the good that was in it and discarded the rest. After all, not all intellectual and aesthetic excellence was to be found in the Greek and Roman classics. The trouble lay in the fact that there was a class of people who hated German literature, philosophy, and theology, a dislike which rested more upon prejudice and ignorance than upon a knowledge of facts. Before these judges Goethe and Schiller, Kant and Hegel, Leibnitz and Arndt, Heine and Boehme were brought up and condemned as mystics, infidels, or pantheists—in one word, as Germans.

It was high time, Parker thought, that we look German literature squarely in the face, and allow it to speak for itself. In spite of the blasts of criticism it had weathered, German literature remained "the fairest, the richest, the most original, fresh and religious literature of all modern times." Parker did not contend that Germany had produced a great poetic genius like Shakespeare; to say, however, that German literature was narrow, superficial, and poor when compared with that of England was pure nonsense. After all, it was from Germany and not from England that we got the only editions of the classics worth reading, as well as the commentaries, grammars, and lexicons. The Germans even had written a quite readable and instructive history of English literature, while the English lacked such a book. Who had written grammars and lexicons by which the Hebrew and Greek Testaments were read, and who had written critical introductions to the Bible? Only contemporary Germans studied theology, or even the Bible with the aid of enlightened and scientific criticism. In English there was not even a history of theology available. German strides in philosophy were just as astounding. Within less than sixty years four philosophers—Kant, Fichte, Schelling, and Hegel—had appeared in Germany, who would hereafter rank with Plato, Aristotle and the other great names. In poetry and belles-lettres there was also no peer of Wieland, Lessing, the Schlegels, Herder, Jean Paul, Tieck, Schiller, or Goethe.

More important, Parker continued, was the religious character of these German writings. That all the Germans were immoral voluptuaries was the greatest of all the falsehoods. "Truth is possessed entire by no sect, German or English," he said. "We cannot predict the result of the German movement in philosophy; but we see no more reason for making Henry Heine, Gutzkow, and Schefer the exponents of that movement,—as the manner of some is, than for selecting Bulwer, Byron, Moore, and Taylor the infidel, to represent the church of England."

Parker then proceeded to flagellate Menzel's views of Goethe in particular. In the first place, he said, the book gave no faithful picture, since it was specked with prejudices. His hostility to Goethe, in fact, amounted to an absolutely pathological hatred. "When a writer attempts, as Menzel does, to show that an author who has a reputation which covers the world, and rises higher and higher each year; who is distinguished for the breadth of his studies and the newness of his views, and his exquisite tastes in all matters of art,—is only a humbug, what can we do but smile, and ask, if effects come without causes?" Parker accused Menzel of a false standard of measuring literature. Instead of judging literature by its own laws he passed sentence on the political complexion of the author. He also stooped to personal abuse and censured works of art according to a moral rather than a critical or artistic criterion.[2] Parker took special issue with Menzel's criticism of Kant, which he considered exceedingly unjust. He pointed out that Menzel never could have reached such a decision if he had read Kant's *Kritik der reinen Vernunft*. "Forgetting to look into these books," Parker said, "in his abhorrence of scholastic learning and 'study, that makes men pale,' Menzel cut the matter short, and rode over the 'high priori road,' in great state to the conclusion." In his chapter on religion Menzel's phobia of book-learning became even more rabid. His knowledge of the Catholic writers remained as narrow as his philosophy was superficial, and his comments on Protestantism and Luther were hasty and inaccurate. Parker finally concluded his criticism with this remark: "We are glad to welcome the book in its English dress, but we hope it will be read with caution, as a guide not to be trusted."

Not until 1843 did Parker travel to the country whose scholars had interested him for so many years. There he visited as many centers of learning as possible: Berlin, Halle, Heidelberg, Bonn, Leipzig, Stuttgart, Freiburg, Tübingen, Zurich, Geneva, and Basle. He sat in on lectures under the men whom he had long admired—De Wette, Gervinus, Ewald, Baur, and Paulus.[3] When he returned to America, he brought back

2. Parker himself did not always adhere to this rule, as we have already seen in the comments on Goethe which he wrote in his journal.

3. Parker's German biographer Altherr goes into detail on this subject as is evident from this passage: "Die Weiterfahrt durch Deutschland gestaltete sich zu einem ununterbrochenen Visitenabstalten bei Gelehrten, die Parker durch ihre Schriften kennen

countless books on every subject imaginable for his ever growing library. His collection flooded every inch of his study walls from floor to ceiling, overflowed to the chairs and tables, and into all the other rooms of the house. Ripley's library, which Parker had purchased when Brook Farm was disbanded, had now doubled many times over. This is not surprising if we remember that Parker was familiar with approximately twenty languages and dialects, and in his library were to be found grammars and dictionaries of many more. Of the almost 14,000 volumes and 2,500 pamphlets which he bequeathed to the Boston Public Library, a substantial number were of German origin. In his zeal for collecting these German writings, Parker was discharging a debt to "the great souls" of Germany, who by their work had sowed New England "with fruitful seed." [4]

When we examine the interests of these theologians in German culture, we find that their tastes were not particularly different from those of the Concord men of letters. Their knowledge of the German language, philosophy, and theology, however, was superior, and unlike the men of letters, Ripley, Hedge, and Parker based their conclusions upon more tangible evidence than mere intuition. Yet the fact that they reached almost the same conclusions in their defense and praise of German culture, gives us the right to consider them as an influential factor in the Transcendental group. Indeed, the influence had a mutual effect. Emerson and Alcott increased their knowledge and enthusiasm for German philosophy and theology by their contacts with these more learned gentlemen. On the other hand, the inspiring conclusions of Emerson's essays and lectures helped to free such men as Ripley and Parker from the restraining bonds of New England Unitarianism.

C. THE CRITICS
JAMES FREEMAN CLARKE AND MARGARET FULLER

"Margaret was to persons younger than herself, a Makaria and Natalia. She was wisdom and intellectual beauty. . . . To those elder than herself she was like the Euphorion of Goethe's drama, child of Faust and Helen,—a wonderful union of exuberance and judgment,

---

gelernt hatte. Nirgends auf der ganzen Fahrt erscheint er innerlich so tief ergriffen wie bei den Luthererinnerungen in Erfurt, Eisenach-Wartburg und Wittenberg, denn Luther galt ihm als Verkörperung des allein in Gott ruhenden Gewissens einer noch grössern Macht, als das 'gewaltige, allmächtige' Rom ist. . . . Von Gelehrten, die er zu Hause besuchte oder in ihren Vorlesungen kennen lernte, nennen wir Schlosser, Gervinus, Paulus, Ullmann, Umbreit, Hävernick, Delitsch und Creuzer in Heidelberg; Tholuck und Erdmann in Halle; Schmidt, Ewald, F. Chr. Baur und Ed. Zeller in Tübingen; De Wette in Basel; Schenkel in Schaffhausen; Follen in Bern; Ferd. Hitzig und Oken in Zurich." See *Theodor Parker in seinem Leben und Wirken* (St. Gallen, 1894), p. 113.
4. Weiss, *I*, 269–70.

born of romantic fullness and classic limitation." [1] With these names chosen from the pages of Goethe, James Freeman Clarke drew the portrait of his friend and fellow critic, Margaret Fuller. No one was more eligible than Clarke to pass judgment on her intellectual abilities, for as students and critics of German literature, it is amazing how parallel their careers ran.

Clarke said that both he and Margaret Fuller were attracted to German literature in 1832 after reading Carlyle's articles on Richter, Schiller, and Goethe, which had appeared in the *Foreign Quarterly Review* and the *Edinburgh Review*. "It was like being introduced into another world: a world of new thoughts, hopes and opportunities." Since he could take little interest in any other books, he would walk from Cambridge to the Athenaeum in Boston, where the periodicals were available, so that he could read them over again. He knew Carlyle's name but nothing more about him, and this scanty information he passed on to Emerson, who also had read the articles but as yet had not even learned the name of the writer.[2]

Clarke first discovered German literature during his student days at the Harvard Divinity School, where he met Hedge, Emerson, Everett, and Ticknor. Dr. Follen's influence also affected him, because Follen had introduced gymnastic exercises along with German into the college curriculum during Clarke's freshman year.[3] At Harvard Clarke first read the writings of Coleridge, who confirmed his longing for a philosophy higher than that of John Locke and David Hartley. Coleridge proved to him from Kant that though knowledge begins with experience it does not come from experience. Then he discovered that he was a born Transcendentalist.[4]

Perhaps Margaret Fuller, more than the Harvard professors, awakened Clarke's enthusiasm for German literature. Clarke wrote in his "Journal of People and Things" on September 12, 1831: "I called this afternoon on S.M.F. I am puzzled by her. I am disposed to believe her the most remarkable of women. . . . She seems to me at her early age to have already attained a thorough knowledge of human character, a consistent system of life, by which all their intricacies are to her like an open book." Yet he thought she was not happy, that she lacked a sphere of action.[5] With this comment began a literary friendship which lasted till Margaret's death.

1. See Margaret Fuller, *Works, 1, 97.*
2. This paragraph is quoted from material in Chapter 4 of James Freeman Clark's MS autobiography owned by the Clarke family. Part of the MS is included in E. E. Hale's biography of Clarke. For a complete list of Clarke MS material used in this Chapter see Bibliography.
3. MS autobiography, ch. 4, p. 12.
4. *Ibid.*
5. This MS journal was also not completely reproduced by Hale.

In his diary on October 16, 1832, Clarke set down his wish to write a good deal, to get an individual style, to read little—and that principally German. He actually carried out this resolution, for until Margaret moved to Groton in 1833, they read and discussed German literature almost every day. In his "Journal of Understanding" one finds passages such as this:

> J[ames]. "I think Dr. Follen did not catch the true interior character of Göthe."
> M[argaret]. "Could you expect he would? He has not a philosophic, only a tasteful mind.[6]

One day he would be hastily reading Goethe's *Tageheft* "to see what was in it" and was struck with the wonderful energy of the man.[7] Another day it would be the study of Fichte or a talk with Miss Peabody on the subject of Goethe. She had condemned the German for having no ideal, no moral standard of perfection, but Clarke maintained that what she was offended with was Goethe's perfect truth.[8] A month later (December 5, 1832) he mentioned a conversation with Emerson on Goethe, German literature, and Carlyle.[9] The Germans, he wrote in his diary, had become for him invaluable because they taught him the necessary connection between life and thought. Since they had rescued him from an unmeaning world and transferred him into one full of significance, they merited his highest gratitude.[1]

In his letters to his family Clarke showed the same enthusiasm for German literature. Sister Sarah, for instance, mentioned in 1834 that their grandmamma thought it "ridiculous" for him "to have German books" when his "grandfather did without them." [2] Nor could Sarah refrain from describing Emerson's future wife, Lydia Jackson of Plymouth, as "a regular enthusiast, an adorer of Carlyle and Goethe." [3] Even a sermon by Henry Hedge she described to her brother as an illustration of "the doctrine of mutual attractions," based on some "things from the 'Elective Affinities' [*Die Wahlverwandtschaften*]; but it was deeply religious." [4]

To William Henry Channing, Clarke wrote in 1835 of the Emerson-Carlyle correspondence, adding that there were some, even in Kentucky,

6. P. 132.
7. *Ibid.*, p. 135.
8. *Ibid.*, p. 155.
9. *Ibid.*, p. 159.
1. *Ibid.*, p. 160.
2. MS letter, Sarah Clarke to James F. Clarke, January 26, 1834.
3. *Ibid.*, January 22, 1835.
4. *Ibid.*, April 28, 1836.

who admired Carlyle's patriarch Goethe. Then he instructed Channing to purchase for him in Germany a long list of German books. Schleiermacher, Fichte, Herder, Goethe, Schiller, Tieck, Richter, and A. W. Schlegel were just a few of the names he listed.[5] No wonder that he could say at this time, "If I am in the 'enthusiasm' period with respect to Göthe & Schiller I fear I shall always stay in it." [6]

Margaret Fuller likewise had made up her mind to study German, and surrendered herself completely, reading no other language, even in the newspapers.[7] Before a year had passed, both Clarke and Margaret were on speaking terms with such works as Goethe's *Faust, Tasso, Iphigenie auf Tauris, Hermann und Dorothea,*[8] *Die Wahlverwandtschaften,* and *Dichtung und Wahrheit,* all of Schiller's principal dramas and lyric poetry, Tieck's *William Lovell* and *Prinz Zerbino,* Novalis' *Heinrich von Ofterdingen* and *Hymnen an die Nacht,* the poetry of Körner, and selections of Richter.

Schiller, Tieck,[9] and Novalis remained among their idols, but none of these entranced them so much as Goethe. Afterward in referring to those happy days Clarke would always speak of the larger life which was opened for them under Goethe's lead.[1] Margaret's letters to Clarke were larded with comments about these German authors. One day she wrote to him: "I wish to talk about such an uncommon person,—about Novalis! a wondrous youth, and who has only written one volume. That is pleasant! I feel as though I could pursue my natural mode with him, get acquainted, then make my mind easy in the belief that I know all that is to be known. And he died at twenty-nine, and, as with Körner, your feelings may be single; you will never be called upon to share his experience, and compare his future feelings with his present. . . . Then it is a relief, after feeling the immense superiority of Goethe." [2] In August, 1832, she spoke again of "the good Novalis . . . most enlightened, yet most pure; every link of his experience framed—*no beaten*—from the tried gold." She read thoroughly Novalis' *Die Lehrlinge zu Sais* and *Heinrich von Ofterdingen,* and believed that she understood the plan and treatment of the latter work. She even considered keeping a Novalis-

5. MS letter, James F. Clarke to William H. Channing, October 22, 1833.
6. MS letter, James F. Clarke to Ephraim Peabody, July 6, 1835.
7. Fuller, *Works, 1,* 114.
8. In the year of Goethe's death, Clarke made a partial translation of *Hermann und Dorothea* with an introduction covering very briefly Goethe's major works and reputation. The MS is still among the Clarke papers.
9. Clarke once wrote to Margaret that Tieck's character was "beautifully harmonious" and his life "warm with self-consciousness and appreciation of others." See MS letter, September, 1832.
1. E. D. Cheney, *Reminiscences of Edna Dow Cheney* (Boston, Lee and Shepard, 1902), p. 419.
2. Fuller, *Works, 1,* 118–19.

journal for Clarke's benefit.[3] Clarke answered Margaret that same
month: "I hope dear Margaret, that you are communicating to me the
impression & the idea you have gained of Novalis. I imagine you constantly meditating and writing this for my delight when I return, & I am
scrupulously careful to write a sort of piecemeal journal of my own
proceedings for you." [4] Again the following year he begged Margaret to
discourse to him "of the good Novalis" according to her own idea since
he felt "a deep interest in him." Clarke had already urged William Eliot
to read Novalis as "one in whom the poetical & profound are completely
blended, & produce entirely a peculiar effect." [5]

The following year Margaret switched her interest to Lessing's plays.
Miss Sarah Sampson she could hardly plow through, but *Emilia Galotti*
and *Minna von Barnhelm* she considered satisfactory. In her letters to
Clarke she praised Lessing's well-conceived and sustained characters and
the interesting dramatic situations, but she thought that he lacked profound knowledge of human nature, "those minute beauties, and delicate
vivifying traits, which lead on so in the writings of some authors, who
may be nameless." She summed up Lessing with these words: "easily
followed, strong, but not deep." [6]

Richter also took high honors among the prized authors of Margaret
Fuller and Clarke. Margaret wondered at her own indolence or shallow-
ness which could have resisted him so long. She thought it was a mistake
to call his riches lack of system; there was a system or plan, but on so
broad a base that she herself could not at first comprehend it. Every
page forced her to make annotations, and she rejoiced in the thought
that she "must have improved to love him" as she did.[7]

Yet in May, 1833, she told Clarke that she was uncertain whether
she should have accepted Richter without question. "His infinitely varie-
gated and certainly most exquisitely colored web fatigues attention," she
said. She chose wit to humor, and daring imagination to the richest
fancy. Besides, his philosophy and religion seemed to be of the plaintive
sort, and, having some tendency that way herself, she wanted an op-
posing force in a favorite author.[8] She showed no hesitation of this sort,
however, in the following poem addressed to Richter and printed in the
Dial:

> Poet of Nature! Gentlest of the Wise!
> Most airy of the fanciful, most keen

---

3. *Ibid.*, pp. 120–1. The influence of Novalis on Margaret Fuller is apparent when she
typified the mysteries of the soul as "Leila" in the *Dial*, and wrote verses about herself
under that name in her diary.
4. MS letter, August, 1832.
5. MS letter, James F. Clarke to W. G. Eliot, December, 1833.
6. Fuller, *Works, I,* 121.
7. *Ibid.*, p. 130.
8. *Ibid.*, p. 147.

Of satirists, thy thoughts, like butterflies,
Still near the sweetest-scented flowers have been;
With Titian's colors thou canst sunset paint,
With Raphael's dignity, celestial love;
With Hogarth's pencil, each deceit and feint
Of meanness and hypocrisy reprove;
Canst to Devotion's highest flight sublime
Exalt the mind, by tenderest pathos' art,
Dissolve in purifying tears the heart,
Or bid it, shuddering, recoil at crime;
The fond illusions of the youth and maid,
At which so many world-formed sages sneer,
When by thy altar-lighted torch displayed,
Our natural religion can appear.
All things in thee tend to one polar star,
Magnetic all thy influences are! [9]

Margaret also recommended Richter to her other friends. In a letter to Sarah H. Whitman, she wrote: "I send you a book of mine, one of Richter's finest works. I think its fancy, humor, and sweet humanity will delight you. You can keep it till April, you will find it quite a study, for Richter loves to coin words, and seeks his thought even in the most distant mint." [1]

In 1836 Margaret hoped for a periodical in which she could write a series of articles on German literature, at least eight numbers of which were to be devoted to Tieck. She especially wanted to translate Tieck's *Little Red Riding Hood* and have it adorned with illustrations, but she doubted whether it could be done in Boston. Margaret also desired to review Heine's *Letters on German Literature* [*Die romantische Schule*], and include at least two articles on Novalis and Körner. Her wish was partly granted when Clarke became editor of the *Western Messenger*, for in this periodical Margaret got an early opportunity to articulate the ideas that she had been expounding in her private letters to Clarke and others. Her article on Körner finally appeared in the *Western Messenger* in January, 1838. [2] Other German names were also prominent in this periodical. Schiller's *Joan of Arc* [*Die Jungfrau von Orleans*], for instance, Clarke considered superior to Voltaire's play on the same sub-

9. The *Dial, I* (July, 1840), 135.
1. *American Literature, I* (January, 1930), 420.
2. As a poet, she thought that Körner could hardly claim immortality, since the interest of most of his poems was local and temporary, but the beauty of his life and the dramatic catastrophe of his early death were bound to impart interest to the feeblest of those poems in which he had recorded its impulses. *4, 372–3.* In a letter to Clarke Margaret said of Körner: "He charms me, and has become a fixed star in the heaven of my thought; but I understand all that he excites perfectly." See Fuller, *Works, I,* 120.

ject,[3] and a translation of *Wallenstein* he praised as a splendid poem.[4] Even the *Philosophical Letters* were lauded as good specimens of powerful thinking and writing, but were recommended to be read "as a fine poem" rather than for the opinions expressed.[5]

Although the *Western Messenger* featured the names of Schiller, Richter, Herder, Uhland,[6] and Körner,[7] a defense of German theology remained its main objective. Clarke believed that there could be no greater mistake than to categorize all German theology as rationalistic and atheistic. In the issue of November, 1836, Clarke satirized the orthodox writers who printed two articles by Tholuck and Olshausen in the *Biblical Repository,* apparently not realizing that these German writers represented liberal Christianity.[8] Clarke also translated in the *Western Messenger* De Wette's book, *Theodore, or the Skeptic's Conversion.*[9] His first interest in this work seems to have been awakened in 1835 when he wrote to Margaret Fuller: "I have been reading a book which has cleared up my mind a great deal with respect to theology—namely, De Wette's *Theodore.* It is an account of the progress of a young theologian's opinions from ultra rationalism to a warm & pure faith, equally

3. *Western Messenger, 2* (November, 1836), 230–2. We can observe in Margaret Fuller's letters that she was in complete agreement with Clarke. She wrote to him that Schiller gave her "great pleasure," and that when she looked upon Schiller's works in her bookcase, she thanked the friendly heart who put all this genius and passion within her power. At times she even preferred Schiller to Goethe, since Goethe did not always make her happy. See Fuller, *Works, 1,* 148.

4. *Western Messenger, 3* (April, 1837), 643. In 1830 Clarke translated a few scenes from *Die Jungfrau von Orleans,* and Margaret corrected them adding this note: "I feel as if taking a liberty in making so many petty corrections. But 'tis what you asked and they would all occur to me in reading these scenes very carelessly. Do not adopt *one* that you do not approve." This translation and note are to be found among the Clarke papers. On June 14, 1833, Clarke again mentioned in a letter to Margaret that he regretted the lack of time to continue a Schiller translation which he desired as "a suitable companion and friend" to her "beautiful Tasso in his Orphic pilgrimage through our deserts." MS letter.

5. *Western Messenger, 3* (April, 1837), 623.

6. In a letter to Margaret dated April 12, 1835 Clarke praised certain lines of Uhland as "beautiful and orthodox."

7. Clarke, as we know, worked hard at his poetic translations. He wrote to George Ripley in February, 1833: "I wish to show you some specimens of translation of German poetry. I am aware that they by no means come up to the high requisitions of a true translator. A translation of the highest sort changes the *form,* the *figures,* and even the thoughts, in order to preserve the *spirit* of the original, and in order to maintain the life and unity of the translation. Mine are merely honest versions—the life of the original is not in them, yet you may guess at it—they are but the reverse of a Gobelin tapestry." MS letter, February 21, 1833. Charles Brooks and John Dwight as well as Margaret Fuller often translated German poems for the *Western Messenger.* Clarke requested such short translations in a letter to Margaret. On July 26, 1837 he wrote: "Can you not send me some of your German translations—some of those from Tieck or Richter or Novalis? Pray now do not neglect this, for I really need them. Our Messenger has come down on my poor shoulders and I shall have to write the whole." MS letter, July 26, 1837.

8. *Western Messenger, 2* (November, 1836), 288.

9. The complete translation appeared in 1841 in Ripley's *Specimens of Foreign Standard Literature.*

remote from vigorous orthodoxy and the cold and lifeless creed of the mere understanding. I should like so much (as they say here) to talk to you about it. I think however of publishing it chapter by chapter in our *Messenger*." [1] The importance of this book from a theological standpoint cannot be overestimated. Joseph Henry Allen said that it was the first book he remembered which showed "clear traces of German influence on critical opinion." [2]

Goethe, however, remained the most beloved German author treated in the *Western Messenger*. Soon after he arrived in Louisville, Clarke wrote to Margaret: "Art thou aware that my love for Goethe is changing into rash anger, because I cannot understand his poetry as I fancied I did his prose? Those little *lieder,* proverbs, etc are darkness visible to me. Perhaps I look for too much—perhaps I have no taste for the purest kind of poetry, having been early used to the sort whose beauty was in words & phrases & turns of speech. I really wish you would tell me why & how you like his poetry. Some how I can not rightly *auffassen* [3] it." [4] But Margaret's answer did not suffice. On November 12, 1833 he informed her that he had to give up Goethe's lyrics and be content with the ideas he had already gained. He had, however, by no means put Goethe out of his mind. Two months later he quoted to Margaret a letter from his friend William Eliot who had been reading *Wilhelm Meister* and was "enraptured" with it. [5] Clarke was openly pleased with the fact that he had urged Eliot to read German and Goethe. [6] The following year Clarke was proud to call Goethe "the greatest poet and philosopher of modern times" without being afraid of Mr. Norton's opinion. [7] Translation after translation passed between Clarke and Margaret Fuller for criticism. With one went these words: "And here too you will find Göthe—as indeed how can we escape from the influence of such an intellect—once having come under it. We must go on reproducing Göthe, I suppose, to the end of our natural lives, either consciously or unconsciously." [8]

In February, 1836, Clarke answered Margaret's request for knowledge of metaphysics in order to understand Goethe. In three long pages of explanation and description, he tried to state the general nature of the intellectual movement in Germany from Kant's time to their own. To

1. MS letter, November 16, 1835.
2. See Chadwick, p. 82.
3. Clarke, like all the Transcendentalists, loved the game of putting German words into his informal correspondence. Thus he often talked of his *"Wandertage"* or found himself torn from his *"Umgebung."*
4. MS letter, September 9, 1833.
5. Two months earlier Clarke had written to Eliot urging him to read Goethe and Schiller rather than Kant and Fichte, Eichhorn and Tieck rather than Schleiermacher and Jacobi. See MS letter, December, 1833.
6. MS letter, James F. Clarke to Margaret Fuller, February 24, 1834.
7. *Ibid.,* May 12, 1835.
8. *Ibid.,* August, 1835.

study Fichte and Schelling, he felt was not necessary since Goethe himself paid little attention to them. Such was his admiration for the German literary giant.[9] In 1837 Clarke, together with his friend George Keats (brother of the poet), first read the second part of *Faust* and was most enthusiastic, finding it "if less interesting . . . even more elegant and graceful than the first." He had to write of this experience to Margaret and describe in detail several scenes from the play.[1]

Goethe's religious views were of special interest to Clarke and Margaret. At one time Clarke decided to accept Heine's opinion that Goethe "leaned close upon Pantheism." [2] In the very first volume of the *Western Messenger* and with unusual candor Clarke, however, defended Goethe's opinions of the *Book of Ruth:*

> It may be interesting to some of our readers to be made acquainted with the views of the greatest of modern critics, with respect to the literary merit of certain parts of scripture. God's word is beautifully adapted to all parts of man's complex nature; it can move not simply his conscience and reason; it also acts on the Imagination, and the sentiment of Beauty. With respect to these latter traits, the judgments of a great poet and chief in literature like Göthe, are of more value than those of the theologian and divine, whose taste and imagination, as has been well remarked by John Foster, are too frequently wholly uncultivated and dormant.[3]

Clarke was determined to shield Goethe from charges of scepticism and infidelity. America seemed to him to lag behind the times, when almost throughout all Europe—not only where German was spoken but also in France, Italy, Sweden, and Russia—Goethe was looked up to as the great poet and philosopher of the age. Moreover, Clarke said, no ultimate harm could possibly develop from reading the thoughts of this German writer, for Goethe was a true eclectic philosopher who had been open to the best influences of all systems. These were daring statements to make. Here was a minister of the gospel advising people to read a poet who had often been called an atheist rather than to concentrate upon the theologians and divines who upheld the orthodox faith. Was it any wonder that these Transcendentalists could not be trusted? [4]

9. *Ibid.,* February 26, 1836.
1. *Ibid.,* November 20, 1837.
2. *Ibid.,* March 28, 1836.
3. *Western Messenger, I* (January, 1836), 457–8.
4. Clarke also translated Goethe's lines on the death of Euphorion from *Faust, Part II* (*ibid.,* pp. 474–5), and in his obituary notice for Charles Emerson he closed with Goethe's lines on Schiller (*ibid., I,* 863–4). Later he translated some of Goethe's *Orphic Sayings* to show the philosophical and religious views of this writer. In a letter to Dwight, March 25, 1837, Clarke spoke of the *Orphic Sayings.* He preferred to deal with Goethe rather than Schiller, he said, since Goethe required less enthusiasm and more study. See MS letters of Dwight, Boston Public Library. Additional material on Goethe appeared in subsequent issues of the *Western Messenger,* such as "A Tale from

To Goethe more than to any other writer Margaret Fuller also returned with delight. Her letters to Clarke spilled over with plaudits of him whose mind, she thought, encompassed the universe. It seemed to her that he comprehended every feeling she had ever had, and expressed it so beautifully that when she shut the book she felt as if she had lost her personal identity. She hoped for the time when she would not be so overwhelmed, and could leave off the habit of wishing to grasp the whole. Perhaps she could be contented to learn a little every day, as became a pupil.[5] Again she wrote to Clarke in June, 1833: "Three or four afternoons I have passed very happily at my beloved haunt in the wood, reading Goethe's 'Second Residence in Rome.' Your pencil-marks show that you have been there before me. I shut the book each time with an earnest desire to live as he did,—always to have some engrossing object of pursuit." [6] She regretted that she could never have the opportunity of seeing Goethe and telling him her state of mind. She would have asked him for guidance, for *he,* understanding her, would have shown her how to rule circumstances instead of being ruled by them.[7]

Only one year from the time that she was introduced to Goethe's writings, Margaret harbored the idea of writing a biography of him. She denied this fact to Clarke, but then added: "I shall need a great deal of preparation before I shall have it clear in my head. I have taken a great many notes; but I shall not begin to write it, till it all lies mapped out before me. . . . I wish to look at the matter from all sides. . . . To whom shall I write to choose my materials? I have thought of Mr. Carlyle, but still more of Goethe's friend, Von Muller. I dare say he would be pleased at the idea of a life of G. written in this hemisphere, and be very willing to help me." [8]

The more she read the writings of Goethe, the more she found to learn, and she became one of the staunchest advocates of Goethe in her time. Although her life of Goethe was never completed, she made translations of his lyrics which she sent to her friends, and in 1834 she com-

---

Goethe" (*4,* 217), and quotations (*4,* 379; *5,* 108, 124, and 392). A review of Dwight's volume of Goethe's and Schiller's Poems appeared in Vol. *6,* 259–60, and excerpts or complete poems of Goethe appeared frequently in Vols. *7* and *8.*

Clarke did not visit Germany until 1849, but the account of his journey, which he published under the title *Eleven Weeks in Europe* demonstrated that so far as Goethe was concerned, he was more enthusiastic than ever. Having studied his writings for approximately twenty years, it seemed to him that a more profound and creative intellect had not visited the earth in these latter days (p. 128). He praised the healthy realism, the clear understanding and the sharp observations of Goethe's mind. He censured those who professed to admire Schiller more, because "no man loved and respected Goethe more than did Schiller himself." Frederic Henry Hedge made a similar statement in his Schiller Oration when he said: "Let no one attempt to disparage either of these great spirits by invidious comparison. . . . Sie wohnen beide auf der Menschheit Hoehen."

5. Fuller, *Works, 1,* 119.
6. *Ibid.,* p. 121.
7. *Ibid.,* p. 122.
8. *Ibid.,* pp. 128–9.

pleted a metrical translation of *Torquato Tasso*. While it was not published until the collected edition of her works in 1874, a number of the Transcendentalists, including Emerson, read it in manuscript.[9]

So late as 1836, however, she had still not made up her mind about Goethe. She told Clarke that she had changed her opinion about his religious views many times. Sometimes she was tempted to think that only his wonderful knowledge of human nature excited in her such reverence for his philosophy. Yet her admiration for the genius of Goethe was in nowise dimmed, and she admitted that she was ready to try his philosophy.[1]

Nor had she abandoned the idea of completing her life of Goethe. George Ripley suggested that she write the biography for his *Specimens of Foreign Standard Literature;* [2] Emerson referred to this ambition of hers in a letter to Carlyle dated September, 1836: "I read Goethe, and now lately the posthumous volumes, with a great interest. A friend of mine [Margaret Fuller] who studies his life with care would gladly know what records there are of his first ten years after his settlement at Weimar, and what Books there are in Germany about him, beside what Mrs. Austin has collected and Heine. Can you tell me?" [3]

To broaden her knowledge of Goethe, Margaret borrowed German books from all her friends, especially from Emerson. On April 11, 1837, she gave back to Emerson Goethe's letters to Merck and the first two volumes of the letters to Zelter, saying: "I look to Concord as my Lethe and Eunoë after this purgatory of distracting petty tasks." [4] In 1840 at Margaret Fuller's request Emerson wrote for the *Dial* the article, "Thoughts on Modern Literature," and her steady backing of the "old Heathen" did more to weaken his animus than Carlyle had been able to do in the earlier years. Emerson said that Margaret Fuller knew German books more cordially than any other person,[5] and "nowhere did Goethe find a braver, more intelligent, or more sympathetic reader." [6]

When Margaret published as part of Ripley's series her translation of Goethe's *Conversations with Eckermann,* Sarah Whitman praised it in the *Boston Quarterly Review* as an important link in the chain of memorials to Goethe and as a work which would assist the American people toward a better interpretation of his character. More important

9. Margaret Fuller sent the translation of Goethe's *Tasso* to Hedge with the suggestion that he transmit it to Emerson for criticism. See T. W. Higginson, *Margaret Fuller Ossoli* (Boston, Houghton Mifflin, 1884), p. 64.

1. Fuller, *Works, 1,* 167.
2. *Ibid.,* p. 177.
3. *Emerson-Carlyle Correspondence, 1,* 100.
4. Higginson, *Margaret Fuller Ossoli,* p. 69.
5. Fuller, *Works, 1,* 204.
6. *Ibid.,* p. 244.

than the translation itself was Margaret Fuller's preface, which made a magnificent case for Goethe, and won praise from all who read it.[7] She called attention to the fact that much of the hostile criticism was addressed to translations of *Wilhelm Meister* and *Faust,* two works which "above all others, require a knowledge of the circumstances and character from which they rose, to ascertain their scope and tendency." She summed up the objections to Goethe in four phrases; he was not a Christian, he was not an idealist, he was not a democrat, and he was not Schiller. "If by Christian," she said, "be meant the subordination of the intellectual to the spiritual, I shall not deny that with Goethe the reverse was the case. . . . His God was . . . the creative and uplifting rather than the paternal spirit, his religion, that all his powers must be unfolded; his faith, 'that nature could not dispense with immortality.' . . . Those who cannot draw the moral for themselves had best leave his books alone; they require the power as life does."

That Goethe was not an idealist, she did not deny. "He thought not so much of what might be as what is. He did not seek to alter or exalt Nature, but merely to select from her rich stores. . . . Had his views been different, his peculiar powers of minute searching, and extended observation would have been much injured; as, instead of looking at objects with the single aim of ascertaining the properties, he would have examined them only to gain from them what most favored his plans." On the contrary, Margaret Fuller was satisfied that "he went the way that God and Nature called him."

That he was an aristocrat she also conceded, but she added this proviso: "A minority of aristocrats is needed to keep these liberals in check and make them pause upon their measures long enough to know what they are doing; for as yet the cauldron of liberty has shown a constant disposition to overboil. . . . To be sincere, consistent, and intelligent in what one believes is what is important; a higher power takes care of the rest."

As for the last accusation, that Goethe was not Schiller, neither was Shakespeare Milton, nor Ariosto Tasso. "It would be well," she said, "if the admirers of Schiller would learn from him to admire and profit by his friend and coadjutor, as he himself did. . . . No one who has a higher aim in reading German books than mere amusement . . . can leave aside either Schiller or Goethe; but far, far least the latter. It would be leaving Augustus Caesar out of the history of Rome because he was not Brutus."

7. Clarke, for instance, wrote to Margaret from Louisville: "I found a copy of your Eckermann, which in the slow progress of spiritual light has not yet shone into our darkness in these parts—these outermost parts of civilization. . . . Your preface seemed to me a masterpiece of composition, clear yet cogent, dignified yet playful, with *point* to attract attention & weighty matter to occupy the thought. I was delighted especially with the answers to those who find fault with Goethe." MS letter, October 8, 1839.

Having dismissed the main objections to Goethe, Margaret Fuller proceeded to discuss what Goethe meant to her personally. She found him most valuable as a means of balancing the judgment and as a means of suggesting thought. She considered him one of the finest lyric poets of modern times and the best writer of the German language. As a critic on art and literature he was also not surpassed in independence, fairness, powers of sympathy, and largeness of view. Margaret denied that she was a blind admirer of Goethe, for she had been disturbed by "his aversion to pain and isolation of the heart," but she was content to describe him in the terms by which Hamlet described his father:

> He was a man, take him for all in all,
> We shall not look upon his like again.

This preface was the first of the famous defenses which Margaret Fuller devoted to Goethe. In her book *Woman in the Nineteenth Century* she had much to praise in Goethe's delineation of the female characters, Margaret, Leonora, Iphigenia, Mariana, Philina, Natalia, and Mignon. "What woman needs," she wrote, "is not as a woman to act or rule, but as a nature to grow, as an intellect to discern, as a soul to live freely and unimpeded, to unfold such powers as were given her when we left our common home." These qualities she discerned in Goethe's women. By continual efforts at self-culture Goethe had elevated the human being, caring for women as well as men, for he aimed at "a pure self-subsistence and a free development of any powers with which women may be gifted by nature, as much for them as for men."

Margaret Fuller's most important comments on Goethe appeared in the *Dial*.[8] Her first critique answered an attack upon Goethe by the German critic Wolfgang Menzel.[9] His view of Goethe, she said, was that of a philistine in the least opprobrious sense of the term. The heart of the trouble lay in the fact that Menzel was only a man of talent, and talent could not comprehend genius. She further accused Menzel of

8. George Willis Cooke said that Emerson's account of Margaret Fuller's connection with the *Dial* was a generous testimony to the modesty with which she undertook the task and the skill with which she carried it forward. Cooke believed that she produced nothing better than the articles she wrote for the *Dial*. At least she wrote nothing better in criticism than her comments about Goethe. See *Introduction to the Dial, 1,* 87–9.

Clarke, on the other hand, made only a few minor contributions to the *Dial*. In April, 1841, he submitted two poems on art. The first, "The genuine Portrait," he said, was inspired by a remark of Lessing, and a second poem, "The Real and the Ideal," he subtitled "On the marble bust of Schiller." Throughout his life, however, Clarke amused himself by making translations of German verse. In 1876 he published a collection of these poems under the title *Exotics*. Goethe was not the only poet included. We also find the lyrics of Heine, Geibel, Schiller, Herder, Bürger, Rückert, and Körner, as well as translations from Hafiz and Saadi, which probably came through the German of von Hammer.

9. The *Dial, 3* (January, 1841), 340.

speaking partial truths which had all the effect of falsehood. Such denials of the crown, she observed, would only have the effect of fixing it more firmly on the head of the "old Heathen."

Then she proceeded to refute each and every argument against Goethe, including her own earlier criticism. Historically considered, she said, Goethe needed no apology, since his so-called faults merely fitted him the better for the part he had to play. If he were too much the connoisseur and attached too great an importance to the cultivation of taste, we could afford to overlook it, since German literature needed to be refined, polished, and harmonized. If he were too skeptical and too much the experimentalist, how else could he have formed himself to be the keenest and most nearly universal of observers? Why ask Goethe to be that which he was not? If one demanded a moral enthusiast, there was Schiller. If piety or pure mystic sweetness, there was Novalis. If exuberant sentiment, one could look to Richter. For literary criticism there were the Schlegels. None of them, however, was able to fill Goethe's place.

Most men in judging another man ask whether he lives up to their standard. But she preferred to ask whether Goethe lived up to his own. She even denied that his private life was immoral; no man could have produced so many volumes without severe labor, steady forbearance, and an almost unparalleled intellectual growth. Although he may have fallen short of the highest fulfillment of his vocation, if we consider his life as a whole, he was neither epicurean nor sensualist. His serenity alone, she said, in such a time of skepticism and sorrowful seeking, gave him a claim to all our study. And it had to be a very slight survey which could confound this calm self-trust with selfish indifference of temperament.

This was not her last word on Goethe. In July, 1842, a second article appeared in the *Dial,* this time not so much a defense as an analysis of Goethe's character and writings.[1] It is also significant that, in spite of her idolatry of the man, she was affected by the puritanical New England conscience. She appeared inconsistent, therefore, when she asserted that Goethe's intellect was too much developed in proportion to his moral nature. "Pardon him, World," she said, "that he was too worldly. Do not wonder, Heart, that he was so heartless." She censured his "perpetual dangling after the royal family," and his "verse-making for the albums of serene highnesses." She compared him to his own character, Tasso. Like him "Goethe had not from nature that character of self-reliance and self-control in which he so long appeared to the world. It was wholly acquired and so highly valued because he was conscious of the opposite tendency." She even commented on an apparent coldness in his nature, but she seemed to take back all this censure

1. The article has often been called Margaret Fuller's finest piece of criticism.

when she said: "Yet never let him be confounded with those who sell all their birthright. . . . He was kind, industrious, wise, gentlemanly, if not manly."

Margaret Fuller believed that *Faust* contained the great ideas of Goethe's life. His other works were but "chapters to this poem, illustrative of particular points." Answering the criticism of readers of *Faust, Part II,* she said: "When the world shall have got rid of the still overpowering influence of the first part, it will be seen that the fundamental idea is never lost sight of in the second. The change is that Goethe, though the same thinker, is no longer the same person." This statement was a prophecy which time has proved correct. Yet she found *Faust* as a whole inferior to Dante's *Divina Commedia.*

Wilhelm Meister, which in her estimation ranked second only to *Faust,* she considered one of the greatest educational works that the world had ever produced. She underscored the *Wanderjahre,* or the second part of *Wilhelm Meister,* merely because it was not so well known as the *Lehrjahre. Iphigenie auf Tauris* she also pronounced one of Goethe's most beautiful dramas. She called it "a work beyond the possibility of negation; a work where a religious meaning not only pierces but enfolds the whole; a work as admirable in art, still higher in significance, more single in expression."

Unlike most American critics she stood up for *Die Wahlverwandtschaften* against charges of gross immorality. The reason for the general interpretation of this work, she thought, was probably the subject, for any discussion of the validity of the marriage vow makes society tremble to its foundation. All that was in the book would have been bearable to most minds if the writer had not displayed such a cold, objective manner, and "had larded his work here and there with ejaculations of horror and surprise." In the character of Ottilie she saw an organizing power of genius greater than in Shakespeare. Others, she said, exclaim, "What an immoral book!" but her only thought was: "It is a work of art!" With each perusal of the book, her admiration and delight grew at the wonderful fulfillment of design. It gave her an insight into the reason why Goethe was content to be called artist, and his writings works of art rather than revelations.

In her conclusion Margaret Fuller blamed Goethe's experiences for distorting the development of his nature. Yet she felt ashamed in finding even this much fault with such a Titan. She was inclined to dismiss all her negations of Goethe as mere "stuff," and look upon herself for uttering them with as much contempt as Mr. Carlyle, Mrs. Austin, or Mrs. Jameson might have done. The only criticism which could be valid, she said, would be to do all he omitted to do, and those who cannot should not be entitled to say a word.

Perhaps the reason why Miss Fuller's puritanical conceptions of morality were finally replaced by an attitude resembling Goethe's more tolerant ethical principles was that, like Goethe, she had devoted her own life to self-culture and development of her intellect.[2] Like Goethe she never gave way to her feelings, "but lived active, thoughtful, seeking to be wise." [3] In this respect she differs from some of the other Transcendentalists. In fact, it might be a misnomer to define her as a Transcendentalist in spite of her connections with the *Dial*.[4] She stated in a letter as early as 1835, when the *Dial* was proposed, that she felt honored to be deemed worthy of lending a hand, although she feared that she was "merely 'Germanic' and not 'transcendental.' " [5] Even

2. Professor Harris once said: "Individual development was the great inspiration of her life, and in this she could appreciate Goethe. But she did not sympathize with German thought, and it seems to me that she has done more harm than any other American to our interpretation of German literature." See Margaret Fuller Editorial, August 23, 1883, Boston Public Library MS, No. 10. I think that the latter part of this statement is biased. We can still read her criticism of Goethe and benefit by her searching analysis. Nor are her comments on many of the other German writers far from the truth. She was not infallible, but she certainly did not misguide the public interpretation of German literature.

3. Fuller, *Works, 1*, 197. Margaret Fuller was also attracted to Goethe's correspondence with Bettina von Arnim. In the *Dial* she praised these letters for their "fullness of original thought and inspired fidelity to nature" (7, 313). Yet she admitted that the relationship of Bettina to Goethe was not a beautiful one, a fact which many of the Transcendentalists did not immediately realize. She expressed the underlying fault in these words: "Were Bettine, indeed, a child, she might bring her basket of flowers and strew them in his path without expecting even a smile in return. But to say nothing of the reckoning by years, which the curious have made, we constantly feel that she is not a child. She is so indeed when compared with him as to maturity of growth, but she is not so in their relation, and the degree of knowledge she shows of life and thought compels us to demand some conscious dignity of her as a woman." *Ibid.*, p. 316.

Margaret Fuller found the letters of Bettina to the Canoness Günderode more satisfactory, for it was a relationship between woman and woman, adorned by great genius and beauty on both sides. Miss Fuller began to publish these letters in translation but was forced to discontinue the project. There is an unsigned letter in the Duyckinck Collection at the New York Public Library concerning this work. The letter, dated January 27, 1845, and addressed to Wiley and Putnam, New York City, reads as follows:

"Miss S. M. Fuller now connected with the New York Tribune, made some years since a partial translation of the celebrated correspondence between Bettina von Arnim and her friend Günderode. It was to have been published in 4 Nos: of which one appeared and being admirably executed, found favor, but owing to the circumstances of the publisher (E. P. Peabody) only resulted in expense to Miss Fuller and was discontinued, much to the regret of many in these parts; and she has never consented to renew it since. The 1st part is to be had: and it has been suggested it might prove worth your while to take it up, for the credit of America, at least. Two of your numbers might probably get the whole in; it is of more value and more likely to be popular than the larger part of the translations you have published."

4. In addition to the articles already mentioned, Margaret Fuller contributed to the *Dial* a series of sketches on the German composers (October, 1841), a translation of the "Epilogue to the Tragedy of Essex" by Goethe (January, 1842), and a long article on Romaic and Rhine Ballads (October, 1842). She also translated German poems with the following titles: Goethe's "Eins und Alles," "Dauer im Wechsel," "Prometheus," "Eagles and Doves," "The Consolers," Schiller's "To my Friends," Körner's "Dissatisfaction," and Uhland's "Justification."

5. See F. A. Braun, *Margaret Fuller and Goethe* (New York, Henry Holt, 1910), p. 75.

when she became editor, she did not consider the *Dial* as belonging to any one sect. Unlike the majority of Transcendentalists, Margaret Fuller had a high appreciaton of aesthetic beauty in the writings of the German authors, and although she attended the meetings of the Transcendental Club, she never contributed to its philosophical discussions. Never claiming to understand the German metaphysicians, she seemed contemptuous of them to some extent. She even admitted that this paucity of knowledge at one time narrowed her interpretation of Goethe. In regard to German philosophy she wrote to Clarke:

> I have long had a suspicion that no mind can systematize its knowledge, and carry on the concentrating processes, without some fixed opinion on the subject of metaphysics. But that indisposition, or even dread of the study, which you may remember, has kept me from meddling with it, till lately, in meditating on the life of Goethe, I thought I must get some idea of the history of philosophical opinion in Germany, that I might be able to judge of the influence it exercised upon his mind. I think I can comprehend him every other way, and probably interpret him satisfactorily to others,—if I can get the proper materials. When I was in Cambridge, I got Fichte and Jacobi; I was much interrupted, but some time and earnest thought I devoted. Fichte I could not understand at all; though the treatise which I read was one intended to be popular, and which he says must compel *bezwingen* to conviction. Jacobi I could understand in details, but not in system.[6]

Like that of most of the Transcendentalists, however, Margaret Fuller's interest in German literature reached beyond the desire of mere personal development. Almost as soon as she had mastered the language, she tried to teach it to her friends, including Emerson. In 1836 she taught German in Mr. Alcott's school with such success that after three months her pupils could read twenty pages of German at a lesson. With more advanced pupils she read in twenty-four weeks Schiller's *Don Carlos* and *Das Lied von der Glocke;* Goethe's *Hermann und Dorothea, Goetz von Berlichingen, Iphigenia, Clavigo,* and the first part of *Faust;* Lessing's *Nathan der Weise, Minna von Barnhelm, Emilia Galotti;* parts of Tieck's *Phantasus;* and nearly the whole first volume of Richter's *Titan.*[7]

From November 6, 1839, to April 28, 1844, she gave a series of lectures—or as they were then called, Conversations—in Boston, for the benefit of a group of twenty-five young ladies. These conversations were saturated with Goethean ideas such as the development of personality, the study of man and character, of God and the universe, and emphasis on life and activity. The group met at the home of Dr. Nathaniel Pea-

6. Fuller, *Works, I,* 127.
7. *Ibid.,* p. 174.

body, whose daughters Elizabeth, Mary, and Sophia were enthusiastic students of German.[8] In addition to shouldering these burdens, Margaret translated De Wette, Herder, and other German writers one evening a week for the benefit of Dr. Channing.

Margaret Fuller's contributions to the radiation of German literature both in and out of the Transcendental circle are not to be underestimated. First with the help of Clarke, and then independently, she produced a body of criticism which did much to domesticate the German writers here as well as to alleviate the acid comments made by their foes in our journals and newspapers.

D. THE TRANSLATORS
JOHN SULLIVAN DWIGHT AND CHARLES TIMOTHY BROOKS

One of the most significant contributions of the Transcendentalists was their attempt to render into English German works from almost every major field of knowledge. Theology, philosophy, metaphysics, poetry, fiction, biography, and letters claimed their attention. They realized that so long as Americans would not stir to learn German, German thought would remain unknown. Once these works were translated, however, scholars could no longer excuse their neglect and ignorance of this branch of European literature.

We have already mentioned that Emerson, Hedge, Clarke, Parker, Ripley, and Margaret Fuller indulged in the hobby of translating German literature, philosophy, and theology. Two Transcendentalists, however, who remain for consideration and who were unlike the other Transcendentalists in that they were concerned solely with the task of translating German belles-lettres were John Sullivan Dwight and Charles Timothy Brooks.[1] Their introduction to the German language follows the Transcendental pattern so closely that it hardly requires repetition. Exposed to the same influences at Harvard, they read the works of Madame de Staël, Coleridge, and Carlyle. In fact, Dwight dedicated his first German translations, published in 1839, to the Scottish writer.[2]

8. These three girls all became famous either in their own right or through marriage. Elizabeth studied German methods of education and is often considered the founder of the American kindergarten; Mary married Horace Mann, another great name in educational circles; and Sophia married Nathaniel Hawthorne.

1. Yet we should not underestimate Dwight's work as a critic, especially in the field of German music.

2. On December 2, 1838, Carlyle wrote to Emerson: "A Mr. Dwight wrote to me about the dedicating of some German translations: *Yes.* What are they or he?" After the book was published, Carlyle wrote to Emerson again, saying: "I received Dwight's Book, liked it, and have answered him: a good youth, of the kind you describe; no Englishman, to my knowledge, has yet uttered as much sense about Goethe and German things." See *Emerson-Carlyle Correspondence, 1,* 207 and 231–2.

On April 17, 1839, Carlyle thanked Dwight for this courtesy in a most laudatory letter. "With great pleasure," he wrote to Dwight, "I recognize in you the merit, the rarest of all in Goethe's translators, yet the first condition, without which every other merit is impossible, that of understanding your original." It seemed to him that Dwight had actually deciphered for himself and unriddled the lineaments of Goethe's great mind. From no other English writer had he heard so much truth as Dwight wrote in his notes of Goethe. Carlyle especially praised Dwight's versions of the songs. "On the whole," he added, "I must congratulate you on getting through so handsomely. It was an enterprise wherein failure to a very high degree need not have been dishonorable." [3]

These translations were published as the third volume of George Ripley's *Specimens of Foreign Standard Literature,* and bore the title *Select Minor Poems from the German of Goethe and Schiller.*[4] Dwight gave to this volume a great deal of thought and preparation. He told James Freeman Clarke that his first aim was to present a faithful translation of the most characteristic and important lyrics, and to arrange them in such a manner as to exhibit as much as possible of their spirit. Secondly, he wished to mark the different phases through which the minds of these German writers passed, and "to show them as they were acted upon by terrestrial education." From Schiller he would present specimens of the earliest, most impassioned poetry as well as the later poems, which were more tinged with philosophical speculations; and from Goethe he would include the pantheistic pieces, although he believed that these poems would be very difficult to accomplish. As to the method of translation, he hoped to preserve the form as well as the spirit, since he believed that in lyric poetry the form is part of the substance. "To retain the very idea of the author, with the exact rhythm and rhyme, and the fervor and grace of expression," he concluded, "is the ideal to which we ought certainly to aim." [5]

Dwight's finished product was not equal to this high ideal, for Ger-

3. G. W. Cooke, *John Sullivan Dwight* (Boston, Small, Maynard, 1898), pp. 27–8.

4. A number of Dwight's friends contributed to the volume. On March 10, 1837, Dwight asked James Freeman Clarke's assistance. He mentioned among other translators who were contributing versions of German poems Longfellow, C. C. Felton, Charles Brooks, and Margaret Fuller. See MS letter, Boston Public Library. Bancroft, Hedge, Channing, and Cranch also submitted a number of poems. Margaret Fuller wrote Dwight that she was discouraged with her translations of Goethe and Schiller. Yet she submitted a few including "Eins und Alles" and "Dauer im Wechsel." See Fuller MS letter, May 3, 1837, Boston Public Library.

Dwight himself not only translated all the poems selected from Goethe's works and approximately half of the selections of Schiller, but also added eighty pages of notes which did much to explain the nature of German poetry in general. Ripley proposed to Dwight two other volumes for the *Specimens,* but they never materialized. The first was to have been a volume on Herder and Spinoza, and the second, a volume of Goethe's prose. On August 6, 1840, Ripley inquired about Dwight's translation of Herder's *Seele und Gott.* See MS letter, Boston Public Library.

5. G. W. Cooke, *John Sullivan Dwight,* pp. 20–2.

man lyric poetry, especially that of Goethe and Schiller, is difficult to translate. Although Dwight usually found an accurate English meaning for the German word, he often lacked, even in his best translations, a lightness of touch, a delicate finish—indeed, the magic grace of style.[6] Dwight caught the desired tone in his versions of *Der Zauberlehrling*, *Der Wandrer*, and *Der Musensohn*. Many other lyrics, however, such as *Neue Liebe*, *neues Leben*, *Das Blümlein Wunderschön*, and Mignon's *Song* are devoid of charm in their English dress. Let us compare, for instance, Goethe's *Mailied* with Dwight's version:

> Zwischen Weizen und Korn,
> Zwischen Hecken und Dorn,
> Zwischen Bäumen und Grass,
> Wo geht's Liebchen?
> Sag' mir das!
>
> Fand mein Holdchen
> Nicht daheim:
> Muss das Goldchen
> Draussen sein.
> Grünt und blühet
> Schön der Mai,
> Liebchen ziehet
> Froh und frei.
>
> An dem Felsen beim Fluss,
> Wo sie reichte den Kuss,
> Jenen ersten im Grass,
> Seh' ich etwas!
> Ist sie das?

Dwight's version:

> 'Twixt the barley and corn,
> 'Twixt the hedge and hawthorn,
> 'Twixt the grove and grass-plat,
> Where goes Sweetheart?
> Tell me that!
>
> 'Found my Dearie
> Not at home;
> Sure, the Faerie
> 'S gone to roam;
> Greener daily

6. Theodore Parker noticed these faults in the volume. In a letter dated January 10, 1839 (Boston Public Library), Parker criticized a number of details in the *Select Minor Poems*.

Grows the May;
Lone, she gayly
Trips away.

On the rocks by the brook,
Where she gave me that look,
In the grass, all to me,
Something I see!
Is it she?

The words are translated accurately enough, but all the melodious smoothness of the German is missing in the English version. In its place one finds a series of jerky, semi-humorous lines, which read almost like a parody of the original.

Dwight was more successful in retaining the vigor of expression and condensation of thought in Goethe's and Schiller's "Epigrams," although his metrical technique limped rather badly at times. For example, we find this "epigram" by Goethe:

Goods gone,—something gone!
  Must bend to the oar,
  And earn thee some more.

Honor gone,—much gone!
  Must go and gain glory;
  Then the idling gossips will alter their story.

Courage gone,—all's gone
  Better never have been born!

The translations were evidently uneven in poetic quality, but their variety and freshness assured them a favorable reception. All the leading periodicals reviewed the volume, and the critics, especially the Transcendentalists, were most generous. Orestes Brownson in the *Boston Quarterly Review* inserted this plea for German poetry:

All true lovers of poetry will gratefully welcome the little volume Mr. Dwight and his friends have prepared from these great masters of German Art. . . . Some of these little pieces will not, at first sight, commend themselves to the general reader of English poetry. . . . The German lyrics, and especially Goethe's, differ essentially from the productions of the great masters of the divine art among us. English poetry overflows with thought. Its thoughtfulness is its most striking trait. It is profound. Metaphysical treatises pass for good, genuine English poetry when translated into verse. . . .
The German song is quite different; it is filled rather with pro-

found sentiments than profound thoughts. Yet sometimes vast meaning is condensed in a few words. . . . But there is a simple freshness in German poetry, especially in lyric composition. . . . The careless reader will perhaps sometimes pass over the beautiful little pieces of Goethe, not discovering what deep meaning lies under them. But the true poetic Argus will be at no loss to penetrate their depths.[7]

While other reviews remained more objective in their criticism, the *New York Review* reserved special praise for the translation of Schiller's *Song of the Bell* [*Das Lied von der Glocke*], calling it at the same time "the finest lyric existing in any modern language, and perhaps the happiest of Schiller's composition." [8] The *North American Review* cited Dwight's notes to the poems, commending him as a good German scholar and a writer with generous impulses and warm poetical sensibility. "His admiration of Goethe," the reviewer added, "seems unbounded; we should have said extravagant, were it not that our own half-knowledge of that famous man, makes us diffident about applying that epithet to the views of one who has studied him thoroughly." [9] The editor of the *Christian Examiner* used his review of the volume as a weapon to slaughter Goethe's reputation, but praised Dwight himself as an admirable scholar who understood the poems he translated and who possessed ready skill in his own language as well. In spite of inequalities, the volume as a whole, he believed, was superior to any English volume of translations from the German.[1]

Dwight's name also appeared in the pages of the *Dial*, his most important contribution being the following original poem called "Rest":

> Sweet is the pleasure,
>   Itself cannot spoil!
> Is not true leisure
>   One with true toil?
>
> Thou that wouldst taste it,
>   Still do thy best;
> Use it, not waste it,
>   Else 't is no rest.

7. *Boston Quarterly Review*, 2 (April, 1839), 188–90.
8. *New York Review*, 4 (April, 1839), 394.
9. *North American Review*, 48 (April, 1839), 514.
1. The criticism of Goethe and Schiller in the article is in no way essentially different from the general run of criticism during the previous thirty years. The editor began by calling Goethe and Schiller an antithesis. Schiller, he thought, was a plebeian but industrious, poor but proud, soft-hearted but disciplined. Goethe, on the other hand, he designated as an aristocrat in the worst sense of the word, unscrupulous, immoral, and having no philosophy, no creed, and no principles. The analysis is not only harsh but also completely superficial. See *26* (July, 1839), 360–78. A similar comparison favoring Schiller appeared in the criticism of the *New York Review*, 4 (April, 1839), 399–400.

Wouldst behold beauty
    Near thee? all round?
Only hath duty
    Such a sight found.

Rest is not quitting
    The busy career;
Rest is the fitting
    Of self to its sphere.

'T is the brook's motion,
    Clear without strife,
Fleeing to ocean
    After its life.

Deeper devotion
    Nowhere hath knelt;
Fuller emotion
    Heart never felt.

'T is loving and serving
    The Highest and Best!
'T is ONWARDS! unswerving,
    And that is true rest.[2]

The style and thought of this poem were so similar to verses of Goethe that for years many people believed Dwight had translated it. There is no doubt, however, of its originality.[3]

Dwight, who also taught German at Brook Farm, contributed a number of translations from German poetry to the *Harbinger*, the Brook Farm newspaper.[4] At Brook Farm he originated the Mass Club to spread the knowledge of German music and composition. A virtuoso on the piano and flute, Dwight became a promoter of the works of Beethoven and Mozart. His enthusiasm was so contagious that Margaret Fuller and others of the group followed his lead, and German music was added to the other branches of German life cultivated by many of the Transcendentalists.

Even before the Brook Farm experiment, Dwight was recognized as an advocate of German music. In a report for the *Dial* on the concerts of the winter 1839–40 he informed his readers that they should hear more Handel, Haydn, Mozart, and Beethoven. "The works of true

2. The *Dial, 1* (July, 1840), 22.
3. Edna Cheney spoke of Dwight's translations as being so felicitous that they were adopted by the public as original poems. See *Reminiscences,* p. 189. Henry Theodore Tuckerman, editor of the *Boston Miscellany,* also asked Dwight to contribute translations from the German poets. See MS letter, November 2, 1842, Boston Public Library.
4. See the *Harbinger, 1* (July 12, 1845), 74.

genius," he went on to say, "which cannot be too familiar, since they are always new like nature, should salute our ears until the nobler chords within our souls respond. We should be taught the same reverence for Bach and Handel as for Homer; and, having felt the spell of their harmonies upon us, should glow at the mention of their names." [5]

Dwight did not publish the first number of his *Journal of Music, A Paper of Art and Literature*, until April 10, 1852. Although he preferred the German classical composers, he did not slight the works of such moderns as Richard Wagner. He translated articles by Franz Liszt on Chopin, as well as a study of Weber's *Freischütz* by Berlioz. In 1859 he translated H. Wahlfahrt's *Guide to Musical Composition* and the words to Bach's *Saint Matthew Passion Music*. In 1865 he adapted a number of Heine's songs in *Buch der Lieder* to selections from Schumann's *Dichterliebe,* as well as a number of German lyrics to accompany the vocal music of Robert Franz.

These translations and criticisms may not be considered so profound as the philosophical and reflective works by other members of the Transcendental group, but in belletristic forms of German culture Dwight's contributions are important. How much German culture meant to him can easily be seen in his correspondence with his friends. In the letters of George W. Curtis written to Dwight in 1844 and 1845 we find a series of discussions dealing with such works as Goethe's *Tasso, Werther, Egmont, Iphigenie auf Tauris, Die Italienische Reise, Die Wahlverwandtschaften,* and finally Bettina von Arnim's *Correspondence with Goethe.* Curtis could not have chosen a more astute person to listen to his comments. Dwight, like all the Transcendentalists, recognized these books as part of his cultural heritage.

A more important translator of German literature was Charles Timothy Brooks. Attracted to German while still a student at Harvard, he attempted translations of German ballads, attended concerts of German music, and began a systematic reading of his two favorite authors, Richter and Goethe. His letters to his friend, Dwight, during these undergraduate days were a delightful combination of German and English vocabulary and full of enthusiasm for German literature. On March 12, 1834, he wrote to Dwight from Cambridge:

My dear Friend—
How is it with you now in the *City of mead?* It is "schönes, hübsches Wetter" with us. We are congratulating ourselves with the thought of having cheated winter out of his due—but I tremble. . . . I have heard the "Vöglein" for several mornings past. Cranch's flute—"die bekannte Stimme" wakens every lonely, pleasant Saturday—"schmerzlich süsse Erinnerung." When I sat down to write I meditated, as

5. The *Dial, 1* (July, 1840), 125.

you may already imagine—"einen deutschen Brief"—but I fear I shall hardly be able to express all that I wish to in German, and besides I should hardly dare to intrude my Hund-deutsch upon the neighborhood of German Purity—Dr. Follen has resumed his German Lecture —He is now on German Belles Lettres. He has lately been relating to us the "Nibelungen Lied"—Romance on a large scale—Romance seen through a magnifying glass—what a queer compound of good sense and marvellousness the Dr's face presents. I have read and translated very little German lately. . . . Our Debates and philanthropy and Ecclesiastical History and City goings etc will hardly allow much leisure for the "Dutch muse." [6]

At graduation his progress won the praise of Professor Follen, who stated that Brooks was "thoroughly acquainted with the principles of the German language and able to read with precision and ease the standard German authors." [7]

During the late 1830's and 1840's Brooks published his translations in periodicals connected with the Transcendental circle.[8] His version of Schiller's *Wilhelm Tell,* however, appeared independently in 1838.[9] Dwight in the *Christian Examiner* called it a "just reproduction . . . of the beautiful original," and commended Brooks for having caught almost unconsciously "the characteristic *Naïve* of German writing." [1] The popularity of *Wilhelm Tell* stemmed in part from the teachings of Rousseau, whose worship of simplicity and the "noble savage" was still reverberating throughout Europe. For New Englanders who had rebelled against reactionary England and who were now fostering the Abolition Movement at home, Schiller's play symbolized freedom from persecution. The legend itself was not new to theater goers. English adaptations had appeared on the stages of New York, Philadelphia, and

6. A letter from Brooks to Dwight, dated August 20, 1833, is written completely in German script. Other letters as charming as the one printed above are dated January 20, 1834, May 26, 1834, July 11, 1836, and June 7, 1839. These letters are now in the MS collection of Dwight material at the Houghton Library, Harvard University.

7. Follen wrote a similar letter for John S. Dwight. See MS letter, July 17, 1832, Boston Public Library. For letter concerning Brooks see published form in C. W. Wendte's *A Memoir of Charles T. Brooks* (Boston, Roberts, 1885), p. 22.

During his pastorate in Newport, Rhode Island, Brooks continued his interest in the German language and organized a class for its study. Again on a visit to Mobile in 1842 he taught German to Southern friends in return for lessons in French. Camillo von Klenze records that on his trip to India in 1853 Brooks taught German to "gloomy Calvinistic missionaries" in return for Hindustani. See von Klenze, p. 4.

8. He published various poems in the *Western Messenger,* such as Stolberg's *To the Sea* [*An das Meer*], Herder's *The Completion,* and Uhland's *Shepherd's Sunday Song* [*Das Schäfers Sonntagslied*]. *The Emigrants* [*Die Auswanderer*] and *The Moorish Prince* [*Der Mohrenfürst*] by Freiligrath and short poems by Rückert, Gleim, and Schiller appeared in the Boston and Cincinnati *Dial.*

9. Brooks followed his version of *Wilhelm Tell* with translations of *Die Jungfrau von Orleans* and *Maria Stuart,* although he published only excerpts from these works.

1. 25 (January, 1839), 385.

Boston, but Schiller's version was first appreciated only when Carlyle championed it in his biography. It was Follen rather than Carlyle, however, who first awakened Brooks to the beauty of the play.

Brooks's earliest translations of German poetry appeared in Ripley's *Specimens* under the title *Songs and Ballads: Translated from Uhland, Körner, Bürger, and Other German Lyric Poets.*[2] In preparing this volume Brooks translated sixty poems and wrote the notes for them. Still not satisfied with the results, he turned to his friends for additional translations. Dwight contributed eight,[3] Frothingham seven, Sarah Whitman four, Cranch two, Longfellow one, and Follen one.

The leading poets in this collection reflected the influence of Follen's teachings and the taste of the Transcendental circle. These New Englanders were attracted by the ethical, patriotic, and religious sentiment in the poems of Uhland and Körner. Unfortunately, Uhland often sank from sincere feeling into commonplace sentimentality. Brooks, who was not always able to estimate the quality of Uhland's poems, included such extremes as the wholesome *Song of the Mountain Boy* [*Des Knaben Berglied*] and the mawkish *Poor Man's Song* [*Lied eines Armen*]. Körner's patriotic fervor was fully represented in such selections as *My Native Land* [*Mein Vaterland*], *Summons* [*Aufruf*], and *Song of the Black Hunters* [*Lied der schwarzen Jäger*]. At first glance it seems surprising that this volume contained so few of the famous and popular poems of the German classics. Brooks knew, however, that many of them had already been adequately translated, although he still included his own versions of Goethe's *Kennst du das Land, Erlkönig,* and *Der Fischer.*[4] The translations were not always accurate or successful. In the *Erlkönig,* for instance, he translated the line, "Lass sausen durch den Hagedorn, Lass sausen, Kind, lass sausen" as "Let the wind whistle through the thorn; Child, what have I to fear?"

Too much had been left out of Brooks's first volume of lyrics for it to be a representative collection of German poetry. In 1845, therefore, he wrote the following letter to James Munroe & Co., Booksellers and Publishers, Boston, Massachusetts:

My dear Sir

I did not find you at your store when I was last in Boston. I wanted to say to you that I have another collection of songs and little poems

2. The volume, furnished with ample notes, appeared in 1842. It contained altogether eighty-three poems, almost a third of them by Uhland. It also contained eighteen poems by Körner, ten by Schiller, six each by Bürger, Goethe, and Hölty, five by Rückert, three by Klopstock, and two by Follen.

3. Brooks asked Dwight for these contributions to his volume. See MS letter, April 13, 1841, Boston Public Library.

4. A manuscript version of "Der Fischer" is to be found in the Speck Collection of Goetheana at Yale University. The version differs markedly from the printed poem and is probably a first attempt.

from the German, mostly of living authors, quite a miscellaneous one in style and subject, nothing too light nor too heavy, I think, and which, it seems to me, would make a very good book for the Holidays. It would probably make not more than from 100 to 150 pages in the style of Wiley & Putnam's *Hood's Poems*. . . . Frothingham and Longfellow encourage me greatly.

Now will you not undertake this? I should call the volume "Schiller's Homage of the Arts with miscellaneous songs and other pieces, mostly from living German Poets." The Homage of the Arts is a very graceful Dramatic Poem and I think would make an appropriate main piece for such a volume.

Will you do me the favour to let me hear from you soon on the subject. The verses are all written off ready for the press. Nothing more is wanted than a few lines here and there of explanation or biography. I remain

Yours truly
Charles T. Brooks [5]

The volume proposed in this letter was issued under the title *Schiller's Homage of the Arts, with Miscellaneous Pieces from Rückert, Freiligrath, and other German Poets*. The book reached the public in time for the Christmas holiday. Brooks's final volume of poems, *German Lyrics*, which appeared in 1853, included selections from many of the less important writers such as Anastasius Grün,[6] Platen, Lenau, Herwegh, Würkert, Claudius, Nicolai, and Klopisch.[7] Some of the minor poets in this volume are now so completely forgotten that Professor von Klenze could find no trace of their writings in available German anthologies.

Brooks's translations of lyric poetry reflect only one aspect of his liaison with the Transcendental group. Typical also is the fellowship of taste which he shared with them. The boom, for instance, in the popularity of Jean Paul Richter increased during the 1840's, when a new biography, compiled by Mrs. Eliza Buckminster Lee, appeared. The book became an incentive for Brooks, whose enthusiasm for Richter grew with the years. Brooks once wrote of him:

> Of all the German writers and men Richter is the one whom we are most eager that our countrymen should appreciate and understand. . . . He is to us by far the most suggestive, soul-stirring, improving of German minds. . . . He is the Shakespeare of Germany.

5. MS letter, October 7, 1846, New York Public Library.

6. Although Anastasius Grün was never particularly popular, Brooks devoted almost a third of the volume to his work.

7. One reviewer said of this work and its author that he had "fully maintained by this publication the credit for himself by his former labors as a translator of German poetry." See the *Athenaeum* (London), No. 1476 (February 9, 1856), 166–7.

. . . Jean Paul's heart embraced everything, while Goethe's held everything at a distance. . . . Goethe's *all-sidedness* has always seemed to us to be a cold indifference of heart to the many forms of humanity . . . while Richter seems to us, with his large and glowing bosom, to meet all the aspects of human life and lot with a profound and tender and immortal interest.[8]

Although Brooks did his best to popularize the writings of Richter, they never took firm hold in this country. In an age when utilitarianism and pragmatism were being fostered in America, more reality in literature was demanded than that which Richter offered. His sentimentalism and obscurity also warded off any lasting appreciation. Brooks published a translation of Richter's *Titan* in 1864.[9] *Hesperus* followed in 1865, and *Selina* [*Selina, oder über die Unsterblichkeit der Seele*], *The History of Fibel* [*Leben Fibels*], and *The Invisible Lodge* [*Die Unsichtbare Loge*] in 1883.[1]

No one could have been more suited to translate Richter's works than Brooks. Richter was at times one of the most obscure and involved of German writers, but nevertheless displayed a lively, romantic imagination, tender sentiment, grotesque humor, and intense moral enthusiasm. If a translator ought to be kindred in spirit to the person whom he wishes to reproduce, then Richter and Brooks shared much in common. Thomas Carlyle, who had also translated Richter's stories, recognized this similarity in Brooks's character. After reading the English version of *Titan* Carlyle wrote to Brooks:

You have been wonderfully successful: have caught a good deal of the *tune* of Jean Paul, and have unwinded his meaning, in general, with perfect accuracy, into comfortable clearness, out of those coils he involves it in. I did not keep the original open all the way, but had a feeling that I was safe in your hands. . . . In conclusion I will congratulate you on having added a highly recognizable new item of good reading for the whole English genealogy of us (now a most extensive Body of People in this world) ;—and with the hope of perhaps seeing a *Hesperus* from you some day. . . .[2]

Of all his translations the one which brought Brooks the most fame was his version of *Faust, Part I,* published in 1856. Brooks was not the

8. *Christian Examiner, 33* (November, 1842), 245–6.
9. Next to *Faust, Part I,* it was Brooks's most ambitious attempt at translation.
1. Although these dates fall long after the period of our interest, these publications germinated many years earlier, when the Transcendental movement was strongest. In some cases, the manuscripts were completed in the late 1830's and 1840's, but for many years Brooks had difficulty finding a publisher. Some translations of Richter still remain in manuscript form. See von Klenze, p. 100.
2. Wendte, pp. 61–2. As we know, Brooks published a translation of *Hesperus* in 1865.

first to attempt a translation of this work. Abraham Heywood's prose version (1833 and 1834) and Anna Swanwick's in verse (1840) were read in New England, especially by the Transcendentalists. Brooks's version could not have come at a more suitable time, for in the previous year George Henry Lewes' *Life of Goethe* created a renewed interest in *Faust*. Superior to all the previous translations, Brooks's version became so popular that by 1880 fifteen editions had been called for.

Of course there were weaknesses in the translation. Brooks did not always grasp the exact meaning of the German, and even when the meaning was clear to him, his poetic endowment was not sufficiently strong to render the verse into suitable English. Brooks wished to imitate the changing meter and the mixture of masculine and feminine rhymes, but he did not always succeed. This attempt to retain the artistic effect of the change in meter detracted from the poetic value of his work, because he was led thereby to padding. Yet, for the most part, his translation was accurate.[3] He was especially felicitous in translating the humorous and popular scenes. Even Bayard Taylor, whose translation of *Faust* supplanted Brooks's version, owed him a debt. In fact, when we analyze and compare individual passages, Taylor's version is not particularly superior. He improved upon some verses but wrote some equally bad ones.[4]

Among German writers not so well known today, but whose works were made available to English-speaking people through the efforts of Brooks is Berthold Auerbach. Auerbach, who had inherited from Gessner the reputation of being a "moral" writer, found many admirers in New England, but none so ardent as Brooks. Moreover, his interest in humble folk and his delight in the simple life delighted the Transcendentalists. Brooks translated three of Auerbach's *Schwarzwälder Dorfgeschichten* [*Aloys, The Convicts and their Children,* and *Lorley and Reinhard*] and the novel *Dichter und Kaufmann* [*Poet and Merchant*]. The latter work dealt with the tragic life of the Jewish epigrammatist, Ephraim Moses Kuh, friend of Lessing and Moses Mendelssohn. These Germans had been popular in Unitarian and Transcendental circles, since they believed that true Christianity contained the elements of liberty, equality, and toleration.

Brooks also translated two works by Leopold Schefer, *The Layman's Breviary* [*Laienbrevier*] in 1867 and *The World Priest* [*Weltpriester*] in 1873. Unlike Schefer's other works, such as the rather offensive *Koran der Liebe,* these two volumes presented him as a teacher of wisdom and moral discipline. *The Layman's Breviary,* Brooks believed, had "helped more souls to the understanding of themselves than any

3. For comparisons and parallels, particularly with Taylor's version, see Frantz, pp. 208–10.
4. See von Klenze, p. 32.

other book of German poesy," and he commended this "work of love
and reverence to the thoughtful, poetic, and pious spirit." [5]

The humorous works of German literature attracted Brooks's atten-
tion early in his career, although his published translations of Carl
Kortum and Wilhelm Busch did not appear until the 1870's and 1880's.
The significance of these translations was that by their publication
Brooks disproved the idea that the Germans lacked a sense of humor.
His selections, however, were not wise. Von Klenze points out that in
the works he chose—Kortum's *Jobsiade* [6] and Busch's *Plisch und Plum,
Der lange Student,* and *Max und Moritz*—we find a sunny, childlike,
occasionally infantile delight in odd or absurd situations, but much too
innocent to be shared by American readers accustomed to the "tall"
joke.[7] Although Brooks may not have chosen the best in German humorous literature, the fact that he considered it at all was a step in the
right direction. Once more he proved to be a pioneer among the translators in New England.[8]

Many of Brooks's translations, published in his later years, were
actually written, if not completed, when the Transcendental movement
was at its peak. Brooks's biographer, Wendte, believed that he was by
nature a Transcendentalist, who could hardly, with his mental con-
stitution and antecedents, have been anything else.[9] This assumption is
based not only on the fact that he contributed to the *Dial* and to Ripley's
Specimens of Foreign Standard Literature. More important, his selection of such authors as Goethe, Richter, Rückert, and Schefer for translation reflects the tastes of the Transcendentalists. In the writings of
such poets as Uhland and Körner, he, like his contemporaries, was impressed by the rebellion against tyranny,[1] the stress of ethical and religious motives, and the emphasis upon homely sentiment and emotion.[2]

5. Brooks again defended Schefer against charges of Pantheism in the preface to
The World Priest.

6. Brooks reproduced by means of English doggerel verse *The Jobsiade,* which was
originally written in rough *Knittelvers.*

7. Von Klenze, p. 45.

8. Another German whose writings delighted Brooks as well as his contemporaries
was Friedrich Rückert. Brooks attempted to translate Rückert's *Die Weisheit des
Brahmanen* but never completed its publication. In 1883 a partial rendition called *The
Wisdom of the Brahmin, A Didactic Poem, Books I–VI* appeared. Two additional
volumes of his version remained in manuscript. It was perhaps the most difficult literary
task of his career, but in spite of its mystical nature, Oriental imagery, and involved
construction, Brooks reproduced it with remarkable accuracy and skill.

9. Wendte, p. 24.

1. Anastasius Grün also appealed to Brooks, because like Körner, he showed sympathy for the struggle for freedom.

2. These qualities explain Brooks's choice of such poems as Platen's *Harmosen*
(printed in the *Boston Transcript,* June 21, 1858), which deals with the magnificent
generosity of a Moslem conqueror. German sententious literature popular among the
Transcendentalists also found an outlet in Brooks's translations of numerous aphorisms
by Goethe and Herder, as well as by the lesser writers Angelius Silenius, Hippel, and

Although this choice of theme was bound to include much didacticism, it did not shut out the humorous element in German poetry of which Brooks was particularly fond. This affinity accounts for his attraction to the writings of many of the minor voices such as Pfeffel, Langbein, and Gellert.

Among the Transcendentalists Brooks contributed most in the form of translations from the polite literature of Germany. With no flair for metaphysical and ethical theories, he shunned the German philosophers. Perhaps he was most successful in his rendition of shorter poems, ballads, and lyrics from the pen of such men as Uhland, Chamisso, and Freiligrath. Yet his translations of Richter and Goethe must be judged at least for their quantity. Brooks's tastes were dictated by the trends of the time. "He never surmounted Victorian reticences or one-sided moral, social, and sentimental standards." [3] He lacked equality of taste and was apt to make no distinction between the mediocre and the best of German poetry. Yet his unflagging zeal and his complete devotion to the beauties of German literature profoundly influenced the men of his time. No statement could better sum up Brooks's contribution than the following written in a letter by E. P. Whipple to John S. Dwight, October 30, 1883 : "What good that man has done, considered simply as a translator of Goethe and Richter! Yet his patriotism in making us familiar with great works of the German mind is hardly yet appreciated—except by men like you." [4]

Grabbe. Brooks selected them from the German book *Buch der Sinnsprüche,* and published many of them in the *Boston Transcript.* See issues of February 5, 1838, and October 17, October 31, and November 21, 1874. See also von Klenze, "German Literature in the *Boston Transcript, 1830–1880,*" *Philological Quarterly, 9* (1932), 12–13.

3. Von Klenze, p. 76.
4. G. W. Cooke, *John Sullivan Dwight,* p. 288.

Summary

ALTHOUGH the Transcendentalists were among the fervent supporters of German literature in this country, they were by no means the first. Much of the spade work had been accomplished in the eighteenth and early nineteenth centuries without which the task might have been far more difficult. Indeed the history of German literature in America can be traced to a period long before the birth of the Transcendentalists and to regions many miles distant from the Boston area. In cities like Philadelphia and New York, where the people were not hemmed in by a Puritan heritage, a new tongue and a new literature could find a warm soil in which to grow. The situation in New England, however, was radically different. Although there was evidence of German scholarship in the earliest colonies and, throughout the seventeenth century, ardent students of German theology and science like Winthrop, Ward, and the Mathers, there was little appreciation for German literature. Harvard and Yale, in the eighteenth century, still remained impervious to German ideas, and refused to pollute their libraries with so-called ungodly and immoral books. A few edifying volumes of Gessner, Klopstock, and Lavater were accepted in the Boston area, but the righteous wrath expressed against the authors of *Werther* and *Die Räuber* was almost unanimous.

This attitude did not continue indefinitely, for by the turn of the century New England began to waken from its stupor. With the publication of reliable texts and accurate translations, and with the frequent defenses which began to appear in the popular magazines, the trend of criticism gradually took a favorable turn. The *North American Review,* the *Christian Examiner,* and the *Athenaeum* were especially kind in their judgments. Hostile editors like Joseph Dennie and Andrews Norton, on the other hand, fought a losing battle, for they had to combat the united forces of a new generation of scholars, men who had studied in Europe and who had undergone a thorough grounding at the German universities. Among these early scholars John Quincy Adams had the advantage of studying the language while traveling in Germany. Others, like William Bentley, James Gates Percival, Moses Stuart, and James Marsh, taught themselves German with little more than a Lutheran Bible and an inferior dictionary.

The idea of studying at the German universities did not really flourish before 1815. Soon after this date a group of young men including George Ticknor, Edward Everett, George Bancroft, and Joseph G.

Cogswell crossed the ocean to find out for themselves about this new literature. They not only attended classes at the universities of Göttingen, Berlin, Heidelberg, and Bonn, but they also visited the leading German thinkers of the time. Their meetings with Bürger, Goethe, Tieck, and other literary giants of the day gave them a wider outlook on life and taught them to be tolerant of ideas not in keeping with their New England background.

To these Americans more than to any other group we also owe the fact that our educational system has been dominated by German methods of instruction. The reforms at Harvard instituted by Ticknor and Everett and the experiments at the Round Hill School deserve special recognition. With the additional aid of the competent German instructors, Charles Follen, Carl Beck, and Francis Lieber, the basis for German knowledge was established, and German literature became fashionable in Boston. Under the influence of Follen, German poetry, in particular, took on new luster and aroused the interest of such students as John Lothrop Motley, George Calvert, and Henry Wadsworth Longfellow. Motley's and Calvert's defenses of Goethe and Longfellow's study in Germany bear testimony to this fact.

Support for the German movement came also from other sources. Henry E. Dwight in his *Travels in the North of Germany* praised highly the German universities and the quality of their libraries. Conservative editors and college officials rebuked him for this, but their scorn of German literature, particularly their dislike for the writings of Goethe, had little effect. A set of Goethe's works, the gift of the author, was welcomed by the Harvard Library, and a few years later Longfellow added Goethe's *Faust* to his course on modern European literature. By the 1830's the language barrier had also been eased by means of Follen's and Beck's elementary text books. Meanwhile the voice of Carlyle in favor of Goethe was heard over the waters, and America gave heed to his words.

As for the Transcendentalists who were enrolling at Harvard during these years, events could not have been timed more accurately. From approximately 1817 to 1842, they carried on the work of their predecessors. Although they began by reading the commentaries of Madame de Staël, Coleridge, and Carlyle, it was not long before they turned to more primary material. At first they too lacked a knowledge of German, but in a short time almost every one of them learned enough of the language to read the popular literary works of their favorites Schiller, Goethe, Novalis, or Richter. Nor did they wait very long before expressing their opinions to the public. The *Western Messenger,* the *Dial,* the *Harbinger,* as well as the *North American Review* and the *Christian Examiner,* overflowed with their comments.

We must remember, however, that the members of the Transcendental group were not cut from the same pattern. Their backgrounds, their education, their objectives were by no means alike. The most homogeneous group, perhaps, was the Concord group—Emerson, Alcott, and Thoreau. They did not study in Germany and they had no early instruction in German philosophy; yet Transcendentalism seems to be represented best in the writings of these men. We realize now that they found the sources of their inspiration in the literature of many countries, particularly in the popular literature of Germany. First on the advice of teachers at Harvard, like Ticknor and Everett, and then on the advice of Carlyle they read the works of the German poets, dramatists, and novelists.

Goethe was the first and remained the main attraction for the Concord group.[1] Even Thoreau could not resist him, and under the influence of Emerson, Thoreau read his Goethe along with the Greek and Latin classics and the Oriental mystics. Alcott, who knew no German, had to depend upon available translations; when he found these unsatisfactory, he turned for aid to his friends Emerson, Parker, or Margaret Fuller.

It remained for Emerson among the Concord group to make a more thorough study of German literature. Beginning with the complete works of Goethe, he read a surprisingly large number of German books in fields as varied as drama and philosophy, poetry and theology, fiction and history. The results of his wide reading finally appeared in such essays as "Thoughts on Modern Literature" and "Goethe." [2] These essays show clearly how limited Emerson's appreciation of German literature really was. In his comments on Goethe, for instance, Emerson expressed some of the finest sentiments, as well as some of the most biased opinions. He paid respect to Goethe's intellectual power, although he felt bound to stress also what appeared to him Goethe's moral delinquencies. If Goethe had taken part in politics, he said, if his soul had been disciplined by contact with more practical life, his character might have acquired greater firmness and vigor. In addition, Goethe showed a lack of sympathy with the creatures of his imagination. Thus Emerson judged him, as he judged almost everything else, in the light of the moral ideal. That is why he could not accept Goethe completely. Emerson's ideas were firmly rooted in the ethical traditions of Puritanic Calvinism, Goethe's in the aesthetic traditions of the Renaissance. Emerson was attracted to Goethe, because he found in him a broad and quick sympathy with life in all its forms, but having viewed the world from the threshold of the spirit, Emerson saw in all things a

---

1. Emerson once said that Goethe "was the cow from which all their milk was drawn." See Emerson, *Journals, 8,* 214.

2. Even more revealing are his numerous comments on the Germans in his journals and letters.

moral aim. The primary criterion in his mind was always the religious conscience. Between Goethe and himself he erected unconscious barriers, which, except in moments of enthusiasm, he was not able to overcome. Emerson, therefore, never attained the freedom from convention for which he continually asked.

Other scholars among the Transcendentalists, however, were more broad-minded and did not hesitate to accept the teachings of these Germans. This is especially true of the theologians Hedge, Parker, Ripley, and Clarke. Although they were primarily interested in German theology and philosophy, they did not neglect German poetry and drama.[3] They were also far more advanced than the Concord group in their comprehension of the German language. Frederic Henry Hedge, for example, has never been given sufficient credit for his leadership in the Transcendental movement. One of the few Transcendentalists to be educated in Germany, he became the most important teacher of German literature and philosophy in the group. His influence at the meetings of the Transcendental Club and his personal friendships with the other Transcendentalists bolstered up the strength of the movement. Even more important were his interpretations of German philosophy, which were among the first clear and concise explanations to be published in the *Christian Examiner* and other periodicals.

The effect of Ripley's efforts also has not been fully realized. Yet all the younger writers in the Transcendental movement were indebted to him for his editorship of the *Specimens of Foreign Standard Literature*.[4] This series of volumes, which contains some of the earliest and most important English versions of the German classics, raised the standard of accuracy for translation. During the Brook Farm experiment Ripley was also the leading advocate of German philosophy, and he encouraged the wealth of German commentary which appeared in the Brook Farm publication, the *Harbinger*.

Ripley gave us German literature in English versions, but James Freeman Clarke, Margaret Fuller, and Theodore Parker were its greatest defenders. In the pages of the *Western Messenger* and the *Dial* they gained their opportunity. Margaret Fuller castigated her fellow Americans, including even some of the Transcendentalists, for misinterpreting the genius of Goethe, Schiller, Novalis, and others. Parker dealt with a more serious problem, the defense of the German theologians and philosophers. His review of Menzel's *History of German Literature* in the *Dial* marked a milestone in the effort of the Transcendentalists for the recognition of German thought. No one could have been more capable than this dynamic preacher from West Roxbury, who owned one of

3. Parker, for example, gave as much attention to the lyrical poetry of Heine as he did to the intellectual poetry of Schiller.
4. Margaret Fuller, Parker, Dwight, and Brooks acknowledged this fact.

the finest collections of German books in the country. Parker, later to play such an important role in the abolition movement, fought heart and soul for the acceptance of the progressive ideas emanating from Germany.

It would be far from the truth to say that in their study of German literature the Transcendentalists displayed much unity of taste. Parker himself admitted that it produced some confusion when Leibnitz, Spinoza, Kant, Goethe, Herder, Schleiermacher, Richter, Jacobi, and the rest all "sailed at once into Boston Harbour, and discharged their freight," [5] for here were crops not grown in New England. "The wharves were littered in a day with the spoils of a century," [6] and like men distracted, the Transcendentalists rushed in to help themselves. As a result, their preferences among these writers were as varied as their conceptions of German thought. A few of the Transcendentalists even ignored the philosophers and studied almost exclusively the writers of *belles-lettres*. Variations in age and background among the Transcendentalists caused these differences of opinion. William Ellery Channing, who was of an older generation than John Dwight and Charles Brooks, had to wrestle with answers which by the 1830's the younger men were already able to take for granted. Emerson's lack of knowledge of the German language made his situation far different from that of Hedge, who had studied in Germany. Margaret Fuller's interest in German literature for its own sake likewise set her apart from the theologians in the group. Admitting frankly that she had no talent for pure philosophy, she put aside Kant, Fichte, and Hegel, and read almost exclusively the writings of Goethe, Schiller, Novalis, Tieck, and Körner. John Dwight and Charles Brooks were also not attracted to German theology and philosophy. Yet their great contributions in the form of numerous translations from the German give them a leading position among the Transcendentalists. In fact, many of their translations are still in use.[7] The differences of taste among the various groups in the Transcendental circle, however, did not outweigh their overwhelming appreciation for German thought. German literature became a passion for the Transcendentalists, and what they lacked in knowledge of the deeper German thinkers, such as Kant and Fichte, they made up for by reading the writers that they did know. Emerson in his essay *English Traits* summed up the opinion of the Transcendentalists, when he said that the Germans, "those semi-Greeks," and not the English, thought for Europe.[8]

5. Weiss, *1*, 238.
6. *Ibid.*
7. In the latest edition of *Readings in European Literature* by Gerald E. Seboyar and Rudolph F. Brosius (New York, 1947), John Dwight's translations of Goethe's poems are used.
8. Emerson, *Works, 5*, 254.

We must finally ask ourselves how the reading of these Germans actually influenced the nature of Transcendental thought. William Henry Channing once defined New England Transcendentalism as "an assertion of the inalienable integrity of man, of the immanence of divinity in instinct." Then he added to this statement a comment of special interest to us: "On the somewhat stunted stock of Unitarianism, whose characteristic dogma was trust in individual reason as correlative to supreme wisdom, has been grafted German idealism as taught by masters of most different schools,—by Kant and Jacobi, Fichte and Novalis, Schelling and Hegel, Schleiermacher and De Wette; and the result was a vague, yet exalting conception of the godlike nature of the human spirit." [9] Like the older Transcendentalists, he too was vague as to the exact contribution which the Germans had made. One fact, however, was abundantly clear. That the German Transcendentalists approached the problem of general truth from the standpoint of emotional, pietistic religious experience caused them from the start to be admired by their American cousins, who also had grown to maturity thinking that religion and Christianity were essential to a normal, well-ordered existence.

To be sure, it was the fashion for these New Englanders to claim philosophical descent from Kant, for Kant had coined the term by which they were known, and they were unanimous in considering him "the greatest" and "the most profound," whether or not they had read or understood his writings. After all, they were not primarily concerned with philosophy for its own sake. An examination of the evidence revealed the fact that they imported and modified the thought of Kant and his successors merely as a basis for their own attitude toward religion and conduct. It is true that, at least at the start, they thought they were followers of Kant, since they accepted a distinction between reason and the understanding, and they attributed to reason the power of knowing the truth directly. But what they really valued from the Germans was summed up by Orestes Brownson when he said: "For their freedom, for their bold and uniform assertion and maintenance of the independence of the reason, we respect the whole body of German metaphysicians, whatever the systems they may have severally arrived at, or supported; in this particular they cannot be praised too warmly." [1]

Moreover, like the great Germans of the late eighteenth and early nineteenth century, the New England Transcendentalists upheld an absolute freedom from traditional authority, a deep interest in man, a belief in moral freedom, and a confiding trust in the perfectibility of the race. Emerson's definition of the scholar as being not a thinker, but man thinking—a definition acceptable to all the Transcendentalists—was

9. Fuller, *Works*, 2, 12.
1. *Christian Examiner*, 22 (May, 1837), 185.

essentially a German conception. Finally, a strongly developed sense for the spiritual unity of all things formed a kinship between the German writers and the New England Transcendentalists which remained as long as the movement itself.

Appendices

Appendix A

IN any analysis of the factors which quickened the enthusiasm of the Transcendentalists for German culture, one must consider the German books accessible to them in public and private collections. To know merely that German books were printed in this country in the original language or in translation, or that such books were imported from Europe is not enough. One must in addition discover the places where collections of such material were housed, examine their contents, and if possible prove that they were used by the Transcendentalists during the years when they were forming their doctrines. Such an analysis is hindered by these problems: the libraries seldom printed catalogues; accessions lists were not always safeguarded; private collections were often dispersed at the death of the owner; and even where they were kept together, careless use of the books has helped to destroy much of the evidence. Yet a surprising amount of information can still be gathered concerning the accumulation of German library collections in and around Boston.

That the shortage of German books actually hampered the popularity of German literature in New England is obvious from the evidence found in the letters and journals of the time. I have already spoken of Ticknor's secret loan of John Quincy Adams' copy of *Werther,* and have quoted Peabody's account of the first German course at Harvard when the students had to share one German book. Edward Everett Hale gave similar evidence in his book *Memories of a Hundred Years:* "I cannot remember the time when she [his mother] did not read it [German] with ease. This is now a common accomplishment, but as late as 1830 she could not buy a German book in Boston. . . . In 1843 I tried in Philadelphia to buy some German books for her, but I could find only Goethe, Schiller, the German Bible, and the German hymn book." [1]

We must remember, however, that not merely German books were scarce. It was not until the middle of the nineteenth century that our famous libraries began to collect books on a large scale. The library at Harvard, although even then the largest college library in the country, was totally inadequate. The first thing that struck American scholars

1. *Memories of a Hundred Years* (New York, 1902), *1,* 254.

upon visiting foreign university libraries was the lack of library facilities in their own country. Göttingen with its two hundred thousand volumes contrasted so sharply with Harvard's twenty thousand volumes
that Ticknor dubbed the latter "a closetful of books." In a letter to
Stephen Higginson, he wrote from Göttingen:

> I cannot . . . shut my eyes on the fact, that one *very* important and
> principal cause of the difference between our University and the one
> here is the different value we affix to a good library, and the differ-
> ent ideas we have of what a good library is. In America we look on
> the Library at Cambridge as a wonder, and I am sure nobody ever
> had a more thorough veneration for it than I had; but it was not
> necessary for me to be here six months to find out that it is nearly
> or quite a half a century behind the libraries of Europe, and that it
> is much less remarkable that our stock of learning is so small than
> that it is so great, considering the means from which it is drawn are
> so inadequate. But what is worse than the absolute poverty of our
> collections of books is the relative inconsequence in which we keep
> them. We found new professorships and build new colleges in
> abundance, but we buy no books; and yet it is to me the most ob-
> vious thing in the world that it would promote the cause of learning
> and the reputation of the University ten times more to give six thou-
> sand dollars a year to the Library than to found three professorships,
> and that it would have been wiser to have spent the whole sum that
> the new chapel had cost on books than on a fine suite of halls. The
> truth is, when we build up a literary Institution in America we think
> too much of convenience and comfort and luxury and show; and too
> little of real, laborious study and the means that will promote it. We
> have not yet learnt that the library is not only the first convenience
> of the University, but that it is the very first necessity,—that it is the
> life and spirit,—and that all other considerations must yield to the
> prevalent one of increasing and opening it on the most liberal terms
> to *all* who are disposed to make use of it. I cannot better explain to
> you the difference between our University in Cambridge and the one
> here than by telling you that here I hardly say too much when I say
> that it *consists* in the Library, and that in Cambridge the Library is
> one of the last things thought and talked about,—that here they have
> forty professors and more than two hundred thousand volumes to in-
> struct them, and in Cambridge twenty professors and less than twenty
> thousand volumes.[2]

It was at this time that Harvard began to build up its German collection. In May, 1817, the *North American Review* printed the follow-

2. Long, pp. 12–13.

ing item : "A small addition of about 80 volumes, of German works, and German editions of the classicks, was made to the Library, the last October. A considerable number of books likewise was received from Germany for the use of gentlemen of the government, and recent graduates in divinity. A large importation for the Library, and for the use of gentlemen connected with the University, is expected this season." [3] This notice refers in part to the books which Edward Everett brought back with him from Göttingen in 1817 and which were to form the nucleus of the German collection at Harvard.

The famous collection of Professor Ebeling of Hamburg also came into Harvard's possession at this time. After his death in the summer of 1816 Ebeling's tremendous library relating to America and consisting of over thirty-two hundred items (including eighteen portfolios of manuscript collections and ten thousand maps) was purchased by the Boston merchant, Israel Thorndike, and presented to Harvard. Although the collection contained little German literature, it displayed a great amount of German scholarship in the scientific fields.[4]

Another acquisition, and in many respects the most important one made by Harvard, was a set of Goethe's works in thirty volumes presented with the compliments of the author.[5] They were accompanied

3. 5, 139.
4. The King of Prussia had bid against Mr. Thorndike for the Ebeling collection, but was unsuccessful. See A. B. Faust, *The German Element in the United States*, p. 212. See also the *North American Review*, 7 (July, 1818), 288.
5. The history of this gift is extremely interesting, and has been recorded in the *Goethe-Jahrbuch*, 25 (1904), 3-37, by Leonard L. Mackall. Although Edward Everett was the first to suggest to Goethe the presentation of his works to Harvard, it was really Joseph Cogswell who persuaded Goethe and made all the necessary arrangements. He wrote to Goethe from Dresden, August 8, 1819: "You ask where you can send the copy of your poetical & scientific works, which you design for the 'Library of Harvard University Cambridge New England.'—If you will permit me to take charge of them, please to address them to me, care of Bassenge and Co. Dresden—I remain here till the middle of September. Allow me to express to you in advance that gratitude, which I am confident, not only the Governors and Senate of that University, but the whole literary community of my country will feel for the distinguished honor you confer upon them. This library has long been the medium, thro' which the friends of learning in the old world have expressed their zeal for its advancement in the new; it enrols among its patrons many of the most liberal Maecenases and finest scholars, which Europe has had during the last two centuries, but there is no name upon its records, which it will be more proud to point out among its benefactors, than that of your Excellency." See p. 14.
The books contained in this gift as listed in Goethe's note were as follows :
Goethe's Works, Vols. *1-20*
Doctrine of the Colours, Vols. *1-2*—Plates 4
The Propylaea, Vols. *1-3*
Life of J. G. Hackert, *sic*.
Travels in Italy, Vols. *1-2*
Art and Antiquity, Vols. *1-2*
On Natural Science
Bohemian Mountains (3 Copies)

with this brief note: "Weimar, 11. August 1819. Die Beifolgenden dichterischen und wissenschaftlichen Werke schenke ich der Bibliothek der Universität zu Cambridge in Neu-England als Zeichen meiner tiefen Theilnahme für ihren hohen wissenschaftlichen Charakter und für den erfolgreichen Eifer, den sie in einer so langen Reihe von Jahren für die Förderung gründlicher und anmuthiger Bildung bewiesen hat. Mit der grössten Hochachtung der Verfasser J. W. Goethe." [6]

It has already been pointed out that the Harvard library catalogue of 1790 lists no important volumes written in German. This is not singular when we remember that twenty times as many pages were devoted to theology as to drama and poetry combined, and sixty-five times as much to theology as to mathematics and science. The University of Virginia actually outstripped Harvard, since by 1826 it owned the available works of Goethe, Schiller, Lessing, and other German writers. The 1830 and 1834 Harvard catalogues, however, showed a great improvement, although as late as 1856 no copy of *Faust, Part II,* seems to have been available. The sudden increase of Harvard's German collection can be partly attributed to the work of Professor Follen. Turning to the 1830 Harvard catalogue, we see that German literature was represented by the names of Eichhorn, Gessner, Goethe, the Grimm brothers, Herder, Klopstock, Kotzebue, Lachmann, Lessing, Musaeus, Schiller, and the Schlegels; theology and philosophy were represented by the works of J. C. Eckermann, Herder, Kant, Luther, Niemeyer, Schaller, and Schleiermacher; classical scholarship and philology by Adelung, Blümner, Böttiger, Heeren, Müller, Schelle, and Voss. Numerous dictionaries were listed not only as aids in translating German into English, but also German-Latin, Hebrew-German, and German-Greek wordbooks.

The 1834 catalogue showed a decided increase. It included the names of Arndt, Bürger, Engel, Fichte, Fouqué, Gellert, Herder, E. T. A. Hoffman, Jacobi, Körner, Mendelssohn, Niebuhr, Novalis, Richter, Hans Sachs, Schelling, Tieck, Uhland, and Wieland. Additional works by Goethe, Jacob and Albert Grimm, Lessing, Musaeus, Nicolai, Schiller, and the Schlegels, as well as many new dictionaries and commentaries on the German language and literature were also available.

Harvard was not the only source of German books in Boston. The Boston Athenaeum, in many respects, surpassed Harvard in its German collection, or at least possessed many of these German authors at an earlier date. In 1827 the Athenaeum listed in its catalogue not only the majority of the authors named above in the Harvard library, but also

---

Iphigenia translated into Modern Greek (3 Copies)
Occasional Poems
6. *Goethe-Jahrbuch, 15,* 288–289.

works by Feuerbach, Grillparzer, Humboldt, Lavater, Müllner, Schubart, Schulze, Werner, Winckelmann, and many minor figures.[7]

The Boston Public Library was not founded until approximately 1851, and issued no catalogue until 1854. Consequently, it hardly concerns us here, but the Mercantile Library instituted in 1820 subscribed to various London, New York, and Philadelphia periodicals which stressed German literature, and it also had in its collection numerous German titles.[8]

Perhaps more important than these public libraries were the private collections in the vicinity of Boston. We know from first-hand accounts that Ticknor's library was exceptionally comprehensive. Although his German collection was inferior to his Spanish one, it was still among the finest in the country.[9] We have already mentioned that Follen used many of Ticknor's books in compiling his reader. We know that Ticknor also owned virtually all the fine German editions of the Latin and Greek classics. Not only did he purchase them for himself, but recommended and sent copies of them to Thomas Jefferson who was pleased with the accuracy of German scholars.

7. Everett and Ticknor were listed as proprietors in the 1827 catalogue of the Athenaeum.

8. Its 1839 catalogue showed few German books, but according to the 1854 catalogue German literature was well represented. William Emerson and B. F. Fuller were members of the Mercantile Library. It seems only logical that the Transcendentalists had access to this collection.

9. In fact, the only private collection among the Transcendentalists which could equal or surpass it was that of Theodore Parker.

Appendix B

Aeschylus, *Aeschyli Tragoediae*. Leipzig, Tauchnitz, 1819.
Anderson, Hans Christian, *Bilderbuch ohne Bilder*. New York, 1869.
Arnim, Bettina, *Correspondence of Fräulein Günderode und Bettine von Arnim*. Boston, 1861.
———, *Die Günderode*. Leipzig, 1840. 2 vols.
———, *Dies Buch gehört dem König*. Berlin, 1843.
———. See Goethe.
Arnim, Gisela von, *Alt Schottland*. Drama in 5 acts.
———, *Wie es unterdessen Daheim war*. Berlin, 1875.
———, *Dramatische Werke*. Bonn, 1857. Vol. *1*.
                      Bonn, 1857. Vol. *2*.
                      Bonn, 1865. Vol. *3*.
Atlantis. Eine Monatschrift zur Vermittlung des deutschen und amerikanischen Kultur und Literatur. 1858.
Austin, Sarah, *Fragments from German Prose Writers*. New York, 1841.

Barchou de Penhoen, Le Baron, *Histoire de la Philosophie Allemande depuis Leibnitz jusqu'à Hegel*. Paris, 1836. 2 vols.
Bechstein, Ludwig, *Märchenbuch*. Leipzig, 1857.
Bible, New Testament in German. Hamburg, 1718.
Boehme, Jacob, *The Remainder of Books written by Jacob Behme*. English by John Sparrow. London, 1662.
———, *Theosophisch Philosophy* . . . abridged . . . by Edward Taylor. London, 1691.
———, *Works*. London, 1764. 4 vols.
Bodenstedt, Friedrich, *Die Lieder des Mirza-Schaffy*. Berlin, 1859.

Cabinets-Bibliothek der deutschen Classiker. Anthologie aus den Werken Jean Pauls. *Bändchen*. Hildburghausen und New York, 1829. Anthologie aus Johann August Musaeus. *Volksmärchen*. 1829.
Caird, Edward, *A Critical Account of the Philosophy of Kant, with an historical introduction*. London, 1877.
Carlyle, Thomas, *History of Friedrich II of Prussia*. London, 1865. 2 vols.
———, *Life of Friedrich Schiller*. London, 1869.
———, *Translations from the German*. London, 1866. 3 vols.
Christliche Harmonika in einer Auswahl von geistlichen Liedern.

Dante et Goethe, Dialogues. Paris, 1866.
Dictionaries
    Feller, F. E., *Neuestes Taschen-Wörterbuch Deutsch, Englisch und Französisch.* Leipzig, 1877. Vol. *3.*
    ——, *Nouveau Dictionnaire de Poche Français, Allemand, Anglais.* Leipzig, 1877. Vol. *2.*
    ——, *A New Pocket Dictionary English, German and French.* Leipzig, 1877. Vol. *1.*
    ——, *ibid.* Leipzig, 1870. 3 vols.
    Flügel, J. G., *Complete Dictionary of the English and German Languages.* London, 1830. 2 vols.
    Grimm, Jacob and Wilhelm, *Deutsches Wörterbuch.* Leipzig, 1854–78. 5 vols.
    Hossfeld, C., *New German-English Dictionary.* Liverpool, n.d.
    Neugriechisch-deutsches und deutsch-neugriechisches Wörterbuch . . . von M. T. A. E. Schmidt. Leipzig, 1825–27. Vol. *1,* Greek-German. Vol. *2,* German-Greek.
    New English-German and German-English Dictionary; containing all the words in general use . . . compiled from the dictionaries of Lloyd, Nöhden, Flügel, and Sporschil. Philadelphia, 1838. 2 vols.
    Schul-und Reise-Taschen-Wörterbuch der französischen und deutschen Sprache. German-French volume.
    Gibbs, Josiah W., *Hebrew and English Lexicon of the Old Testament including the Biblical Chaldee from the German works of Prof. W. Gesenius.* Andover, 1824.

Edda, *Die Edda* . . . Stuttgart, 1855.
Edinburgh Review, from October, 1829 to January, 1830. Vol. *40.*
Encyclopaedia Americana, ed. Francis Lieber. Philadelphia, 1829. Vols. *1–13.*

Feuerbach, Ludwig, *Essence of Christianity.* Translated from the German by Marian Evans. New York, 1855.
Fichte, Johann Gottlieb, *The Nature of the Scholar and Its Manifestations.* Translated from the German, with a memoir of the author, by William Smith. London, 1845.
Follen, Charles, *Practical Grammar of the German Language.* Boston, 1826.
Fouqué, Friedrich, Baron de la Motte, *Undine.* New York, 1846.
Furness, William H., *Gems of German Verse.* Philadelphia, 1860.

Goethe, J. W., *Auto-Biography. Truth and Poetry.* Translated by John Oxenford. London, 1848.
——, *Conversations of Goethe with Eckermann.* Translated by John Oxenford. London, 1850. 2 vols.
——, *Conversations of Goethe with Eckermann.* Bohn's Library, London, 1875.
——, *Correspondence with a Child.* London, 1839. 3 vols.
——, *Correspondence with a Child.* First American, from London edition. Lowell, 1841. 2 vols.

Goethe, J. W., *Correspondence between Goethe and Schiller from 1794 to 1805*. Translated by George Calvert. New York, 1845. Vol. *1*.

——, *Essays on Art*. Translated by Samuel Gray Ward. Boston, 1845.

——, *Faust*. Translated by Bayard Taylor. Boston, 1871. 2 vols.

——, *Faust, Part II . . . with other poems*. By Leopold J. Bernays. London, 1839.

——, *Faust*. Translated by Charles T. Brooks. Boston, 1856.

——, *Faust*. Translated by A. Hayward, first American from third London edition. Lowell, 1840.

——, *Letters from Switzerland and Travels in Italy*. London, 1849.

——, *Roman Elegies*. Translated by L. Noa. Boston, n.d.

——, *Sämmtliche Werke*, Vol. *3, Sprüche in Reim und Prosa*. Stuttgart, 1840.

——, *Sämmtliche Werke*, Vol. *6, Vollständige Ausgabe in fünfzehn Bänden*. Stuttgart, Cotta'schen, 1872.

——, *Sämmtliche Werke*, Vol. *15, Die Wahlverwandtschaften*. Stuttgart, 1840.

——, *Sämmtliche Werke*, Vol. *24, Naples Rome Italy*. Stuttgart, 1840.

——, *Sämmtliche Werke*, Vol. *36, Morphologie*. Stuttgart, 1840.

——, *Sprüche in Prosa*. Berlin, 1870.

——, *Werke. Vollständige Ausgabe letzter Hand*. Stuttgart, Cotta'schen, 1827–31. Vols. *1–40*.

——, *Werke. Nachgelassene Werke*. Stuttgart, Cotta'schen, 1832–33. Vols. *41–55*.

——, *Unterhaltungen mit dem Kanzler Friedrich von Müller*. Stuttgart, 1870.

——, *West-Easterly Divan*. Translated by John Weiss. Boston, 1877.

——, *Wilhelm Meister's Apprenticeship*. Translated by Thomas Carlyle. London, 1839.

Grimm, Hermann, *Armin. Ein Drama in fünf Aufzügen*. Leipzig, 1851.

——, *Aus dem September-Heft der preussischen Jahrbuch*. Berlin, 1870.

——, *Bettina von Arnim*. Weimar, 1880.

——, *Cornelius und die ersten fünfzig Jahre nach 1800*. Berlin, 1875.

——, *Das Leben Raphaels von Urbino*. Berlin, 1872.

——, *Die Venus von Milo. Raphael und Michel Angelo. Zwei Essays*. Boston, n.d.

——, *Engel und Liebesgötter*. Berlin, 1875.

——, *Essays*. Hanover, 1859.

——, *Fünfzehn Essays*. Berlin, 1875.

——, *Goethe in Italien*. Berlin, 1861.

——, *Goethe und Luise Seidler*. Berlin, 1874.

——, *Goethe und Suleika*. Berlin, 1869.

——, *Hamlet*. Berlin, 1875?

——, *Leben Michelangelo*. Hanover, 1863. Vol. *2*.

——, *Life and Times of Goethe*. Translated by Sarah Holland Adams. Boston, 1880.

——, *Über Künstler und Kunstwerke*. Berlin, 1865.

——, *Unüberwindliche Mächte*. Berlin, 1867.

———, *Voltaire und Frankreich*. Berlin, 1870?
———, *Vorlesungen gehalten an der Kgl. Universität zu Berlin*. Berlin, 1877. 2 vols.
Günderode, Caroline von. See Bettina von Arnim.

Hammer, Joseph von, *Der Divan von Mohammed Schensed-din Hafis*. Stuttgart, 1812 and 1813. 2 vols.
———, *Geschichte der schönen Redekünste Persiens*. Wien, 1818.
Heeren, Arnold H. L., *Reflections on the Politics of Ancient Greece*. Translated by George Bancroft. Boston, 1824.
Hegel, Georg W. Friedrich, *Vorlesungen über die Aesthetik*. Berlin, 1842. 3 vols.
———, *The Philosophy of Art*. Translated by William M. Bryant. New York, 1879.
———, *Naturphilosophie und die Bearbeitung derselben durch den Italienischen Philosophen A. Vera. Von Karl Rosenkranz*. Berlin, 1868.
Heine, Heinrich, *Letters auxiliary to the History of Modern Polite Literature in Germany*. Translated by G. W. Haven. Boston, 1836.
Humboldt, Alexander von, *Aspects of Nature*. Philadelphia, 1849.
———, *Cosmos*. 1847.
Humboldt, William von, *Religious Thoughts and Opinions*. Boston, 1851.

Kant, Immanuel, *Critick of Pure Reason*. Translated. London, 1838.
Kerner, Justinus, *Seeress of Prevorst*. Translated by Mrs. Crowe. London, 1845.
Kestner, J. C., *Goethe et Werther*. Traduites par I. Poley. Paris, 1855.

Lessing, Gotthold Ephraim, *Laocoon*. Translated by E. C. Beasley. London, 1853.

Michaelis, Johann David, *Beurtheilung der Mittel, welche man anwendet, die ausgestorbene Hebraische Sprache zu verstehen*. Göttingen, 1757.
Müller, Falk von, *Characteristics of Goethe*. Translated by Sarah Austin. London, 1833. 3 vols.
Müller, John von, *Universal History*. Translated from the German. Boston, 1831. 4 vols.
Mundt, Theodor, *Literatur der Gegenwart, Geschichte der*. Berlin, 1842.
Musaeus, J. A. See *Cabinets-Bibliothek der Deutschen Classiker*.

Neues Taschen-Liederbuch. New York, 1855.
Novalis, *Henry of Ofterdingen*. Translated from the German. Cambridge, 1842.

Richter, Jean Paul. See *Cabinets-Bibliothek der Deutschen Classiker*.
———, *Campaner Thal: or Discourses on the Immortality of the Soul*. Translated by Juliette Baner. London, 1848.
———, *Titan: A Romance*. Translated by C. T. Brooks. Boston, 1862. 2 vols.
———, *Walt und Vult, or the Twins*. Translated from *Flegeljahre* by the author of the *Life of Jean Paul*. Boston, 1846. 2 vols.

Ripley, George, ed., *Specimens of Foreign Standard Literature*.
   Vol. *1, Philosophical Miscellanies from the French of Cousin, Jouffroy and Benjamin Constant*. Boston, 1838.
   Vol. *2, Philosophical Miscellanies*.
   Vol. *3, Select Minor Poems of Goethe and Schiller*.
   Vol. *4, Conversations with Goethe*.
Roelker, Bernard, *German Reader for Beginners*. Cambridge, 1854.

Schelling, Friedrich von, *Sämmtliche Werke*. Stuttgart, 1857.
Schiller, J. C. F. von, *Song of the Bell*. Translated by W. H. Furness, with poems and ballads from Goethe, Schiller, and others, by F. H. Hedge. Philadelphia, 1850.
———, *The Historical Works of Frederick Schiller*. From the German, by George Moir. Edinburgh, 1828.
———, *Wallenstein's Camp*. Translated by George Moir. Boston, 1837.
———. See Thomas Carlyle.
Schlegel, A. W. *Course of Lectures on Dramatic Art and Literature,* Translated by John Black. Philadelphia, 1833.
Schlegel, Friedrich von, *Philosophy of History*. Translated by James Burton Robertson. London, 1835. 2 vols.
Staël, Madame de, *L'Allemagne*. Paris, 1850.
———, *Germany*. Translated from the French. New York, 1814.
Stirling, James Hutchison, *The Secret of Hegel*. London, 1865. 2 vols.

Tiarks, J. G., *A Practical Grammar of the German Language and Exercises*. London, 1846.

Varnhagen von Ense, K. A. *Tagebücher von Friedrich von Gentz*. Leipzig, 1861.

Watson, John, *Kant and his English Critics*. New York, 1881.
Werder, Karl, *Vorlesungen über Shakespeare's Hamlet*. Berlin, 1875.
Winkelmann, John, *History of Ancient Art*. Translated by G. H. Lodge. 2 vols.

Appendix C

BORROWED	FROM BOSTON ATHENAEUM	RETURNED
Apr 29, 1831	Schiller, *Wallenstein* (tr. Coleridge)	May 11
May 3, 1831	Herder, *Outlines of a Philosophy of Man* (1) *	May 6
May 28, 1831	Schiller, *Wallenstein* (tr. Coleridge)	June 25
Aug 1, 1831	Herder, *Outlines of a Philosophy of Man* (1, 2)	Aug 26
Dec 23, 1831	Mueller, *History and Antiquity of Doric Race*	Jan 3
Aug 13, 1832	Goethe, *Wilhelm Meister's Apprenticeship* (1)	Aug 16
Aug 16, 1832	Goethe, *Wilhelm Meister's Apprenticeship* (2)	Aug 23
Aug 20, 1832	Goethe, *Memoirs*	Sep 5
Feb 20, 1834	Austin, *Characteristics of Goethe* (3)	Feb 22
Feb 20, 1834	Austin, *Characteristics of Goethe* (1, 2)	Apr 17
Apr 8, 1834	Wieland, *Sämmtliche Werke* (5–6, 21–22)	Apr 9
Apr 9, 1834	Wieland, *Sämmtliche Werke* (13–14, 17–18)	Apr 9
Apr 23, 1834	Wieland, *Sämmtliche Werke* (11–12)	Apr 25
Nov 25, 1834	Luther, *Commentary upon Galatians*	Dec 11
Mar 15, 1835	Austin, *Characteristics of Goethe* (1)	May 4
May 28, 1835	Goethe, *Memoirs*	July 22
May 28, 1835	Schlegel, *Sämmtliche Werke* (1)	June 23
May 28, 1835	Wieland, *Sämmtliche Werke* (9)	July 22
Feb 2, 1836	Pückler-Muskau, *Tour in England,* etc.	Mar 1
Apr 5, 1836	Grimm, *Kinder und Haus Märchen* (3)	Apr 21
Apr 21, 1836	Musaeus, *Volksmärchen der Deutschen* (1, 5)	Apr 28
Aug 2, 1836	Hardenberg, *Schriften*	Oct 10
Aug 22, 1836	Biber, *Henry Pestalozzi*	Oct 3
Mar 7, 1837	Wieland, *Sämmtliche Werke* (21)	Mar 8
Mar 8, 1837	Wieland, *Sämmtliche Werke* (43–44)	Mar 8
Mar 24, 1837	Austin, *Characteristics of Goethe* (1)	May 20 ?

* Arabic numerals in parentheses refer to numbers of the volumes which Emerson withdrew; Roman numerals refer to the number of the series. I am grateful to Kenneth Cameron for the form of the identifications in this list. However, I made an independent check of the German references in the library records.

BORROWED	FROM BOSTON ATHENAEUM	RETURNED
Mar 24, 1837	Jacobi, *Werke* (2)	Apr 24
Apr 24, 1837	Austin, *Characteristics of Goethe* (2)	May 10
Jan 30, 1840	Beyle, *Lives of Haydn and Mozart*	Apr 23
Mar 6, 1845	Wieland, *Sämmtliche Werke* (7–8)	May 12
Apr 16, 1845	Wieland, *Sämmtliche Werke* (33–34)	May 10
Nov 4, 1845	Schlegel, *Lectures on History of Literature* (1, 2)	Jan 28
Jan 7, 1851	Goethe, *Werke* (21)	Feb 20
Sep 12, 1851	Hardenberg, *Schriften* (1, 2)	Dec 5
Sep 12, 1851	Schiller, *Correspondence . . . with Körner* (2)	Sep 25
Sep 25, 1851	Schiller, *Correspondence between Schiller and Goethe* (2)	Oct 30
Sep 27, 1852	Luther, *Life Written by Himself* (ed. Michelet)	Dec 16
Nov 21, 1853	Grimm, *Correspondence* (II. 1)	Nov 29
Nov 30, 1853	Grimm, *Correpondence* (2)	Dec 13
Dec 13, 1853	Grimm, *Correspondence* (1, 3)	Dec 20
Dec 20, 1853	Grimm, *Correspondence* (II. 4)	Dec 26
Dec 26, 1853	Grimm, *Correspondence* (I. 5)	Feb 25
Feb 25, 1854	Grimm, *Correspondence* (4, 5)	May 10
July 8, 1854	Lieber, *Manual of Political Ethics* (1, 2)	July 25
Dec 8, 1854	Wieland, *Sämmtliche Werke* (5, 6)	Dec 26
Feb 1, 1855	Niebuhr, *Life and Letters* (1)	Apr 10
Feb 1, 1855	Niebuhr, *Life and Letters* (2)	Apr 11
Apr 11, 1855	Niebuhr, *[Lectures on] History of Rome* (2)	May 4
Mar 28, 1857	Richter, *Sämmtliche Werke* (27, 28)	Aug 15
July 20, 1857	Wieland, *Sämmtliche Werke* (21, 22)	Aug 7
Sep 5, 1860	Humboldt, *Letters to Varnhagen*	Sep 7
Feb 21, 1861	Goethe, *Theory of Colours* (Eastlake)	June 5
Apr 10, 1861	Welcker, *Alte Denkmäler Erklärt* (1)	Apr 24
Apr 18, 1861	Welcker, *Alte Denkmäler Erklärt* (2)	Apr 24
Sep 10, 1861	Mueller, *History of Ancient Sanskrit Literature*	Nov 27
Feb 20, 1861	Mueller, *Lectures on the Science of Language*	Mar 5
Apr 17, 1862	Hafiz, *Eine Sammlung persischer Gedichte*	June 2
Feb 12, 1863	Fichte, *Popular Works* (tr. Smith) (2)	Feb 28
Mar 5, 1863	Varnhagen von Ense, *Tagebücher* (1)	Apr 6
Mar 10, 1863	Varnhagen von Ense, *Tagebücher* (2)	Mar 19
Apr 6, 1863	Varnhagen von Ense, *Tagebücher* (5)	May 15
Apr 13, 1863	Varnhagen von Ense, *Tagebücher* (3, 4)	May 15
Oct 1, 1863	Varnhagen von Ense, *Denkwürdigkeiten* (8)	Oct 2
Oct 2, 1863	Sadi, *Lustgarten*	Mar 11
Feb 10, 1864	Varnhagen von Ense, *Tagebücher* (5)	Mar 16

BORROWED	FROM BOSTON ATHENAEUM	RETURNED
Mar 19, 1864	Sadi, *Rosengarten*	Mar 30
July 9, 1864	Varnhagen von Ense, *Denkwürdigkeiten* etc. (6)	Aug 18
Sep 10, 1864	Lieber, *Reminiscences of . . . Niebuhr*	Oct 29
Oct 15, 1864	Auerbach, *Gesammelte Schriften* (7, 8)	Oct 26
Aug 19, 1865	Buechner, *Force and Matter*	Sep 18
Aug 19, 1865	Grimm, *Life of Michael Angelo* (2)	Aug 23
Nov 4, 1865	Hegel, *Lectures on Philosophy of History*	Mar 10, 1866
Apr 4, 1866	Forster, *Sämmtliche Schriften* (9)	May 22
July 5, 1866	Homer, *Werke* (ed. Voss)	Aug 17
July 23, 1866	Beethoven, *Letters* (1)	Jul 28
Aug 25, 1866	Grimm, *Life of Michael Angelo* (2)	Aug 30
May 29, 1867	Lessing, *Sämmtliche Schriften* (10)	June 5
Aug 17, 1867	Lessing, *Sämmtliche Schriften* (10)	Sep 3
Aug 17, 1867	Herschel, *Familiar Lectures on Scientific Subjects*	Aug 20
Sep 3, 1867	Herschel, *Familiar Lectures on Scientific Subjects*	Sep 10
Oct 11, 1867	Mueller, *Lectures on the Science of Language* (2d Series)	Nov 19
Apr 4, 1868	Mueller, *Chips from a German Workshop* (1)	Apr 13
Nov 21, 1868	Stahr, *Weimar und Jena*	Dec 29
Mar 29, 1869	Tholuck, *Blüthensämmlung*	Apr 22
Apr 10, 1869	Wieland, *Sämmtliche Werke* (47, 48)	May 30
May 1, 1869	Wieland, *Sämmtliche Werke* (15, 16)	May 4
May 4, 1869	Wieland, *Sämmtliche Werke* (27, 28)	May 8
May 4, 1869	Heyse, *Vier neue Novellen*	May 5
May 8, 1869	Wieland, *Sämmtliche Werke* (5, 6)	May 11
May 11, 1869	Wieland, *Sämmtliche Werke* (21, 22)	May 26
Aug 9, 1869	Wieland, *Sämmtliche Werke* (29, 30)	Aug 30
Aug 30, 1869	Wieland, *Handbook of the History of Philosophy*	Sep 30
Nov 25, 1869	Wezel, *Belphegor* (1, 2)	Dec 4
Jan 22, 1870	Schiller, *Correspondence between Schiller and Goethe*	Mar 21
Jan 29, 1870	Varnhagen von Ense, *Blätter* (3)	Mar 7
Feb 17, 1870	Varnhagen von Ense, *Tagebücher*	Mar 7
Mar 7, 1870	Varnhagen von Ense, *Tagebücher*	Apr 23
Apr 25, 1870	Lewes, *Life and Works of Goethe* (2)	May 14
July 7, 1870	Varnhagen von Ense, *Tagebücher* (9)	July 27
July 13, 1870	Varnhagen von Ense, *Tagebücher* (8)	Sep 1
Dec 28, 1870	Hardenberg, *Henry of Ofterdingen*	Feb 8, 1871
Dec 28, 1871	Varnhagen von Ense, *Tagebücher* (10)	Jan 27, 1872
June 13, 1872	Mueller, *Lectures on the Science of Religion*	June 24
Sep 26, 1872	Witte, *Dante-Forschungen*	Jan 11, 1873

BORROWED	FROM THE BOSTON LIBRARY SOCIETY	RETURNED
Feb 13, 1817	Klopstock, *The Messiah* (tr. Collyer)	Feb 28 (?)
Apr 26, 1821	Schlegel (August? or Friedrich?) (1)	June 2
July 21, 1821	Schlegel (August? or Friedrich?) (2)	July 28
Mar 21, 1822	Staël-Holstein, *De l'Allemagne* (1, 2)	May 23
May ?1, 1823	Staël-Holstein, *De l'Allemagne* (1, 2)	June 7
Feb 28, 1824	"Schlegel on Literature" (cf. above)	Apr 10
Feb 2, 1828	Staël, *Memoires de Madame de Staël* (1, 2)	
Apr 3, 1828	Goethe, *Memoirs of Goethe*	May 15
Dec 5, 1829	Schiller, *History of Thirty Years' War* (1)	Dec 12
Dec 12, 1829	Schiller, *History of Thirty Years' War* (2)	Dec 19
Dec 19, 1829	Goethe, *Memoirs of Goethe*	Jan 26
Dec 21, 1830	Humboldt, *Personal Narrative of Travels* (3)	Jan 4
Jan 4, 1831	Humboldt, *Personal Narrative of Travels* (1)	Jan 29
Jan 29, 1831	Humboldt, *Personal Narrative of Travels* (2)	Feb 26
Jan 29, 1831	[? Humboldt, *Political Essay on Kingdom of*] *New Spain*	Feb 5
May 26, 1832	Klopstock, *The Messiah* (tr. Collyer)	May 31
Aug 21, 1832	Goethe, *Wilhelm Meister's Apprentice-ship* (3)	Aug 23
Feb 1, 1840	Carlyle, *German Romance: Specimens* (1, 3)	Feb 8
Feb 1, 1840	Carlyle, *German Romance: Specimens* (4)	Feb 15
Oct 13, 1840	Austin, *Characteristics of Goethe* (2)	Oct 22
Nov 10, 1840	Goethe, *Memoirs of Goethe*	Nov 24
Nov 10, 1840	Roscoe, *The German Novelists* (2)	Dec 8
Nov 24, 1840	Velde, *Tales from the German* (Greene) (1)	Dec 8
Dec 12, 1840	Beyle, *The Life of Haydn . . . Life of Mozart*	Dec 19
Dec 19, 1840	Beyle, *The Life of Haydn . . . Life of Mozart*	Dec 29
Apr 6, 1841	Arnim, *Goethe's Correspondence with a Child* (1)	Apr 13
Dec 11, 1841	Austin, *Fragments from German Prose Writers*	Dec 14
Feb 12, 1842	Taylor, *Historic Survey of German Poetry* (1)	Feb 22
Feb 12, 1842	Austin, *Fragments from German Prose Writers*	Mar 3
Dec 20, 1842	Lee, *Life of Jean Paul Frederic Richter* (1)	Dec 27
Dec 20, 1842	Lee, *Life of Jean Paul Frederic Richter* (2)	Dec 20
Jan 28, 1843	*Specimens of Foreign Standard Literature* (14)	Feb 14

BORROWED	FROM THE BOSTON LIBRARY SOCIETY	RETURNED
Feb 14, 1843	Taylor, *Historic Survey of German Poetry* (2)	Feb 28
Feb 28, 1843	Taylor, *Historic Survey of German Poetry* (3)	Mar 11

FROM HARVARD COLLEGE LIBRARY

Mar 17, 1823	Mosheim, *An Ecclesiastical History* (1)
Feb 17, 1825	Leibnitz, *Essais de Theodicee*
Dec 5, 1828	Goethe, *Werke* (Stuttgart) (3)
Feb 1, 1829	Herder, *Outlines of History of Men* (ed. 1800)
Nov 8, 1848	Schleiermacher, *Introduction to Dialogues of Plato*
Nov 8, 1848	Ast, *Platon's Leben und Schriften*
Mar 14, 1849	Goethe, *Oeuvres d'Histoire Naturelle*
May 18, 1855	Niebuhr, *Lectures on Ancient Ethnography* (1)
May 18, 1855	Niebuhr, *Lectures on History of Rome*
May 18, 1855	Niebuhr, *Life and Letters* (3)
Mar 25, 1868	Preller [*Die Regionen der Stadt Rom*] [*Römische Mythologie*] [*Ausgewählte Aufsätze*]

Bibliography of Manuscripts *

Boston Public Library Manuscripts

Alcott, Bronson. Orphic Sayings on "Spiritualism" (n.d.).
Letter of Charles Follen certifying John S. Dwight's knowledge of the German language. July 17, 1832.
Letter of John S. Dwight to Charles T. Brooks. March 10, 1837.
Letter of James F. Clarke to John S. Dwight. March 25, 1837.
Letter of Margaret Fuller to John S. Dwight. May 31, 1837.
Letter of Theodore Parker to John S. Dwight. January 10, 1839.
Letter of George Ripley to John S. Dwight. August 6, 1840.
Letter of Charles T. Brooks to John S. Dwight. April 13, 1842.
Letter of Henry T. Tuckerman to John S. Dwight. November 2, 1842.
Letter of Margaret Fuller to Ralph Waldo Emerson, April 11, 1837. Fuller MS, No. 64.
Margaret Fuller Editorial. August 23, 1833. Fuller MS, No. 10.

Houghton Library Manuscripts. Harvard University

I examined the following journals and manuscripts of Ralph Waldo Emerson to verify all statements quoted from the published journals and writings.

Houghton
1 Cabot's A January 12, 1820, No. 17.
2 Cabot's D The Wide World No. 1, 1820.
3 Pythologian Journal 1819–21.
4 Cabot's B September 1820—January 1821, No. 18.
5 Cabot's E The Wide World No. 2, October 1820.
6 Cabot's C The Universe Nos. 1–8, 1820–21.
7 Cabot's F The Wide World No. 3, January 12, 1822.
8 Cabot's G The Wide World No. 4, February 22, 1822.
9 Cabot's I The Wide World No. 6, April 14, 1822.
10 Cabot's J The Wide World No. 7, July 11, 1822.
11 Cabot's K The Wide World No. 8, November 6, 1822.
12 Cabot's L The Wide World Nos. 9, 10, 11, 12, 1822–24.
13 Cabot's N The Wide World No. 13, February 1824.
14 Cabot's O? Early Journals No. XV, 1824.
15 Cabot's S Early Journals No. XVI, 1824.
16 Cabot's M No. XVIII, 1823–29.
17 Cabot's Q January 1, 1826—February 1828.
18 Cabot's R August 1826—March 1828.
19 Cabot's U 1827.
20 "Little Journal St. Augustine" Jan–Feb–Mar 1827.

* This list includes only the manuscripts, journals, and letters which I have cited in the text.

21 Sermons and Journals 1828–29.
22 Blotting Book Y 1829–30.
23 Blotting Book No. IV, October 27, 1830.
24 Blotting Book Ψ October 1830.
25 Blotting Book No. III Ω June 1831.
26 March 1832—March 1833.
27 Journals of Travel—Sicily, 1833 (Cabot's 1) (Pocket Note Book).
28 Journals of Travel—Italy, 1833 (Cabot's 2) (Pocket Note Book).
29 Journals of Travel—Italy and France, 1833 (Cabot's 3) (Pocket Note Book).
30 Journals of Travel—Scotland and England (Cabot's 4) (Pocket Note Book).
31 Pocket Note Book 1833 (Cabot's 5).
32 Visits to France and England and fragment of Journal in Maine 1833–34.
33 Journal A 1833–34.
34 Journal B 1835–36.
35 Journal C 1837.
36 Journal D 1838–39.
37 Journal E₂ 1839–42.
38 Journal F 1840.
39 Journal G 1841.
40 Journal H 1841.
69 Journal RO 1835.
91 Journal August 1822.
92 Journal NP 1825.
93 Collectanea 1825.
Letter of George Ripley to Thomas Carlyle. December 29, 1836.
Letters of Theodore Parker to James Freeman Clarke. Nos. 475–95.
Letters of Margaret Fuller Ossoli to James Freeman Clarke. Nos. 462–73.
Letters of Charles T. Brooks to John S. Dwight.
August 20, 1833
January 20, 1834
May 26, 1834
July 11, 1836
January 7, 1839
Letter of Frederic Henry Hedge to Margaret Fuller. June 5, 1843.

New York Public Library Manuscripts
Unsigned letter concerning Margaret Fuller to Wiley & Putnam. January 27, 1845. Duyckinck Collection.
Letter of Charles T. Brooks. October 7, 1846.
Letter of George Ripley. April 6, 1838.

Sterling Memorial Library Manuscripts. Yale University
Letter of Bronson Alcott. Bohton, 1877. Yale Collection of American Literature.
Letter of Ralph Waldo Emerson to Thomas Carlyle. April 22, 1840. Speck Collection.

MS translation of Charles T. Brooks. Goethe's "Der Fischer." Speck Collection.

Manuscripts owned by James Freeman Clarke III
James F. Clarke.
> "MS Autobiography."
> Loose pages from "Journal of Understanding."
> Loose pages from "Journal of People and Things, 1831–33."
> "Journal of Thoughts and Reading 1838."
> "Journal," 1839–40.
> MS Commonplace Book of Poetry.
> MS Translations for *Exotics*.
> MS Translations from Goethe and Schiller.

Letters of James F. Clarke to Henry W. Bellows.
> February 27, 1849
> March 7, 1849

Letters of James F. Clarke to William H. Channing.
> October 22, 1833
> October 13, 1835

Letter of James F. Clarke to William G. Eliot, December 20, 1833.

Letters of James F. Clarke to Margaret Fuller.
> August (n.d.) 1832
> September (n.d.) 1832
> June 14, [1833]
> July 31, 1833
> September 9, 1833
> November 12, 1833
> February 24, 1834
> October 22, 1834
> April 12, 1835
> May 12, 1835
> June 14, 1835
> August (n.d.) 1835
> November 16, 1835
> February 26, 1836
> March 28, 1836
> May 11, 1836
> July 26, 1837
> November 20, 1837
> October 8, 1839

Letter of James F. Clarke to Ephraim Peabody, July 6, 1835.
Letter of James F. Clarke to George Ripley, February 21, 1833.
Letters of Sarah Clarke to James F. Clarke.
> January 26, 1834
> January 22, 1835
> April 28, 1836

Index